FLOURISHING IN A SMALL PLACE

FLOURISHING IN A SMALL PLACE

A Pastor's Journey

PAUL EMANUEL LARSEN

Foreword by Robert K. Johnston

WIPF & STOCK · Eugene, Oregon

FLOURISHING IN A SMALL PLACE
A Pastor's Journey

Wipf & Stock
An Imprint of Wipf and Stock Publishers
199 W. 8th Ave., Suite 3
Eugene, OR 97401

www.wipfandstock.com

PAPERBACK ISBN: 978-1-5326-7427-3
HARDCOVER ISBN: 978-1-5326-7428-0
EBOOK ISBN: 978-1-5326-7429-7

Manufactured in the U.S.A.   OCTOBER 14, 2019

To Elizabeth
My greatest love
and
my deepest mentor

Contents

Foreword

"Every person is the painter of his own life, and choice is the craftsman of the work, and the virtues are the paints producing the image."

—GREGORY OF NYSSA

THERE ARE TWO VERY different reasons for reading Paul Larsen's memoir, *Flourishing in a Small Place*. Either one would be sufficient for me to say regarding this book, "Take and read." But together, they make writing this foreword a real joy. The first has to do with the nature of a good memoir; the second, has to do with the particular events of Paul Larsen's life.

Writing one's memoir is usually done in the hope of making sense of one's life. At its worst this can remain a shallow pursuit, little more than self-promotion. Just as the historical progression of titles of our popular magazines reflects the growing narcissism of our age (from *Life* to *People* to *Us* to *Self*), so an increasing number of authors today who seek to tell the story of their lives never get beyond "me, myself, and I." Such books ring hollow. They are at best page-turners to fill idle time, and at worst, simple trash. But when done well, an author's search for self-discovery through writing his/her story invites readers to reflect on how to strengthen their own journeys. Reading the memoir of another, when it is well told, offers us as readers both community—a sense that we are not alone—and instruction—help in living our lives more fully and more meaningfully. *Flourishing in a Small Place* does just that.

I write this foreword on the day of the State funeral of George H. W. Bush. As all of us, whether Republican or Democrat, heard recounted both by the former President's friend Alan Simpson, and by his son, George W. Bush, the story of a life well-lived—a life in which position was thought less important than family and faith, a life in which the measure of a person was not money, but furthering the community good, and a life filled with humility and humor, not self-aggrandizement—we were reminded of the power that a well-told story of a life well-lived can have. As someone who did not vote for Bush, I nevertheless found myself both inspired and informed by the reflections on his life. His life story affected my life. Here also is the invitation I would offer you as readers of Paul Larsen's self-portrait. His story is both inspirational and insightful, one filled with integrity and a deep care for faith, family, and the disadvantaged. This book offers both community and instruction.

But there is also a second reason for reading this memoir. It has to do with Paul Larsen's lifetime of service within the Evangelical Covenant Church. In today's media-saturated world, being an evangelical has become synonymous with a particular and narrow outlook on life. But the Covenant Church denomination in which Larsen has served for a lifetime, both as a pastor and later as its president, has thrown evangelicalism's sociological net wider than this, embracing and helping to define what might better be described as an inclusive evangelicalism.

The term "inclusive evangelical" might seem oxymoronic to some, but this is only because some are unaware of how the term "evangelical" has functioned historically, sociologically, and theologically. Historically, to be an evangelical was to be a Protestant. In Germany, still today, the Lutheran church is called the Evangelical Lutheran Church. Here is a definition that is perhaps too broad to be helpful in our North American context. Sociologically, evangelicals, regardless of their denomination, all sing the same praise choruses, all read C. S. Lewis and Eugene Peterson, and all support the same parachurch organizations (e.g., InterVarsity and CRU). They also have voted overwhelmingly Republican, strongly opposing abortion and gay marriage. Increasingly their political stance has cast them in the eyes of others as intolerant and legalistic. But such a political definition is also proving unhelpful. It is too narrow to embrace the larger evangelical coalition. Instead, a theological definition is called for.

Theologically, some have said, perhaps tongue in cheek, that evangelicals are those who believe what Billy Graham believed. And they would be correct. But to be more specific, we can say an evangelical today is someone who believes in

1. the need for a personal relationship with God through faith in the atoning work of Jesus Christ,

2. the need to share with others this gospel, or good news, through word and deed, and

3. the need to live under the full authority of the Bible in their faith and life.

Such a definition is at one and the same time inclusive and exclusive, inviting a dozen or more traditions (e.g., Baptist, Pietist, self-consciously Reformed, Dispensational) under its umbrella, while remaining only a subset of those who are Christians.

And it is here that Larsen's autobiographical memoir is important. For the story of Paul Larsen's involvement in the Evangelical Covenant Church provides an important alternative to current understandings of what it means to be an evangelical. From his Stanford friendship with Diane Feinstein to his daily prayer meetings on campus, from his leadership in early marches for racial justice to his continuing commitment to personal evangelism, Paul Larsen has modeled a breadth not typical of much evangelicalism today. His ecumenical leadership in gathering together leaders of all Christian communions (evangelical, mainline Protestant, Roman Catholic, Protestant), his commitment to expositional preaching, his early leadership in making the Covenant Church denomination more racially inclusive, his commitment to helping national leaders overthrow India's dehumanizing caste system – in these and other ways, Larsen has modeled a more holistic and ecumenical, yet biblically-based evangelicalism. The jury, at present, is out as to whether such a theologically motivated definition of the term "evangelical" can rescue the word from it sociological captivity. But if there is a reason to try, Larsen's memoir gives readers both impetus and inspiration. Like the reflections heard today on the life of George H. W. Bush, his memoir helps us envision a better way. May his life prove contagious.

ROBERT K. JOHNSTON
December 5, 2018

Preface

MINE IS THE STORY of a pastor's journey from the last half of the second millennium through the first two decades of the third. Inspired by the lives of great Christian leaders since my childhood, I have yearned to be like them. Such ambitions, of course, are always a mixture of personal ambition and the authentic passion to please our Savior. Eighty-five years has produced little real greatness. But reflection has convinced me that by God's grace I have flourished in the small place he has given me.

The first three chapters of this book describe the years from my birth through my training and education. The next three chapters concern my service as a local pastor in Orangevale, Pasadena, and Redwood City, California. Chapters 7 and 8 cover the years when I was given the privilege of serving the Evangelical Covenant Church for three terms, from 1986 to 1998. Then followed twenty years—chapters 9–11—as a retiree serving as the founding chair of both the William Carey Foundation of India, as well as the Truthseekers International of North America. This includes seventeen trips to India. This period differed from the others in that I kept an exhaustive daily journal of each trip to South Asia. That journal helped ensure a daily record of observation of an emerging Christward movement among the half-billion members of the Other Backward Classes (OBCs) of India.

This memoir may be of interest to my friends and family as well as the people of the Evangelical Covenant Church. It may also have a broader appeal to those beyond the bounds of my former churches and those interested in my involvement in the social and spiritual movements in the world beyond the Covenant.

1

Family Background

> Centuries ago a Danish mother was leading her children through the forest in central Jutland, the peninsula that juts up from Germany into the Baltic Sea. As she journeyed, she was suddenly pursued by a pack of wolves. She ran into a clearing where there were several cows. She cried to heaven, "God please save my children. If you do, one child of mine from every generation will be given to the holy priesthood!" Suddenly the cows circled her and the children with their horns facing outward. In every generation since then, there has been a priest among the descendants.

This is an early myth since wolves and forests had been absent in Jutland since before the Reformation. There is no reason to believe that this really occurred. The story does nonetheless have significance as a founding myth of our family origin.

My mother's family can be traced back to the fourteenth century in Denmark. This founding myth has been handed down over the centuries and has shaped the family identity.

I arrived in this world on October 5, 1933, born to David and Myrtle Larsen in the Swedish Hospital in Minneapolis, Minnesota. My brother, David Leonard, had been born two and one half years earlier, and my sister, Mary Elizabeth, arrived fifteen months after my birth. Both my brother and I have been ministers, as have many close relatives and more distant ancestors. I now look back on more than three quarters of a century. To say that I was graciously sustained and enabled by God the whole time is to grossly understate the reality of these years. I take up the task of expressing my recollections fairly and honestly—a challenge ever before me as I write these words.

MY MOTHER

Born Myrtle Mary Grunnet in 1906, my mother was the fifth child of Nels and Laura Grunnet. They were Danish immigrants who settled in Stewart, a small town near Hutchinson, Minnesota, where other Danish families lived. Her mother was born in Odense, Denmark, and was raised in a Danish Salvation Army background. Her sister Mary and brother Louis also lived in Stewart, Minnesota.

Mother's father came from an old Danish family. They trace back as far as 1360 in parish records; they have a clear genealogy. One of her ancestors was rector of the Danish Cathedral at Ribbe on the west coast and was a contemporary of Martin Luther. In the 1530s, while serving as rector, the church officially became Lutheran. He was known for his compassion and care for the poor.

In the early nineteenth century, the king was an absolute monarch after the pattern of Germany's Fredrick the Great. Danish religion and culture were dominated by German Enlightenment thinking, and rationalists dominated the church. Pontoppidan's famous explanation of *Luther's Small Catechism* was replaced by "Principles of Enlightenment." Thomas Kingo's Psalter was replaced by "Songs of Enlightenment." Moravian missionaries brought awakening to the central peninsula of Jutland. The father of Danish philosopher Søren Kierkegaard was the leader of the Danish Moravians. One cannot understand Kierkegaard apart from his Moravian connections. These movements were soon headed up by a band of fiery lay evangelists who led in the spiritual awakening and the democratization of Denmark. Named the "Strong Jutlanders," they initiated an internal struggle that allowed the churches to return to Pontoppidan's catechism and Kingo's Psalter. They won the right of communities to appoint and dismiss the schoolteachers. The struggle climaxed in 1849, when Denmark adopted Europe's first democratic constitution.

One of the Strong Jutlanders was my great-great-grandmother, Hilda Grunnet. We have learned much about her life of prayer and intense preaching. It was said of her, "She was some woman—she outlived three husbands!" My mother translated much of her writing from Old Danish. It was to the estate and village of Grundet (Grunnet) that King Fredrick VI came and abolished serfdom and granted liberties to the nation's citizens.

This same king issued the official charter for Serampore College near Calcutta, Asia's first Western-style university. The king decreed that Serampore College was empowered to teach any subject that would be of use to the people of India and have the same accreditation as the universities of Copenhagen and Keil in perpetuity.[1] This took the form of a treaty that is binding on the nation of India to this day. In 2005, I was the founding chair of the William Carey Heritage Foundation for India (to be discussed in chapter 9). A chief purpose was to renew the university's original mission. This school is empowered to grant all theological degrees to this day. The theological department of the school grants their theology degrees Oxbridge-style to the more than fifty affiliated Protestant theological schools. The foundation helped to refurbish the campus and increase faculty compensation.

The fiery leader's son, Nels Grunnet, went to the Basel Mission School in Switzerland to prepare for missions. His orthodox Lutheranism conflicted with the school's high Reformed theology. He then pastored at Martinskirken, a church along the canal in Copenhagen, where he is memorialized. He defended the mentally ill and the mistreated, yet he was nonetheless a fierce polemicist. He ultimately formed Denmark's Free Lutheran movement, which survives to this day with a few churches.

Grandfather—named Nels after his uncle—immigrated to Minnesota, where he married. He was a genteel, kindly man who failed at homesteading at Coeur d'Alene, Idaho. He moved with his family to a home in Morningside, a Minneapolis suburb. They lived many years in a home that was a block from his elder sister's, Johanna Leerskov—whose husband had founded the village. He took a modest job at the Leader Department Store and spent his time reading history and novels by authors such as Dickens and Hugo. He struggled with alcoholism, twice taking the cure called Anabuse. Sobered, as he got older, he spent his last years in active and faithful worship.

Mother grew up with a multitude of siblings and cousins. In her teen years she often argued with her male cousins over women's suffrage. She accepted Christ in the little one-room Methodist Church in Stewart, Minnesota. She was often nurtured at the historic Red Rock Camp Meetings each summer outside the Twin Cities. When she came down with tuberculosis, she spent a year in recovery at the Glendale Sanitarium. She was delighted to attend to University of Minnesota for a year. But then, family finances led to the decision that her older sister Helen should attend the university while Mother helped support her and the family. Yet she continually took courses in language, literature, and history. This interest in art, music, literature,

---

1. King Christian VI, *The Royal Charter and Statutes of Serampore College*, p 43.

history, and political science later came to characterize the interests of her three children as well.

Mother taught high school girls at the church. Sixty years later, the same girls would recall her influence on them. Despite our family's Republican sympathies, she went off the reservation and voted for Roosevelt. In later years, she was a volunteer assistant to Audrey Wetherell Johnson, the internationally known founder and leader of Bible Study Fellowship.

Mother was most gentle and caring, following the personality and outlook of her parents. When Father retired in 1951, he brought us to Los Altos, California, and our new home. This was her new home, and adjustment was not that easy, but she would often say, "Life is like a girdle—adjust or bust!" I can never forget the loving care she gave me in times of my acute illness with asthma. Always a people person, she was the epitome of a dancing Dane. She found it difficult to speak ill of anyone. Immersed in the Swedish culture of the Covenant Church, she adapted. The only evidence of any quiet rebellion showed in her steadfast unwillingness to sing the Swedish hymns. She lived only two years after Father's death. David and I moved her to the Northbrook Covenant Village near us on Chicago's North Side. We could then see her often during those last days. She never lost her kindness, cheerfulness, or spiritual passion.

MY FATHER

My father, David Paul Larsen, was born in 1895, twelve years before my mother's birth, to Swen and Anna Larsen (nee Simonson). They arrived in America from Sweden in the 1880s and settled near Fergus Falls, Minnesota. This area is the location of the series of novels by noted Swedish writer Vilhelm Moberg. These novels included *The Emigrants, Unto a Good Land, The Settlers,* and *The Last Letter Home.* Three of these novels were produced for nationwide television audiences. Of interest to me were the struggles between the Lutheran priests and the low-church Pietists, out of which the Covenant Church in America sprang.

Both of my paternal grandparents died before I was born. Grandfather Larsen was a Stockholm Swede. His youth was spent on the family He struggled unsuccessfully to raise his family out of poverty. He attempted to homestead a farm near a Swedish colony near Richvale, California. But arriving in the hundred-degree temperature on the hardpan of California's Sacramento Valley, he soon felt the delay in bringing water to the dry land. He concluded that the promise of a thing called irrigation was a trick by real estate criminals. He sold his parcel for only enough money to buy train fare for his family to the muskeg swamps of Northern Minnesota near Baudette, Minnesota. It seemed like Swedish farmland, but was even less productive. Prematurely blinded by a botched cataract operation, he could not sustain the family, but continued as a blind lay minister of the young denomination we now call the Evangelical Covenant Church.

My grandmother, born Anna Simonson, grew up on a prosperous farm near Arvika, Småland, near the Norwegian border. She became a reader of the Mission Friends. State Lutheran Church friends ridiculed her, and her own parents found it difficult to accept this enthusiasm. A very poor young neighbor boy would occasionally stop by their back door of the farmhouse. At times he had not eaten for long periods. She would feed him from the family kitchen. One day she invited him to a meeting of Mission Friends where he gave his life to Christ. He later became E. August Skogsbergh, the "Swedish Moody." A great revivalist, he built the massive Swedish Tabernacle in Minneapolis seating more than 2,500 people, and was one of the five corporate founders of the Covenant Church.

My paternal grandfather came from an area near Stockholm. Raised on a poor farm, he became a wild young man—drinking and philandering. Yet when a young boy was dying in the farm next door, he joined his family in the neighboring home in a wake anticipating the coming death. As the family wept and prayed, the unconscious boy labored heavily in his final moments. All at once he sat up and cried out to grandfather, "Unless you repent, you shall die in your sins!" He instantly collapsed and died. He was a "Crier," a child who uttered prophecies in the middle of the night. Grandfather was so shaken that he was immediately repentant and transformed. Delivered of his alcoholism and carousing, he ultimately became an early Covenant lay preacher.

Father was the fifth child born to Swen and Anna Larson in 1895. His younger brother, Joseph, became a pastor and evangelist. The two eldest children died before I was born. Esther, his sister, was born earlier. She later became a high school teacher in Minneapolis and authored a book, *The Northwest Forest Fires*, which is still cited to this day.[2] A few years before father's birth, Emanuel Swen was born. They always lived near us.

The impoverished family homesteaded near Richvale, California. Knowing nothing of coming irrigation, they abandoned the property. Years later the coming of irrigation made the land the most productive rice fields in America. Returning to the muskeg swamps of northern Minnesota, the family was penniless. Living in a one-room house with only a blanket suspended for sleeping, Father and Emanuel (Emil) tried to keep the family

---

2. Larson, *Tales from Northwest Forest Fires*.

going by trapping wild animals. Father spoke only Swedish and taught himself to read by watching his mother play from the hymnbook Sions Basson on an old piano. He and his teenaged brother were among the few who remained to fight the great forest fire of 1910 that destroyed both Spooner, Ontario, and Beaudette, Minnesota. They plied hoses on the great lumber shed all night. The next morning that was all that was left of the two towns. The following morning Grandfather Swen was staying in the small family farmhouse nearly a day's walk from town. When the fire came, he crawled into the overhang of a small stream and kept his mouth just on top of the water as the fire raged. Walking to town the next day, he saw other burned farms with a number of burnt corpses along the way. A failed cataract operation blinded Grandfather, and thus the two boys kept the family together.

Poverty kept him from school, but the sawmill superintendent had seen the poverty and took the young teenager to a job in the sawmill. It was the cut-off room, where occasionally flying broken band saw teeth would slash into the workers. He was put to work in that room because it was so dangerous that the union steward was afraid to go in. There it was safe for him to work though underage. Father studied bookkeeping at night, and at age seventeen became head bookkeeper at the Crookston Lumber Company in Bemidji, Minnesota. He still could not make enough to support the family, so he took a second job loading the giant sleighs with goods and supplies that horses would draw into the woods to service the scattered logging camps. He was quickly recognized. Thus, at just over twenty he was sent to the headquarters of the Shevlin group of lumber companies. This group combined fifty-four lumber companies, employing scores of thousands with sawmills and related businesses in the United States and Canada. At twenty-three, he was general auditor for the companies. He had memorized the entire Revenue Act of 1917. The previous general auditor could not understand the war tax and was dismissed. The two finalists for the position were Father and the immediate past head auditor for the Panama Canal, as it was completed. Father got the job. Thus he became the chief financial officer for these companies until his retirement at age fifty-five in 1971.

He survived the stock market crash in 1929—the year he married— but it left him deeply in debt throughout the depression. The coming of World War II brought recovery in the industry. He was named a member of the National Committee on Wage and Salary Stabilization. When the war ended, the Department of the Army held a celebration banquet in Chicago honoring the work of both labor and management in the war effort. Father was honored by being asked to respond on behalf of all US industrial companies.

After conceiving the sale of a large part of the company's sawmills, he retired in 1951. He moved us to Los Altos, California, so that we three children could all go to Stanford University.

Now investing for himself, he earned far more than he would have had he stayed as a senior company officer. Always more than a tither, he told us that he would help each of us with our education plus a small fund for a down payment on a home and other necessities. He did not believe in inherited wealth—because so many of the children of the timber barons ended in failed marriages, insolvency, and alcoholism. He then began to give out of the principle and not just the income from his investments. He stated that the more he gave away, the greater his investments grew. I was in seminary when he one time visited me. He told me that he would give such a large percent of his investments away that he could never recover. Then he wept, telling me as he wept that by the end of the year he had more money than when he made the huge gifts. Settling an adequate amount on my mother, he determined to give away the rest of his means before he died. He had nearly succeeded when he died of a stroke at ninety-four years of age.

MY PARENTS' MARRIAGE AND MY CHILDHOOD HOME

My father married Myrtle Grunnet, my mother-to-be, in 1929. He survived the stock market crash that same year by a miraculous fluke. He had asked my uncle Emil (Emanuel Swen) to arrange for the honeymoon to be a six-week tour of Europe. Since Uncle had arranged the same for the family members of the Dayton family, owners of the department store where he worked, he booked the trip as a grand tour, not informing his brother of the astronomical cost. Arriving in New York, my parents discovered that they had been booked into the Bridal Suite on the Isle de France. The bathroom alone cost an extra $80 per night. They had two waiters and a wine steward assigned exclusively to their dining table. During this long honeymoon, the great stock market crash of 1929 occurred. Father could do nothing, for all his stock certificates were tied up in his safety deposit box. The market had rebounded by the time they returned, but Father had already resolved to liquidate all his investments. He discovered that the rebound had moved his stock above his original costs—and was astounded to discover that this honeymoon extravagance had cost less than nothing. He was out of the market completely before its steepest declines ensued.

This did not, however, resolve an even bigger problem. As Shevlin Pine Companies opened a mammoth timber and sawmill operation in Blind

River, Ontario, the company gave Father a large chunk of stock, to be repaid out of future dividends. Employing thousands of lumberjacks in the woods, the market crash forced the entire operation into bankruptcy. It took years during the depression to finally pay off the debt.

Nevertheless, my parents found the cash to build a lovely home in a suburb of Minneapolis, on Casco Avenue in the Edina Country Club—one of the first lot subdivisions in the country. Noted architect Louis Bersbeck designed an authentic Massachusetts Bay colonial home. The lumber was shipped from the company's sawmills. Covenanter Aaron Carlson provided a beautifully paneled circassia walnut living room. A paneled den and slate roof topped it off. Over the years the home was featured in *House Beautiful* magazine.

It was about six blocks to Grandma's house on Sunnyside. A big, dark, brown-shingled house, it stood next door to the bungalow where my mother's older brother, Leslie Grunnet, lived with his wife, Grace. She was raised by her teenaged brother, Cameron Thompson. Both of her parents died during the flu epidemic of 1917. Wild teenagers, he could not bear to see his siblings sent away, so he got busy. Finally getting a bank position, he rose in the ranks and was the founding president of Northwest Banco, which ultimately became Norwest and more recently bought the Wells Fargo Bank. The Thompson Family Trust generously helps fund my journey to India for missions each year. They had two children. Margaret, nearly our own age, became a top neuropathologist, teaching at the University of Connecticut. Her older brother, Jim, became an aeronautical engineer and lives with his wife in Minneapolis, where he continues to assist our India work.

Less than two blocks away on Bruce Avenue was the home built by my Uncle Emil and Aunt Florence. Mother's older sister, Florence, had married Emil Larsen, my father's older brother. His full name was Emanuel Sewn Larsen, from whom I received my middle name: Emanuel. Aunt Florence had been a schoolteacher. Emil was an officer of the Dayton Company. They had two sons, David and Richard, who were quite a bit older. Thus, their two sons were our double cousins.

Only a few blocks from us lived Mother's older brother, Les, and his family, and he was next door to our grandparents. We spent much of our childhood going back and forth among these homes, especially on holidays. Mother's family was so large that a hundred people would gather at Uncle Louis's summer cottage on Lake Marion every Fourth of July.

DAVID LEONARD

Two and a half years before my birth in 1933, my brother David was born. He was born in Swedish Hospital in Minneapolis, while Father's mother was also there dying of cancer. When the little baby was taken down to see her, she raised her arm and declared that this child would be mightily used of God. This memory has lived in our family ever since. David was extremely bright and even-tempered. As a student he excelled always. He had an ei-detic, or photographic, memory. While no genuinely photographic memory exists, his recall was phenomenal. Even in adult years he could recall the place and sermon he had preached on any given Sunday going back many years. He could remember what was on a given page in a book. He became an avid reader, often devouring at least one book a day throughout his life. He was not aggressive, and my mother had to teach him to hit back at school bullies. He was invariably kind to me and had an unsurpassed influence on my life.

From his early years David had a deep sense of calling to the ministry. When very young, he preached to dolls stuffed into the footboard of his bed, and later he held church services in the basement. We shared a room together from my earliest days. We did not always agree, and I remember a debate during junior high years regarding the interpretation of a verse in 1 John—it lasted for three summer days. Finally, the tears of Mother brought us back to the real world.

David graduated from high school with honors and went on to Bethel College in St. Paul. During his two years there, he also pastored the Calvary Covenant Church in Columbia Heights—an amazing feat for an eighteen-year-old!

When Father retired, he took us to California so that we could live near Stanford University only a few miles away, and fifteen minutes by the back road from our home in Los Altos. While at Stanford David led in the establishment of the Peninsula Covenant Church, which began in Burlingame, but acquired its first property in Redwood City, California. The church grew rapidly, and as I entered Stanford, I became teacher of the high school class as well. Meanwhile, he carried a full load of at least 18 units at Stanford on a straight-A record. He was extremely disciplined. He would begin a term paper promptly on a Saturday morning and type with no more than two corrections per page. He would arise for a brief lunch and return to a completed term paper four hours later. Then he would both teach and/or preach three times on Sunday.

Upon graduation, he attended Fuller Seminary for three years and continued to earn top grades. During this period, he pastored the

Neighborhood Covenant Church in South San Gabriel. Upon graduation, he spent an additional year of studies at North Park Seminary in Chicago. While studying there, he met a Jean Johnson, a nurse at Swedish Covenant Hospital. They were married a year later. Together they raised three children. The newlyweds returned to South San Gabriel and then moved to the First Covenant Church of San Francisco. From there he moved with his family to Minneapolis, where he succeeded Milton Engebretson as pastor of the Elim Covenant Church. He was able to send his children through Minnehaha Academy. The historic First Covenant Church of Rockford, Illinois called him next, and from there he was called to the historic First Covenant Church of Minneapolis. He pastored there until his appointment as professor of pastoral studies at Trinity Evangelical Divinity School in Bannockburn, Illinois. Declared "Teacher of the Year" three times, he spoke on preaching and related themes throughout the United States and abroad. A PhD candidate at Central Baptist Seminary in Kansas wrote his dissertation on David's life and preaching.

With the arrival of the laptop computer, he began disciplined book writing on subjects related to preaching, evangelism, and spiritual formation. Among them, he wrote three books of nearly 1,000 pages each. The first is *The Company of the Preachers*, a single volume on the history of preaching.[3] Then he published a book entitled *The Company of the Creative*, using his encyclopedic knowledge of history, theology, philosophy, and culture to show how the changes in Western history both affected and were affected by Christian preaching.[4] The third volume was *The Company of the Hopeful*, a massive study in the history of Christian eschatology.[5] Additionally, he even wrote a few short mystery novels. He probably is the most published Covenanter in the church's history.

It might seem difficult to live under the shadow of such a gifted brother. Our personalities were quite different, and we did not always agree, but were always at one theologically. I found my own identity in not trying to ape him or resent him, but to exercise my identity in ways that God called me and fulfilled me.

He continued all these years as an active member of Covenant churches and is now in retirement at the Northbrook Covenant Village in Northbrook, Illinois. He continues to write, teach, and preach, even into his eighties.

---

3. Larsen, *Company of the Preachers*.
4. Larsen, *Company of the Creative*.
5. Larsen, *Company of the Hopeful*.

MARY ELIZABETH

Fifteen months after my birth, my sister, Mary Elizabeth, arrived on the scene. Now there were three children. My earliest memory—before I was two years old—is Mary's arrival home in a basket. I distinctly recall her little pink crocheted bonnet trimmed with imitation white rabbit fur. I recall her being taken into the nursery and carefully weighed in the baby scale there. I adored her. She was built more like my father and possessed his athletic skills as well as an incredibly quick mind in math—qualities that neither David nor I possessed.

Early on she developed strong survivor skills in such a male-dominated home. She got top grades in school. She attended Minnehaha Academy in Minneapolis for the first years of high school and finished with top grades at Mountain View High School in California. She also was accepted at Stanford. With all three of us graduates of Stanford, we joined a small handful of families with three graduates in the more than one hundred years of Stanford's life.

She began her career as an assistant buyer for an upscale women's department store chain in San Francisco. Later, she worked as a technical writer for Hewlett-Packard Corporation in its early days. She then met a fine young Christian man who was living in the same Menlo Park apartment complex: David Goerz Jr., who became her husband. He had been among the handfuls of young men that Miss Henrietta Mears had discipled over the years at the famed Hollywood Presbyterian Church. He was doing graduate work at Stanford. He had invented the world's first interplanetary vacuum—he was the first to successfully create the same nearly perfect vacuum as existed between planets in the solar system. He then organized a corporation called Vac-tite and began to sell the devices for both research and industry. After this he worked as an executive of the Bechtel Corporation, the world's largest construction and development company. He became director of development for the company's international business, with major projects in Russia, China, Africa, and the Middle East. Long into retirement years he continued his creative research and enterprises. All this time he was a dedicated husband and father with a devout Christian faith.

Mary often traveled with him and served as international hostess to major political and industrial leaders. When the Chinese Premier paid a visit to Washington, DC, Mary became the official hostess to the Chinese vice premier. Mary was a lifelong leader in the prestigious Menlo Park Presbyterian Church, serving on its leadership over many terms. She was a dedicated, conscientious, and loving mother of three children, all of whom continue to follow Christ with their families. She also served as chair of the

Allied Arts Guild, a development arm of the Stanford Children's Hospital, where she also served as vice chair.

An avid reader, she bore clear witness with a wide group of non-Christian intellectuals in the Stanford area all her life. In later years, she and Dave held video worship services from Menlo Park Presbyterian at the prestigious retirement community to which they moved on the edge of the Stanford campus.

I can never affirm Mary enough—strong church leadership and community service accompanied her stalwart contributions to family. She is one of the most admirable persons I have ever known, demonstrating great strength during our family tragedies.

2

My Arrival

I WAS BORN AT Swedish Hospital in Minneapolis on October 5, 1933. I was frail and underweight from the beginning, then plagued with severe asthma all my life. I grew up in the beautiful house in the Edina Country Club, surrounded by extended family living nearby. The year of my birth, the Great Depression hit bottom.

Here I entered the family—soon to be the middle of three children—at the bottom of the Great Depression. It was an indebted but relatively prosperous household despite the financial crisis. Initially the family employed two maids. A foot pedal under the dining room table would summon one of the maids from the kitchen. The coming of World War II meant that the help could get wages in factories, leaving the burden of washing the dishes to David and me—he washing and me wiping the dishes each evening. But World War II and our dishwashing came after my early childhood.

WOODDALE SCHOOL

The nearest public school was the Wooddale School, just two blocks from home. We could trudge there and back even for the daily lunch. A smaller school, it was a part of the country club subdivision—one of the first in the United States. Brother David could escort me faithfully. My first grade teacher was Miss Bemis. Alarmed when I told her that we passed an anteater on the way to school every day, she summoned my brother from the second grade classroom. David explained that it was not an anteater, but a Scottie dog that had been shaved due to a skin problem—leaving a skinny dog with a long, pointed nose. That was not the last of my misperceptions!

I attended the school through the eighth grade. During this time, I developed many friends in the neighborhood. Ronnie Shirk lived two doors up. Manny Houseboy lived across and two doors up. David Adams lived five houses down. His father was Cedric Adams, the celebrity newscaster and daily columnist for "In This Corner" in the daily *Minneapolis Star Journal.* Feeling myself outclassed, I had to compete by bragging. On his birthday, he told me that his father had given him a five-pound box of candy. I topped that by saying, "My father gave me a box of candy so big it took four men to carry it." I sheepishly listened the next morning at the breakfast as my parents laughed aloud while reading Adams's daily column concerning the anonymous boy down the street and his big box of candy. Later, I announced to David that we had an elephant at our house. He asked, "How come I haven't seen him?"

"Because we keep him in the basement."

David harrumphed, "He is too big for your basement!"

"But it is a baby elephant."

He then demanded that we go at once to see the baby elephant. I triumphantly announced, "We can't go because my father rides him to work every morning!

Again at the breakfast table, my parents laughed out loud as they read the story in the daily column a day or two later. These were timely lessons in truth telling for a first grader.

CHILDHOOD IMAGINATIONS

David and I shared a room from my earliest days until I had completed two years at Stanford. As young children we developed elaborate fantasies. In preschool, David would put stuffed dolls between his mattress and footboard and preach sermons to them regularly. Later, he would hold church in the basement on Wednesday evenings. We also had Sunday morning and evening services—sometimes roping neighboring children into the services. I, of course, was the associate pastor, and Mary served as usher. Later, David also developed a little newspaper, *The Appleton Weekly*, printed from rubber type.

During summers we created a university. David would teach Bible, Latin, and Greek—utilizing texts that Mother had used while taking extra courses at the university. I taught wood shop. David continued to develop his fantasies of preaching and teaching.

I had fantasies of preaching, but dreamed of myself as the leader of a denomination. I would get a big book of noted churches and cut them out, placing their pictures in strategic places. This expanded to a large number as I began to draw simple plans of other small churches. Then I drew a picture of a national headquarters. It was a red-brick colonial two-story building with white pillars on either side of the entrance. I then drew pictures of the seminary, which was also red brick with pillars and two extended wings. I thought that I had saved them in my files, but evidently lost them before I had any idea of becoming president of the Covenant. In fact, I had completely forgotten them until I recalled them one day after a few years in office as Covenant president. Nevertheless, the drawings I remember bore an uncanny resemblance to the Covenant Headquarters building in Chicago and the North Park Seminary building.

These memories puzzle me, my skepticism largely wrote off these fantasies as coincidental. Child psychology experts, however, have long held that childhood fantasies with dolls and games are rehearsals for life. Robert K. Johnston's book, *The Christian at Play*,[1] emphasizes this fact, and says that for many people these are in fact part of the real world and not simply confined to the world of fantasy. Playing childhood church can be the beginnings of life's ultimate vocation. I cannot help but note that David spent his life both as pastor and professor, while I served as a pastor and church leader.

SEVERE ASTHMA

I was always frail and sickly as a child. Often underweight, I developed severe asthma at an early age. The attacks were most frequent during the ragweed season. I would sit up gasping all night with my mother rubbing my back. This also led to frequent colds and flu. Thus, I missed large amounts of school. In the eighth grade my parents finally consulted with Dr. Albert Stoesser, head of Pediatric Allergy at the University of Minnesota. Both Dr. Gilligan and Dr. Stoesser came to our house to examine me. I listened at the staircase as they told my parents that they had to force me to get up and get back to school. I heard Dr. Stoesser say, "Unless we get him on his feet, he will be an invalid." They then prescribed a "parentectomy." No longer used, it was an effort to remove my maternal dependency. Mother was shipped off with her sister, Florence, on a tour of the South. A hard-bitten old nurse came in to get me up and off to school. I was blue in the lips and the school nurse would keep sending me home. Dad would simply drive home from his office and return me to school the same day. The other students would sometimes stand around and watch me struggle. The doctors then put me

1. Johnston, *Christian at Play*.

on both an oral medication and allergy shots. This treatment has allowed me to lead a normal life except for setbacks in college, seminary, and just before retirement. I took these shots for the next seventy years. By that time, my sensitivities had dimmed. I now take only a couple of mild medicines.

CHRISTIAN FAITH

A deeply Christian home was our parents' greatest gift. In the earliest years my parents left the Swedish Tabernacle (First Covenant Church) because every other Sunday the services were in Swedish. They became active at the Oliver Presbyterian Church during the years when Norman B. Harrison and Louis T. Talbot served as pastors. Father played golf with them both during their tenure. Norman B. Harrison was the father of Dr. Everett Harrison, a longtime New Testament professor at Fuller under whom I later studied. Dr. Talbot became the president of the Bible Institute of Los Angeles, now Biola University. Its seminary, Talbot, is named for him. When preaching only in English arrived, my parents returned to the Tabernacle. In those days revival continually swept the church under Pastor Gustaf F. Johnson. The church, which seated 2,500 people, overflowed on Sunday evenings, requiring the fire department to close the doors more than an hour before the service, sending as many as a thousand people away. Father taught young men's Bible classes of more than one hundred. As many as a hundred people were converted every Sunday evening. Father became a very close friend of Gustaf.

In the late 1930s, the church became deeply divided. Due to the bitterness on both sides of the dispute, our parents decided to attend W. B. Riley's First Baptist Church. My earliest remembered church experiences took place there. Dad taught the Baraka class of over a hundred men. Mother had attended First Baptist with her sister-in-law, Grace, before she was married. They both attended the Sunday school class for younger women led by Henrietta Mears, who later became famous as the founder of Gospel Light Press and as education director at Hollywood Presbyterian Church. Pastor Riley became a friend to our family; I remember him reading the funny papers to me on his knee. One of fundamentalism's greatest leaders, his sermons were reprinted in a series of volumes entitled *The Bible of the Expositor and the Evangelist*. We heard guest preachers such as James McGinley, H. A. Ironsides, and Campbell Morgan.

New Birth

In my seventh year, I began to long for the time when I could make my own life commitment to Jesus Christ. My father, seeing that I wished to follow the earlier example of my brother, felt that I was not yet able to understand what such a commitment was. Several times I asked him to show me the way, and he demurred. This whetted my appetite. In early February 1942, shortly after the bombing of Pearl Harbor, Dr. Riley brought noted English evangelist Gipsy Smith to hold citywide meetings in Minneapolis. We would go nightly to hear him preach. Now in his seventies, he would tell his story. Growing up in a band of nomadic Gypsies wandering over the English countryside, he told of his conversion. Father had also taken us out into the countryside near Minneapolis where a group of such Gypsies had stopped their horse-drawn wagons and camped. Smith did not shout or preach judgment. He rather preached the love of Christ. Before each service he would sit at the piano and sing a simple song, "Let the Beauty of Jesus be Seen in Me," repeatedly asking us to join:

> Let the beauty of Jesus be seen in me
> All His beauty and majesty!
> O, Thou Spirit Divine,
> all my nature refine
> 'Til the beauty of Jesus be seen in me.
> —Albert Orsborn

He would close each message by asking for a show of hands: How many would like him to pray for them before he took off his coat that evening at his hotel? I would slip up my little hand, but I was too shy to go forward. Each Sunday at First Baptist, Dr. Riley would begin the sermon, and the Gipsy would finish, closing with the song again. The entire Sunday school primary and junior departments would sit on a large platform beneath the pulpit. On February 11, 1942, I raised my hand. Mrs. Riley, recognizing me, asked whether I really wanted to receive Jesus and bid me to go back to my Sunday school class. There my teacher, Mr. Bass, explained the way of salvation. In that moment I claimed the promise of Christ's gift of everlasting life.

The Return to Park Avenue

Dr. Riley was succeeded in the pulpit at First Baptist by R. L. Moyer, who was then president of Northwestern Bible School, which Riley had founded and housed at the church. While Father was teaching the huge men's Bible class, known as the Baraka class, Moyer discovered that Father was not a Calvinist and did not affirm the so-called doctrine of eternal security. He dismissed my father from teaching. Father then felt that enough time had passed since the split at the Tabernacle. People were no longer obsessed with that controversy. Gustaf Johnson's new church, Park Avenue Covenant, had purchased the venerable old stone First Congregational Church at Park Avenue and Franklin. Up to a thousand would gather to hear the music and preaching. Sunday evenings were particularly moving, as Johnson would often preach on the second coming of Christ.

I soon developed panic attacks during the morning worship services. I was unable to swallow. I was also beset by a long period of doubt. I remember how often in the cold midwinter I would kneel by my bedroom window and look up at the stars, crying out for the assurance that God was real. Occasionally Father would take us back to First Baptist on Sunday evenings when an especially well-known guest preacher was speaking. At my lowest ebb he took us to hear the noted pastor of the Brooklyn Tabernacle, James McGinley. With his heavy Scottish accent he would preach and entertain the congregation with great good will and humor. One Sunday night he preached on the theme: "Arroond the daarrkest corrner there shoines the brrrightest light." I saw a faint hope—and in a couple of weeks both my doubts and swallowing panic had permanently disappeared. This does not mean that I have never had times of doubt and fear. It was, however, a decisive high point in my life. It was not a turning for salvation, but for the gift of full assurance.

ADOLESCENCE

Finishing the eighth grade at the Wooddale School, I joined my brother, David, on the long walk to Southwest High School, as no local high school was completed yet at that time. Here David asked me to join him in the Junior Republican Club. We began to receive propaganda steadily, including fundamentalist John R. Rice's *Sword of the Lord*, a fundamentalist and right-wing political weekly, a regular paper from the South. We also received a periodical called *The Broom* to strengthen our convictions. We were troubled, however, by the tone. It slipped in questions like: "Why do the Jews have kinky hair?" Answer: "Because Moses married a negro." While we were economic conservatives, regarding civil rights we were liberals. Offended by the anti-Semitic and anti-black materials from various periodicals, and by Rice's extremism, we determined to take a clear stand in opposition to these movements, even while we were in high school. Our alienation from that talk ended our interest in this brand of politics. That experience has influenced us to this day.

In the tenth through the twelfth grades, I entered the newly opened Edina-Morningside High School. There were only a hundred or more students on my level in the huge new facility. I helped organize the student government and other activities. I developed some of my best friends there, some of whom I follow to this day.

I likewise became active with the high school group at Park Avenue Covenant. There Eugene Johnson, Earl Fredrickson, and Lester Bloom became great friends, and some of the girls began to attract my interest. During a series of meetings held by Pastor Wesley Nelson he gave a call for those who would give their lives to serve as ministers or missionaries. Not understanding what or why I felt deeply impelled to go forward for prayer, I went nonetheless to offer myself to Christ's service.

As graduation approached, my father announced that he had helped sell the Shevlin Hixson Company at Bend, Oregon, leaving only the Mc-Cloud River Lumber Company among the Shevlin Pine Companies. At fifty-five, he felt he had enough money to retire. He then moved us to Los Altos, California, in the hopes that all of us could attend Stanford University nearby.

3

Higher Education

STANFORD UNIVERSITY

FOUNDED BY LELAND AND Jane Stanford in honor of their deceased son, Stanford University occupied a beautiful, 9,000-acre campus on what had once been their Palo Alto farm. The university was completely secular despite Jane Stanford's wish to keep nonsectarian Christianity at its center. A twenty-minute drive each day through the apricot orchards and hills took David and me to the school from the home my father built for us on a hilltop above Los Altos. It had huge plate glass windows overlooking the San Francisco Bay to the east and Black Mountain and the historic Maryknoll Monastery on the west.

I entered Stanford University as a freshman in the fall of 1951, just short of my eighteenth birthday. My brother, David, entered as a junior. David began the Peninsula Covenant Church in the City of Burlingame immediately. The following year the new church bought the lovely but vacated Redeemer Lutheran Church building in Redwood City.

For my first year at Stanford I was immediately enrolled in the mandatory Western Civilization course. During the first quarter I was asked to join a select group of less than ten students to engage in independent studies for the rest of the year. It greatly challenged my faith as ancient history attempted to debunk biblical authenticity. I spent much time trying to salvage my faith in the university library. By God's grace I held on and grew. It was an interesting group. One bright co-ed was "Jinx" Patterson. No one at Stanford would be a name dropper, yet I asked what her father did. She smiled and said he was a small-town politician in Oregon. Only in my senior year did I learn that Oregon Governor Paul Patterson had spent a weekend at Stanford visiting his daughter "Jinx."

One of many friends was lovely Diane Goldman. I had a number of classes sitting next to her over the next four years—followed by coffee almost daily at the Student Union. She was Jewish, and I felt I should not date a non-Christian, but we were good friends. She eventually married and became Diane Feinstein, California's distinguished senior senator. I read an article about her in Redbook in which she said that her father was Jewish and mother Russian Orthodox. She chose Judaism but mentioned that she had almost become an evangelical Christian. I have often wondered whether I was either the source of or the hindrance to that decision. We have occasionally sent greetings to each over the years.

But infamous connections arose there too. Gene Scott was getting his PhD in the philosophy of education. Trained as a schoolteacher, he had a Pentecostal background. During university days he was active in both InterVarsity and our Peninsula Covenant Church. Some years after graduation he drew huge crowds as a Christian apologist. He took over two television stations—one in Glendale and then in San Francisco. He became more egocentric and bombastic. After a broken marriage and perpetual war with the Internal Revenue Service, he eventually lost his TV licenses, but continued on nationally through thousands of house churches connected by satellite. It was both frustrating and entertaining to watch him carry on disputes with outrage and even profanity while smoking his pipe. He passed away a few years ago.

Courses and Teachers

I had a psychology major. Because so many students wanted an easy major, the department put a brain-killer required course into the curriculum known as Psychological Statistics. I had to get advanced math to take the course, and a professor at San Jose State trying to finish his PhD had to take the course. During the final exam this professor was caught cheating and then committed suicide. For some reason I passed. My project for Experimental Psychology was entitled, "Orthodox Religious Conversion and Manifest Anxiety." I took the Taylor Manifest and Anxiety Scale of the Minnesota Multi-Phasic Personality Inventory and correlated it with a random sample of evangelical students in InterVarsity Fellowship. It passed with flying colors, and demonstrated that the converted Stanford students had a significantly lower level of manifest anxiety than the average population. The statistical formula was complex, but it was highly affirmed by a faculty circle with the suggestion that it would make a good subject for an expanded PhD dissertation.

Teaching my course in Theory of Personality was young Dr. Albert Bandura, who has become one of psychology's foremost scholars. He has done significant work with behavioral change and positive psychology. He also took part in the program of the Pacific Institute of Seattle that trains corporate heads and athletes to perfect their skills. I became a good friend of the institute's founder, Lou Tice, before his death in 2012. Along with the high caliber of the faculty, though, Stanford was rigidly empirical, and the endless use of statistical studies became tedious. One day I passed the huge computer center in the basement of the Cubberly Education Building, I heard my teacher Sid Segal bellowing a string of obscenities. He cried, "More than 90 percent of all psychological studies are statistically invalid!" Although I had already taken enough courses to claim my major, I abandoned these studies for philosophy.

In philosophy, I took to the history of ideas like a duck to water—a tradition that I have made a lifelong hobby. In Greek philosophy, I took a course on Aristotle from John David Goheen, chairman of the department, who was often called "the Great White Father." The going was tedious, but it laid a foundation by which to compare all subsequent philosophic developments. In our four-hour written exam, he simply wrote on the chalkboard, "Write an interesting article on Aristotle." He immediately left the room to catch a plane to Tokyo to deliver lectures.

I took my modern philosophy from Professor Donald Davidson, who has since become regarded as America's most eminent philosopher. He was a militant logical positivist, claiming that any facts that could not be established by the evidence of the five senses were simply nonsense. He was the professor that taught about David Hume and his eighteenth-century attack on the arguments for God's existence. When he concluded, he asked, "Is there anyone here that can now advance a single reason to believe in God?" Intimidated and insecure, I was too cowardly to raise my hand. I did go underground by inserting my hand under my Stanford jacket and slightly lifted my arm.

In my senior year I took a single course in speech. Somewhat emboldened, I entered Stanford's annual Forensic Oratory Contest. My oration presented evidence for the resurrection of Jesus Christ. I won second prize, and my instructor told me that my faith was not the reason for the second placement. Perhaps that success marked a partial comeback from my earlier weakness.

My greatest instructor was John Leland Mothershead. Like Goheen, he had studied the history of ideas under England's famous C. I. Lewis. I took Medieval and Nineteenth-Century Philosophy from him, as well as a course titled Theories of Moral Value. He was a most conscientious and clear teacher. My term papers invariably had nearly as much handwritten notes as the original paper. One day he apologized for not having our papers back. He said, "Mr. Larsen has said something about Kant's famous 'categorical imperative' that puzzled me . . . I stayed up all night rereading the book and concluded that Larsen was right."

When discussing St. Augustine, he took on the entire class defending Augustine's argument for the existence of the soul. Finally even the most vehement skeptics were silent. He said, "Augustine here has advanced the most perfect argument that I have ever found in philosophy." He argued persuasively for any view he was presenting, but warned us not to infer from his spirited defense of Marx any indication that he was a communist. He was an agnostic, but reflected that at the end of their lives, many atheist philosophers had turned to God. I have also been observing this ever since.

I often ate a bag lunch on the lawn at the Stanford Student Union with doctoral student in nuclear physics Whalen George. Other grad students often joined us. From time to time we would be joined by Nobel laureate Wolfgang Panofsky. All of this talk was above my head, so I provided the comic relief. One day I asked "Wolfie," as we called him, about the difference between theoretical physics and experimental physics, "What is the difference?" He gave a brief, clear answer. I then declared, "In that case I should infinitely prefer being a theoretical physicist." He then asked me why, knowing that I was in pre-theology. I replied, "Because theoretical physics is so much like theology—one does not need to be impeded by the facts!" He then rolled over on the ground with laughter. Such is my contribution to the world of physics.

Christ at Stanford

Although thoroughly skeptical and at times antagonistic, the atmosphere at Stanford was the bedrock of my greatest period of spiritual growth. I became active with Stanford Christian Fellowship, which at that time was an active chapter of InterVarsity Christian Fellowship. I became active in the leadership, often spending an afternoon a week visiting followers and seekers on the vast floors of Encina, the men's freshman dormitory. Among others, I became a close friend of Don Lunde, who became active in the fellowship. He later became professor of forensic psychiatry at both the Stanford Law School and Medical School. I would often read of him over the years as a top forensic witness in sensational murder trials.

I became close friends with grad students Ken Lincoln, Don Robbins, and Bruce Forsman, who shared the servants' quarters above the horse stables of a large Woodside estate. We called it the Barn. I joined them in active ministry each Sunday morning at Log Cabin Ranch, the young men's detention facility for delinquents from San Francisco and San Mateo Counties. High in the redwoods behind Stanford, it housed approximately sixty young men. Its director was a man named Shay. With a graduate degree from Harvard, he was a confirmed agnostic. But he saw Christian faith as very important in the rehabilitation of these young miscreants. We would always mingle with the boys for a couple of hours afterward each week. I remembered how troubled many of them were. I think of one young man who broke down, telling me how he went joy-riding, stealing a car. When fleeing the police he ran through an intersection, totally paralyzing the woman driver of another car. He sobbed and sobbed: "I will never forgive myself—I will never forgive myself." While I visited him at his mother's home later in San Francisco, I felt that praying with him for forgiveness and cleansing was at least my feeble effort to turn this young teenager to Christ.

But there is no assured success. I remember another fourteen-year-old. Thad had been at the ranch for some months in deep depression. I asked if he wanted forgiveness and strength in Christ. But he merely looked down without speaking, while shaking his head negatively. Six months later the newspapers reported that he was found hanging by his neck on a tree at Sequoia High School in Redwood City.

I formed deep, lifelong friendships with the team from the Barn, including Ken Lincoln and Don Robbins. Ken and Don were with me all sixteen years I spent as pastor at Peninsula Covenant. Another close friend, Everett Bruckner, went on to Stanford Medical School, later becoming chair of Hematology and Histology at Emory University Medical School. From there he moved to spend some years as a medical missionary for the HCB hospital in Quito, Ecuador. I reconnected with him in retirement as he was finishing his career at Loma Linda University, an hour from our home in the desert. With the initial military victory in the Afghan war, he led a team of physicians in reestablishing that nation's only medical school.

One of the greatest spiritual experiences arose from a daily prayer meeting in an alcove of Stanford's historic Memorial Church. Each day Professor Nanny would play J. S. Bach during the lunch hour on the chapel's massive Victorian organ. Joining me were three brothers: the youngest was Bill Clark, a Methodist from Texas. The second was Phil Getchel, an heir to the Hormel family fortune and National Junior Golf Champion. The third was Bob Evans, captain of Stanford's baseball team and president of the Inter-Fraternity Council. The meeting grew to fifteen, then to twenty each noon. We felt drawn to it, something I had not previously experienced. The four of us then went to a second 8 a.m. prayer meeting each morning in the garden outside the Memorial Auditorium.

The movement began to show real signs of awakening, and soon our young leaders were giving witness in the fraternities on campus. The year after my graduation, that morning prayer meeting continued to meet outside Florence Moore, the women's dormitory. Attendance averaged close to eighty.

Bob and Phil began to feel the burden of mission in Brazil. Bob went on to Princeton Seminary, graduated first in his class, and went on to teach at a Presbyterian seminary in Brazil. Phil joined me at Fuller Seminary—a strange thing for an active Episcopalian in those days, he later confided in me. He said, "I came to my first InterVarsity meeting looking for good-looking girls." You needed a song leader for the Sunday worship at Log Cabin Ranch. I was no Christian, but I came along. He laughed out loud, asking, "You remember that crazy Sunday? You told the story of David and Bathsheba—my face began to burn with embarrassment. I was using my imagination and began to cross the stream toward the story's conclusion—I realized that I should never have started—my metaphor was outrageous." Phil said, "But when you asked if anyone would like to receive Jesus for the forgiveness of their sins, I was afraid to raise my hand. I prayed the prayer—that was my new birth!" Phil went on to run an Episcopal orphanage in the Chaco of Brazil. These men not only influenced me greatly, but also were gallant soldiers of the cross.

SUMMERS IN THE FOREST

Before turning to my days at Fuller Seminary, I would like to tell about how I spent four summers working in the forests of the McCloud River Lumber Company during my Stanford and Fuller years. Father had decided to make a man out of me, feeling that, given my existence at an elite university and a hothouse home environment, I needed exposure to the real world. He insisted I look for a summer job away from home and offered to recommend me for work in the logging operations of the McCloud River Lumber Company on the slopes of Mount Shasta, California. It was one of the companies in the consortium of lumber companies of which my father was CFO. After school was I out, I hopped the Shasta Daylight train to Dunsmuir, California. I was greeted at the station by the McCloud sheriff. McCloud was an entirely company-owned town—all the homes, stores, schools, churches, and the hospital.

He deposited me at Camp Kenyon, the large logging camp twenty miles beyond McCloud. I lived in one of the little two-man cabins with only a wood stove. Water could be gotten at a pipe stand shared by several houses, there being no indoor plumbing. The siren would sound at 4:30 a.m., and we would eat in the cook-house and clamber aboard a steel-clad candy wagon. It would deposit us at the loading site along the railroad where a steam jammer would load logs onto flatcars. We would then follow the D-8 bulldozers to the site of the felled timber. I then worked as a Choker setter and Rigor, fastening steel cable onto thirty-two-foot log sections and hooking them onto the logging arches towed by the tractors. It was hard, dirty, and dangerous work. At first I was afraid it would kill me, and then I was afraid it wouldn't. A Mexican logger working with me shook his head and told me, "Go back home, you fool kid, before you kill yourself."

My cabin mate, "Little Ollie," was the "Bull buck" in charge of the log buckers. During the summer two-week shutdown I was put on the lopping crew, using a double-bitted axe to cut down slash—branches left on the ground. I wore myself through three blisters in one day—and a chronically sore shoulder. I noticed how experienced loggers could sharpen their axes and cut through huge sections of trees with only two bites. I took forever and finally made the cut—but it looked like a beaver had gnawed it. I found I consumed a five-gallon water bag in less than a day. Then I saw how the loggers dumped salt into their water bags as they left breakfast. It was salt thirst—not water thirst—which no amount of water could quench.

Pondosa

I then moved to the huge permanent logging camp known as Pondosa. It was really a small town. I bunked with a hand-bucker who used a huge crosscut saw ("Swede Fiddle"). These were the last of these old-timers in the West who had not yet turned to gas-powered crosscuts. He was a kindly man, but a dedicated communist revolutionary. He dropped candy bars on my bed after work each night and read long history books of the United States and Russia. Since I was a Stanford student, I thought I could easily make mincemeat out of his ignorance. Instead, he was way ahead of me. He possessed exceptional knowledge and argumentation. He never even began to convince me, but I did gain respect for his continual study of history.

I was next assigned to the Survey Crew, laying out p-lines for new rail spurs into the virgin timber. It was in the Bear Creek tract, which was regarded as the most magnificent stand of ponderosa and sugar pine in the West.

Here the bears were always stealing our lunches. We would spring the knapsacks upwards on a bending small tree beyond the bears' grasp. One day, however, the lunches for the entire crew were emptied except for one orange. How the bears accomplished this we could never discover.

Following us were the powder crews, setting dynamite charges to prepare the way for grading and track laying. They could not detonate the charges until after we had all left the site each day. But one day they set them off while we were still exiting. Huge boulders, logs, and stumps kept flying at us until we finally escaped safely. We were no longer called the "Survey Crew." Rather, we became the "Survivor Crew.

Since McCloud did not bother with white fir trees, only the pine, the fir trees were milled at the Pondosa site by Cheney Grant in their small pond and sawmill. The only university student at the entire camp was Richard Dix Jr. He operated the log unloader at the Cheney Grant Mill. We were tablemates in the McCloud cookhouse morning and evening. He was the son of the then-deceased famous movie star Richard Dix (*For Whom the Bell Tolls*). Richard Dix Jr. was a student at UC Santa Barbara. I felt the need to share Christ with him, but found myself too insecure. He was to leave for school a couple of days before me, I went to his cabin over Saturday and Sunday determined to share Christ, but he had taken the weekend in Fall River. Monday was his last day. When I got off the candy wagon, I went immediately to buy a coke and candy bar at the company store. The clerk said, "Did you hear what happened to young Richard Dix today?" He then told me that when Dix pulled the unload lever, the safety lines failed and he was crushed to death under eight logs. I have never forgotten this.

Hackamore

I graduated from Stanford the following year. The commencement speaker was Dag Hammarskjöld, Secretary General of the United Nations. I embarked the next day to work as a firefighter on the Modoc National Forest, the Eastern portion of which was still McCloud River Lumber Company land. I arrived from Alturas the next day to a former Civilian Conservation Corps camp, where there was still a US Forest Service fire suppression crew station. Having now finished the university, I embarked on my career the next day by digging outhouses for the large fire crew training camp!

When all the trainees left, I was to be on a tank truck operation for a five-man crew. Our foreman, Joel Stevens led us, while his wife, Bea, was the cook. Joining me was my Christian classmate Lawson Warburton. We then spent two weeks hardening up by digging fences around water holes on the Modoc Plateau. These stout pillars held the cattle back from the water holes and only allowed the sheep to get under the wires. The reservoirs had a chemical seal that kept the water from seeping down, thus drying up the water holes. Cattle, with their much heavier hooves, could break the seal that prevented seepage, so these fences were needed. It was backbreaking work in 100-degree heat. The dry gumbo was nearly as hard as concrete; holes for the fence anchors could only be drilled by eleven steel pinch-bars. The whole area was sheep country, open-range sheep country. Basque sheepherders from Spain who spoke only the Basque language tended the sheep. They had only a couple of mules and a couple of dogs; they camped as they followed the herds over the rocky, arid plateau of scrub pine juniper trees. They were very shy and tried to hide from us whenever we approached. What a unique lifestyle.

We were trained to use the compass to plot fires on the map, often climbing trees to get bearings from the lookouts by using reflective mirrors. Often we would sleep outside in huge fire camps that also included Arizona Indians and convict labor. We could often go more than twenty hours before relief. An allergist told that I never got ill because physical hardness and my self-administered allergy shots protected me!

White Horse

The next summer I was made foreman of the US Forest Fire Suppression Crew at White Horse. This was a former logging camp of the McCloud River Lumber Company, which had logged all the great timber from this 60,000-acre tract. The town had been moved, leaving only a Forest Service station and a station house for a steam locomotive, together with a house for the locomotive tender on the McCloud River Railroad. I was given a Dodge Power Wagon with a water tank, together with three crewmen. I received a map and a policy manual from the District Ranger. We were stationed more than thirty miles away by dirt road through the forest. We had no electricity. We did have running water, but no water heater. Instead we were given a wood stove with a water pipe running through the stove's firebox. Being a station of less than five, there was no cook. I took on the job of doing the cooking on a wood stove. I even learned to do an angel food cake on a wood stove!

There was a telephone from a crank receiver on which I would call the closest lookout for instructions each day, and we could have the week's groceries and mail sent in once a week. Each morning I began my work at 4 a.m. It was so cold; at that elevation, frost still appears in the month of

August. I would load the firebox on the stove to heat the water for showers and cook breakfast. When the station house was warm, the water hot, and breakfast ready, I would rouse my small crew from bed and begin the day's work, carefully laying out the work to be accomplished on the coming day.

The unpaved roads—former logging runs—were sometimes more than six inches deep in dirt. This created a disgusting and smothering cloud wherever we went. One day on patrol I spotted a mountain lion with two whelps crossing the road in front of us. Without thinking, I stupidly grabbed a brush hook and followed her into the forest. Lava rock walls rose up on either side of the path, and I realized that the mother merely had to double back and could leap on me from behind. Common sense bade me make a hasty retreat. My crew had locked themselves in the pumper with the windows rolled up. Once again discretion was the better part of valor!

We received a call from the lookout one noon that a fire had broken out on land owned by Shasta Forest Products Company adjacent to the White Horse tract. We managed to get there in about two hours. But the climb was steep. I finally had to use the winch to haul us up the steep ascent. The blaze had started at a logging site after the loggers had left that day. I had to use the winch to pull aside some of the logs. We battled all night, but were relieved in the morning when more crew and bulldozers arrived. When released, we discovered that we had to descend an extremely steep grade. Terrified, my crew abandoned our vehicle, leaving me to slowly inch my way down the incline. The next day the district ranger came by with a congratulatory message from the Shasta Forests Lumber Company, thanking us for containing what could have become a major fire. Feeling highly affirmed, I was then humbled by the ranger reminding me how valuable the pumper truck was and that I had no business endangering government property trying to rescue private timberlands!

There were other fire calls and fire camps; I grew in my understanding. Two of my team members were from the Carlsberg Cattle Ranch near Alturas. Years later I discovered that they had come to Los Angeles and had developed one of Southern California's largest real estate development firms. On one fire I was on the line with a mop-up crew together with prisoners from San Quentin. One of my crew had swung his axe in a glancing blow, nearly severing his foot. We tried to stanch the flow, but a huge convict was loaned to me to take him down the mountain and to the hospital. It was difficult to help him hobble along between the two of us. At last the convict, a three-time loser for drug addiction, just picked him up gently and carried him like a large child the rest of the way down the steep incline. We finally got him safely to the little hospital in the town of Tule Lake and went on our way.

Angeles Crest

My final summer in the forest was in the Angeles National Forest in Southern California. I was already attending Fuller Seminary, and it was four miles above Foothill Boulevard emerging from the city of La Cañada—less than six miles from Fuller. It was known as the Angeles Crest Station, a gateway through the steep mountain pass that gave access to that huge mountainous wilderness. It was luxurious by many standards. I was the foreman and I had two tanker operators and a hoseman. Once again I did the cooking. We had a huge initial attack zone. With a mammoth four-wheel-drive Marmon Herrington cab-over pumper, we would respond to calls with red lights and siren over the full range to the desert on the far side. We would also fight fires along the spine of the mountain range. When a fire occurred in the front of the mountain ranges, we would drive forty or so miles on either the East or West Foothill Expressway through the heavy traffic of the Los Angeles basin.

Our spring training took my crew high up on a ridge of Big Tujunga Canyon. From there we were to cut a trail all the way down for miles to where it would hit the river and a dirt road. Such hard labor was extremely difficult in the heat. At the end of the first day we thought it would be easier to leave by descending to the streambed and walking out instead of climbing all the way back up the trail. When going down though, we were faced by impassable thorny thickets that cut us and blocked our way. Before nightfall we finally emerged on the lower road, where we were picked up and taken back to the station.

One morning we received a call from the dispatcher that a target drone had been flying over Mount Pacifico. The trailing jets fired on it and missed, their rockets setting off a mammoth fire—one which was very hard to get to. We were stationed on the ridge top with the fire racing toward us. We received a radio call that sixteen hotshots from the Chilao campground were trapped by the fire below us. (These were all Papago Indian firefighters.) My crew was too frightened to drag the hoses down the canyon for fear of being cut off. I called them to throw me the hose. When I got down the almost vertical slope, I discovered that they had given me the wrong end of the hose. The fire was beginning to send its tongues within a few feet of the hose, so I hurriedly pulled myself up by the hose, and called for another one—this time with the right nozzle. But as I came down I realized the great danger of the hoses being burned off by the encroaching flames. I made it, though, and knocked down the flames surrounding the trapped firefighters and gingerly sprayed my hose as I climbed back up to safety. That evening I was assigned to set a backfire all along the firebreak to halt the fire. It was the most intense heat I had ever experienced as I moved along with a torch for a great distance touching off the inferno that saved the day. The story of the fire was covered in a national men's magazine including a picture of my tank truck operator standing on our pumper while I was over the edge. Thus ended my adventure as a forest fire fighter. I then decided that I liked setting fires rather than fighting them—and committed myself to a lifelong task as a spiritual incendiary.

FULLER SEMINARY

I entered Fuller Theological Seminary in Pasadena three months after my graduation from Stanford in 1955. I was twenty years old at the time. During my three years there, I lived in Taylor dormitory, named for the famous China missionary Hudson Taylor. It was one of several mammoth old houses adjacent to the campus. My roommate for three years was Jim Guier, a basketball star from Seattle Pacific University. Active in Young Life, he joined other Young Life leader students studying at the seminary. I soon was asked to teach a high school Sunday school class at the Eagle Rock Covenant Church. A church of more than two hundred members, the class was so unruly that three teachers had already quit. I met the raucous crowd and began to teach. One student began bouncing a basketball while I was teaching. I simply walked over and took the basketball away. For some reason I never had a bad day after that. The class grew in the second year to more than eighty each Sunday. The student leadership of the Young Life clubs all brought their friends to the class, some became Christians. In my zeal, though, I went too strongly at one young leader and saw him pull away. This has left me cautious for the rest of my life about pressurized commitment to Christ.

The student body at Fuller was under three hundred students at the time, but has since grown to an enrollment of several thousand to become the largest nondenominational seminary in the world. The faculty was superb. The first year entailed a four-day-a-week morning class on the English Bible under Professor Wilbur Smith. Coming from a secular university, it was salutary to proceed through a survey of the entire Bible. Bible majors from schools like Wheaton felt it was redundant. I ate it up. Smith was inimitable in his teaching eloquence. An amazing bibliophile with a private library of 25,000 books, when asked if he had read them all, he would reply with clear evasion: "Some of them twice." He modeled a passionate interest in Scripture and great preaching. Since I was in constant debate with high Calvinists, I one day kept at it without knowing Dr. Smith had entered the room. Stunned into silence, he looked over his glasses and muttered, "And men wonder that Balaam's Ass could speak!" His wry sense of humor left me laughing rather than offended. Years later, Elizabeth and I often had Sunday dinner with him and his wife at the home of Gladys and Milt Moberg. She was his one-time secretary. He was as entertaining at the dinner table as in class.

New Testament courses were taught by Everet Harrison and George Ladd. Harrison, gentle and deeply devout, was a master of the text. He knew the entire New Testament by heart, together with the textual variants. I found his pre-class prayers profoundly moving. George Ladd was the opposite. He was a relentless and demanding scholar. This was too much for some students, but I always thrived under a demanding teacher. He later won acclaim among world scholars of the New Testament for his superb insights and scholarship.

George Ladd was a most disciplined scholar. His research was on the kingdom of God. His book, *A Biblical Theology of the New Testament*, launched a new era of conservative New Testament scholarship.[1] Even liberals see his work as something of a landmark. I took some of his courses, including graduate courses in Apocrypha and Pseudepigrapha and in Christology in later years. The latter kept me grounded in my later studies on the subject.

Studying the Old Testament was more difficult. We had to learn Hebrew, with its entirely foreign alphabet and many cognate words. Dr. William S. LaSor used the inductive method in teaching the subject, startling us during the first class in reading the text. He simply footnoted the rule for the word or point of grammar, teaching us through repetition the rules and language of Hebrew. Second-year Hebrew was another matter as it was taught by Gleason Archer. He had won the Latin and Greek Oratory prize each year he studied at Harvard. He had mastered twenty languages. But he was the opposite of LaSor in that he used the traditional deductive method. It was starting all over with Hebrew. He was meticulous. Instead of letters for the vowels, the Hebrew Bible has small vowel points below or above the consonants. He would take off one-tenth of a point for every missed vowel point in the text. A fellow student was a studious Chinese student, Shim Pei Higuchi. After Archer wrote a text on the board, gentle Shim Pei raised his hand, saying, "Doctor Archer, you have mistaken vowel point in last word." Archer looked twice, erased, and corrected—then dismissed class.

Archer's Old Testament Introduction was a back breaker. He made us memorize the entire history of the documentary hypotheses developed

---

1. Ladd, *Theology of the New Testament*.

in the nineteenth century by Karl Graf and Julius Wellhausen. This history was exceedingly complex and demanding. When he finished teaching the course, he concluded succinctly. He declared, "Virtually every date for the Old Testament and its sources has been claimed and reversed a number of times during the last century and a half. The studies have their value, but they in no way provide us with real certainty about their often destructive theories."

Lars Grasberg taught Pastoral Care. A psychologist, he was the healthiest minded person I have ever met. His daughter later married Wes Michelson Grasberg, who later became head of the Reformed Church of America. These were the earlier days of the pastoral counseling movement. He adapted much of its methodology for a clearly evangelical context.

Carl F. H. Henry taught me both epistemology and ethics. This giant was sometimes difficult for students who, unlike me, had no philosophical background. I remember in Biblical Ethics he argued that abortion would be justified in rape and incest—a position abhorrent to more conservative pro-lifers. He was personally kind and devout, ready to witness to a stranger on a park bench.

The greatest of the teachers was E. J. Carnell. His works on apologetics were the most helpful of all my studies. He lectured without notes on the history of doctrine.

He suffered from bouts of acute depression; I have never quite recovered from his untimely death. His mother and daughter attended my church even after his death.

I sought to continue the benefits of Fuller's Greek and Hebrew requirements that I deeply value. During my Orangevale years I spent a half hour each on Greek and Hebrew each day. The years at Fuller gave me a classical theological education. Though broadly reformed, there was much opportunity for a free Lutheran pietist evangelical like myself to flourish.

EAGLE ROCK

I took my first church assignment a year after my graduation from Fuller. That was 1958. I was only twenty-four years old and single. I had been working as a volunteer youth director at the Eagle Rock Covenant Church, located in a beautiful Tudor-style facility in Eagle Rock, a community between Pasadena and Glendale. Upon graduation I became full-time Minister of Youth and Education. My salary was $300 dollars per month, and I had a studio apartment in Glendale. The church had just over two hundred members. The senior pastor was Lloyd Tornell. He was certainly one of the most kind and devout persons I have ever known. His wife and family were always affirming. The Covenant's California Conference Superintendent, Gordon Nelson, was a member of the church. His three teenage children— Arlys, Gordon, and Jim—were in my youth group. That was a year of learning and mistakes, but lifelong friendships emerged. The families of Dick Bourell, Bob Flanders, Gust Magnuson, Lars Almquist, and Jerry Howard were among those with whom I developed lifelong friendships.

4

Orangevale

DURING THE YEAR I served at Eagle Rock Church, the California Conference held its annual meeting atour church. There I met Dick Sandquist of the First Covenant Church of Sacramento. He had just begun to plant a daughter church in Orangevale near the mammoth new Aerojet General Corporation's solid and liquid rocket plants. The 2,000 new employees had begun a population boom. Dick had begun a weekly Bible study in the near-by community. He asked me if I would be interested in being the first pastor. Superintendent Gordon Nelson, seeing the work I was doing, immediately approved my going for an interview.

Dick Sandquist became one of my closest friends over the years. He and his wife, Isabelle, had seven children, who also have remained friends ever since. During my Orangevale years he and I had a luncheon every week. He was self-educated, with a relentless reading habit that kept him abreast of most things theological, social, and political. He had a gifted sense of humor and splendid preaching skills. His gregarious nature was infectious. When we walked down the streets together in downtown Sacramento, someone would greet us on nearly every block. Often we would stop at the legislature, and would inevitably be greeted by at least one legislator who knew him by name. His death thirty years later has always left a hole in my heart.

On the appointed Sunday I preached morning and evening at the First Covenant Church. Following the evening service I met with the Orangevale Committee from the church. I, of course, was full of youthful confidence and arrogance. I was then asked by a senior engineer from Aerojet, "Young man, just how much experience have you had in starting new churches?" I was advised years before by my father that when caught in a trap, I should tell a funny story. I replied, "That reminds me of a story: A young woman who was something of know-it-all was bragging about her horsemanship skills to her friends. 'I will have you know that I was on the Olympic dressage team!' One of her friends, with a wicked gleam in her eyes, declared, 'That's wonderful! Join us tomorrow afternoon at the local stable where we can all ride together! Let's meet at the stables for a group ride next Friday afternoon.' On that afternoon a terrified young woman arrived early and begged and begged the stable master, 'Please give the gentlest horse you have because I have never been on a horse before.' Replied the stable master, 'I have just the horse for you—it has never ridden before and you both can start out together!'" A senior patriarch who had a stammer as the result of a stroke retorted to me, "You rwrrremind me of PPPaul RRRRood!" Flattered that I should be likened to the great Covenant pulpit master of a generation ago, I said, "Thanks you so much." His answer was quick: "WWWho SSSaid ThThThat was a CCCompliment?" Humbled, I was nevertheless invited to become the founding pastor of the Redeemer Covenant Church of Orangevale.

SEPTEMBER 1959

Dow and Mary Coffman had a lovely home, where I stayed through Christmas. He was the chief engineer on the Hawk guided missile. They were two of the most gentle and godly leaders I had ever met. Though she did not have formal training, Mary was one of the most effective counselors I have known. I would refer troubled women to her after I had met with them two or three times. Ultimately Dow went to work for Covenant Retirement Centers.

The Conference had secured a five-acre olive orchard at 6800 East Main Street in unincorporated Orangevale. It was mixed with modest homes and small pastures. The boom left no rental space for worship. Hence, it was necessary to build a small facility quickly. Two contractors from the First Covenant Church began immediately in September to build a small classroom unit with a central hall seating 150 people. By the first of October, with unpainted walls and no electricity, we gathered for worship. I preached on Psalm 127, "Except the Lord build the house . . ." I preached behind a thirty-inch tall flower stand with seventy-eight people were in attendance. The worship unit began immediately and was finished for occupancy that Christmas. A memorable Christmas Eve prayer service marked the day.

The builders were John Swenson and Harry Gammelgard from the Sacramento First Covenant Church. They soon decided to join the new group. They and their families became lifelong friends. While serving later in Pasadena, John came down with cancer of the lip and spent several years undergoing repeated surgeries at City of Hope. He was noble and positive until he finally succumbed. Their youngest son, Bob, is a cardiologist near Camas, Washington.

I cannot forget Al and Ethel Molen, as well as their children. Al was a manager at Aerojet and a graduate of North Park College. He was also a graduate of the Chicago Conservatory of Music. Ethel played the organ. The music at the new church was excellent, including the choir. I soon came to realize the importance of music and worship in the building of the body of Christ.

ADVENTURES IN EVANGELISM

I was by now living in a small apartment of my own. Being single, I could spend most evenings calling on prospects and newcomers. This was one of the most productive times in my ministry. I would often take a hand-marked New Testament to each home and have them read the Bible verses that take them through steps toward the new birth. I would ask each person what the verse meant after they read it back to me. I would ask at the end whether they wanted Jesus to forgive their sins and grant them eternal life. If the answer was yes, I would then ask them to pray that prayer or repeat after me the sinner's prayer. On one evening I made house calls as scheduled at 7, 8, and 9 p.m. On that evening the entire family in each of those homes gave their hearts to Christ. They all became active and growing believers in our church.

The Engineer

An engineer and his wife came for marital counseling. They had no Christian background. When asked if they would like to become Christ followers, they said yes. When I asked the man to pray with me, he began trembling and shaking. When I asked what was troubling him, he gasped, "I am afraid!" After prayer he found peace. I was struck by the fact that leaving all to follow Christ was a serious and sometimes frightening step. This bright young intellectual knew something of its awesome significance.

Shirley

But life could get complicated. I remember when the senior engineer at the liquid rocket plant at Aerojet and his wife professed faith. Some months later, his wife, Shirley, came to me and said that her husband would throw a fit when she asked for the divorce papers of his previous marriage. She finally hired an attorney. The report was devastating. His list of academic and scientific degrees was totally bogus, and there were four other undisclosed marriages. I prepared for the confrontation by having John Swenson—a man of great size and strength—sit in the adjoining room. When I confronted the man he immediately leaped out of his chair and physically assaulted me. Fortunately, he was unable to make the leap across my desk and John entered the room to calm things down. I told Shirley she was under no obligation to still be married to this man. He professed penitence. They agreed to sit separately in church. I also insisted that he would have to register his prior divorces with the court. This was the crime of serial bigamy. Naturally it made headlines. How would the church react? For some months they appeared separately, and he sat apart from his wife and children. She finally decided that too much trust had been lost. He then rejected further counseling and left the church angry.

Shirley later moved to the East Bay. Years later she met me at a Conference Annual Meeting. She told me she was now happily married and worked as the office manager at a Covenant church. I then responded to her request to counsel with her teenage daughter. During Orangevale days only one person in the congregation ever made any indiscrete comments or questions. When the chips are down, the church so often shows itself as a redeeming community.

Dottie

Even grimmer was the case of a teenage girl who started coming to church. She came some weeks later trembling with fear and stress. Her father was also a senior engineer at Aerojet, yet with the complicity of the mother she was being forced to live in incest with her father. I consulted an attorney friend and we secretly took her down to the police and District Attorney's office. The parents had already reported her missing during the police interrogation. It again hit the papers. The man was charged with seven felonies and three misdemeanors. The wife was also charged on three counts of contributing to the delinquency of a minor. Out on bail, they visited my office three days later. They had a local pastor urging me to forgive them and get their daughter to retract her claims. I bluntly declined. Then began a series of threatening phone calls, including a number of threats to my life. I routinely called the police, who merely took note and said that nothing could be done unless there was a credible attempt. He subsequently went to prison for many years. She continued to be part of the church afterward.

The Inebriates

There could be an amusing side as well. I was studying for my sermon in my office at the church one Saturday evening. I heard the central church doors open and waited for someone to inquire. Hearing nothing, I found a couple kneeling on the floor before the cross. She was crying loudly. She said, "As a young woman I had a call to the mission field. Instead I married a man whose life I ruined. Now I am married again, and am ruining this man's life again—I need forgiveness." They both were drunk. I took them to my study, debating what I should do. I took an irrational chance and presented Jesus Christ. They both prayed the sinner's prayer. They rose up with joy, the woman asking, "Father, What time is 'mash' in the morning?" I mumbled, "Sunday at 11 a.m." They arrived at the service and continued faithfully thereafter! I visited their home adjacent to Phoenix Field, a small airport. They had a small plane right in back of the house. The house was full of white carpet and black walls with two electronic organs in the living room. Five tiny toy poodles paraded out from a bedroom and performed somersaults in sync. When one of them barked, the good lady shamed them and sent them back to the bedroom on command. They remained faithful worshippers until long after I left for the Pasadena Church.

Alice

Alice came to my study for an appointment. Young and attractive, she asked if she could be married in our church. I explained counseling procedures. When I asked her if she was a Christian, she indicated that she was not. I shared Christ with her and asked if she would like him to be her savior. She said yes. I then asked her whether her fiancé was a Christian, and she answered in the negative. I said that unless they were both followers of Christ I could not marry them. I asked if you had to choose between Jesus and Jay, her fiancé, which she would choose. A long silence followed, as great tears fell silently. Finally she said, "I choose Jesus." We had prayer. On the return for premarital counseling, Jay also received Christ—and celebrated the wedding with hope and joy. Fifty years later I returned to the church. There they both were—still active leaders in the church. Their grown children and teenage grandchildren were all likewise active in their Christian faith. The Lord honored that woman's faith.

David

David was brought by his teenage sister. She also brought her twenty-year-old brother. He was short and thin, with buckteeth. He had been dismissed from the army as mentally unfit. His sister told me that he had always been a problem to their mother with whom they lived in a nearby trailer park. When I visited the home, I was told by his angry mother that she found him totally impossible. She forced to him live in a shed outside the trailer. She then threw him out altogether. A few weeks later I exited a meeting at the local Rotary Club and found him staggering around the street. I asked him what the matter was. He replied that he had been sleeping all night in bowling alleys, but he had not eaten in four days. He exuded a noxious stench. I then called the police and asked for assistance, but the officer merely sought to entrap him into confessing to burglaries. I was so incensed that I filed a complaint with the sheriff's office. I took him to a large meal, then to my apartment, where I put him up for the night. Calling county welfare, I was informed that there were no programs for needy males over age eighteen.

I took him to my apartment and had him bathe and gave him the bed in my spare bedroom. He awoke in the middle of the night with violent stomach pains and retching. I again called the sheriff's office, but they refused to come. At that point I lost it and declared if they did not send help I would appear at the police station and take a statement with a reporter from the *Sacramento Bee* and then file it with *Sacramento Bee* and a grand jury. Twenty minutes later an ambulance came, and he was taken to the hospital. The mental health people indicated that he was not technically mentally ill and therefore there was no assistance available through the county welfare system. In desperation I called the State Department of Mental Hygiene. The counselor on the phone told me that section 600 of the State Welfare and Institutions Code required assistance to a dependent male over the age of eighteen. When I called again, the counselor told me to bring him into the state offices. They gave him a psychiatric examination. They then indicated that he was of normal intelligence, but the early rejection by his mother had left him so dependent that he would never be able to survive on his own. They therefore had him committed to the Stockton State Mental Hospital, where I would visit him from time to time. They gave him orthodontic braces, and I wondered what good thousands of welfare dollars spent on the hopeless would ever do. I would converse and pray with him— I could do nothing more.

While I was serving as pastor in Redwood City some fifteen years later, I stopped for lunch at a coffee shop in the City of Belmont. While dining, a well-groomed young man came up to me and asked, "Are you Rev. Larsen?"

I replied that I was, and then he identified himself as the man I had helped so many years before. He said that it helped when they found out he was good with animals. He then left the hospital and became a tender of racehorses in Idaho. He decided he liked people better and took a job as a salesman in a nearby shoe store. He smiled through his perfectly aligned teeth and said, "I am now assistant manager, and I will be married next month." Surely this was a God thing!

The Skeptic

Harvey was a magnificent soloist, singing for us from time to time. He had been a soloist with the Mormon Tabernacle Choir, but was a total skeptic. He was a top engineer at Aerojet General, where he was regarded by all as an exceptional genius. As we talked about faith from time to time, he said he could not accept any religion that rejected the idea that man could achieve salvation by his own efforts. Our conversations grew more personal and profound. He said that he had benefitted from seeing a psychiatrist who helped him to achieve by regressing him into his former incarnations. I said that this story was harder to believe than the resurrection of Christ. I also pointed out that despite his self-sufficiency he obviously needed some outside help. But he finally left us.

I was alarmed that a board-certified psychiatrist would be practicing such an absurd form of psychiatric treatment. I contacted the California State Board of Medical Examiners, who sent an investigator to my office. He took the report, and I later learned that this psychiatrist had left her medical practice. I was amazed that she subsequently ran and was elected Sacramento County Assessor.

Saints, Sinners, and Skeptics

I enjoyed work in the community and speaking to various groups. Most exciting was my experience with a club I started at nearby American River Junior College. I called it the Saints, Sinners, and Skeptics Club. I particularly enjoyed jousting with vocal doubters and skeptics. A number found Christ.

Cassidy

One hot summer afternoon, there was a knock on my study door. A blond teenager, thirteen or fourteen years old, walked in. He introduced himself to me as Cassidy. As he sat down he declared that his older sister had died some months earlier. He had never been to a church, but had been wondering about where she was and if he would ever see again. I shared Jesus with him and the story of the resurrection. When I asked him if he would like to accept Christ as his Savior he immediately said yes. I then led him through the sinner's prayer and prayed that he be given assurance. When we had finished, he sat silently for some time.

Suddenly he declared, "Man, this sure feels wicked!" A strange way to describe the gift of assurance, but the theology and the heart could not have been more eloquent.

Fayetta

Two miles from the church there was a dramatic twenty-acre site on the bluffs overlooking the American River. Its owner was the oldest licensed pharmacist in California. She remembered living through the famous San Francisco Earthquake in 1906. She and her friend were ardent rock hounds, filling every stair, bathroom, closet, and living space with the rocks they had collected from all over California. They belonged to a club of rock hounds known as the Rock Rustlers. She also was an avid student of Shakespeare and had some early folios in her large vault. She had adopted the theory that Shakespeare was only a pseudonym. She declared, "Frances Bacon was the real author of the great plays." The beautiful property of hers also held an historical monument: California's first railway was constructed from the north bank of the American River to what was to be downtown Sacramento, twenty miles away. The engine was brought by ship around the cape. The engine house remained as a monument to that first rail line. Fayetta was determined to establish a retirement home for the elderly on the magnificent site she owned. She and her friend had built three apartment units overlooking the river.

She offered the property to the Covenant, and I got Paul Brandel and Nils Axelson of the Board of Benevolence to look over the site. Covenant Retirement Communities was given the site with a life occupancy agreement for both women. We also acquired five acres down along the highway with a lovely stream running through it. There was a lovely house. We then built five lovely retirement units along the creek. Our first church chair, Dow Coffman, had taken retirement and ran the program for many years both at Hearthstone (the name of the project) and later at our centers in San Diego and Turlock.

Covenant President Milton Engebretson was navigating through tough economic times and ruled that the Covenant could not extend its credit lines further in the multimillion-dollar development plan. The property was sold to a developer. Subsequently the land was developed as one of the luxury home projects overlooking the American River. Not all projects can be completed successfully.

LEAVING

Over those four and a half years of pastoral work at Orangevale, we completed three buildings and had a Sunday morning attendance of approximately 250. We had become self-supporting in two years. God had been good to us throughout that time of fruitful harvest and deep learning.

Then I received a call to the large Pasadena Covenant Church. I felt led to leave Orangevale and I accepted the call from Pasadena Covenant. Subsequently, the hard times brought on by recession and the closing of Aerojet General's two large rocket plants left more than twenty thousand people unemployed. But the church survived and flourishes to this day, in addition to assisting in the planting of several large neighboring churches.

I left in 1963. It was an emotionally wrenching experience. I carry the memories of so many serving co-workers and their families with me to this day. In my farewell sermon I told them they had all been good schoolteachers to me. I declared, "I have learned many things that will be useful as I move ahead to new ministries." Then I added, "And there are some things I have learned never to try again. I would like to one day plant another church—but not too soon!" Gordon Bunnell, a lifelong friend, said as I left, "Learning caution is fine. But never get so cautious that you lose your effectiveness."

5

Pasadena

In 1963, I left the Redeemer Covenant Church in Orangevale after four and a half years. I became the senior pastor of Pasadena Covenant Church and served there until the end of 1970, when I was called to be senior pastor at Peninsula Covenant Church. This pastorate lasted seven years. During these years I married and my two daughters arrived. I took additional courses from Fuller Seminary and taught a variety of classes. I also served as president of the Alumni Association.

In November of 1963, I had completed five years of pastoral service. I was in Springfield, Massachusetts, on a preaching mission at the local Covenant church, then pastored by my close friend Dick Sandquist. Seated in the parsonage living room that Saturday evening, we discussed various denominational matters. We had heard that the pulpit committee of the Pasadena church had thirty members. I laughed, declaring that if those thirty Swedes could ever agree on a candidate, it would be a sign of direct divine intervention! The phone rang. It was Roy Johnston, chair of the church. He stated that the pulpit committee had been meeting one evening a week since the church began—always and fundamentally for prayer. They had just taken a closed ballot to ascertain who were the top most likely candidates. He said that the vote was unanimous for me. I replied, "Roy, I think I had better stop by on my way home from Springfield."

THE CITY OF PASADENA

Pasadena, located at the base of the San Gabriel Mountains in the Los Angeles basin, is well over one hundred years old. It is the crown city of the

San Gabriel Valley. Originally it was filled with orange orchards. It became, however, the winter residence of many prominent people from the Midwest. For more than one hundred years it has been the site of the famous Tournament of Roses parade and the Rose Bowl of football fame each January 1. It is the home of the prestigious California Institute of Technology and Fuller Theological Seminary. The Huntington Library and Museum, and the Norton Simon Museum have helped make it a cultural center. In addition to residences for the wealthy, a growing portion of the city became home to serving classes, including African American, Swedish, Armenian, and Hispanic populations. With a deteriorating core and declining public schools, white flight sent large numbers of people to the adjacent suburbs of La Canada, San Marin, and Arcadia—all within ten minutes of the center of Pasadena. During the Marino 1960s the city began to reinvent itself. This has been largely successful, and the most rundown section of that time has now become a revitalized Old Town, attracting visitors from neighboring cities. In addition, it has always had some of the largest Protestant churches in their respective denominations.

PASADENA COVENANT CHURCH

The church had been founded in 1922 as a daughter church of the Mission Covenant Church Los Angeles. Its first organizers consisted of seven Swedish servant women from the mansions on the south side of the city and two Swedish carpenters. The small congregation, with the help and advice of an older Swedish contractor who wintered each year in the city, bought property on Lake Avenue, a major street running north and south, just six blocks above the historic Colorado Boulevard (of Rose Parade fame). They erected a small building seating 125 people, including the balcony. Above the choir loft was a large picture of a ladder painted from earth to heaven. It read, "This is none other than the House of God, and this is the gate of heaven," a quotation from Genesis 28,[1] the account of Jacob's vision at Bethel. So great a claim from so tiny a Swedish-speaking church! But it grew.

The Great Depression struck hardship on these believers. Despite the hardship, they found a way to meet a need of the church as well as local men without work. They decided to excavate a basement beneath the sanctuary. They dug it all by hand. Unemployed men could work for a dollar a day plus their lunch. The basement is used to this day. It has a good kitchen and an ample-sized room that acted as the first fellowship hall.

1. Gen 28:17.

In 1947, the church built its main sanctuary, a Monterey Colonial-style building directly on Lake Avenue. It seated approximately 500 people. More importantly, the church called a bright young pastor named Arvid Carlson, and his wife, Linnea. A man of consummate cheerfulness, social skill, and pulpit eloquence, he led the church out of an ethnic enclave into the mainstream of Southern California evangelicalism. He was to become a central leader in Southern California. He was the first professor of evangelism at Fuller Seminary. Prayer evangelist Armin Gesswein, a member of the church, led the prayer awakening at the first major Billy Graham Crusade in Southern California. He was also an excellent personal evangelist. He served for seventeen years until my arrival in Pasadena.

Among several prominent members, Dr. Carl F. H. Henry and his wife, Helga, were faithful attendees. She served as the church's director of Christian education. Their son, Paul Henry, grew up in the church and later succeeded Gerald R. Ford in the U.S. Congress. Also active was Bob Bowman, founder of the Far Eastern Broadcasting Corporation, and Paul Peterson, founder of the Eastern European Mission.

The church's Pastoral Search Committee had decided unanimously to call me! I received the call and began ministry in Pasadena in 1963, concluding it at the close of 1970.

DAUNTED

I had just turned twenty-five years old—too young in the minds of a number of members. With my usual bravado and inward trepidation, I acknowledged their apprehension, declaring, "I can assure you that my youth is one problem that time alone will solve!" Brash and bold on the outside, I was trembling on the inside. I was following the much-loved and popular Arvid Carlson, who had served with great passion and skill for seventeen years. The strong lay leadership tended to make me feel insecure rather than comfortable. I asked then-Covenant Secretary Milton B. Engebretson how I might be successful. He said, "Preach the gospel to them for a whole year without changing anything. They will then trust you to lead them in new directions!" Some of the best advice I ever received—and some that I have told younger pastors during my entire lifetime.

The church had about 430 members with a higher attendance. Most helpful to me was the music minister, Roland Tabell, who blessed us with his most important musical support during my tenure. Until his recent passing he gave me the greatest personal support as well. He and his wife, Betty, remained among our closest friends. Since I was single when I began, the church leased out the parsonage and rented a brand-new, one-bedroom apartment. Settling in, I soon found that the congregation had learned well how to love and support Pastor Carlson over his seventeen years with them. They had established a wonderful habit, and I became the object of their love, trust, and affection very soon.

Some did have their uncertainties. The church had a huge group of senior citizens called the Golden Years. Its chair was John Rylander, a retired contractor who sat with an earphone in the second row each Sunday. From time to time he would privately correct my use of the Greek or Hebrew. As chair of the Golden Years, he invited me to speak to the monthly meeting. He introduced me by saying, "I had it on good authority dat Pastor Larsen was sent here by Chicago to make dis into a liberal church. I have listened very carefully to every word he has spoken. I can assure all of you dat I have not heard vun liberal word since he came! I am happy to present him to you this evening!" So hearts opened overwhelmingly.

The church had a morning service as well as an evening service each Sunday. Soon an 8:30 service was added. My preaching was expository, following the traditional *lectio continua* format, covering each book on successive Sundays with occasional topical and holiday series.

The evening service was the most popular in town. Roland Tabell had something of a mini-concert and would sing before my message each week. We added an after-church dessert with a question-and-answer time each summer Sunday night. It was a delightful and successful innovation.

The church had now outgrown its exclusive Swedishness, but clung to the understanding of minorities among us. The local Armenians became anxious that their children find a place among English-speaking young people and so came in significant numbers. One was Paul Tahmisian, a lay preacher who brought his family. He held a Friday morning prayer breakfast at the church each week where businessmen and workers could come for a hearty breakfast and Bible study. This helped build a cadre of strong lay leaders and model fathers. Also present was a Chinese family. The Lowe family consisted of a widowed mother and three children. All the children were brilliant. The two sons were top leaders. Together they owned the prestigious Lowes Furniture store that sold elegant Chinese furniture. The eldest, Albert, became a significant leader and chair of the Pasadena School Board. The younger brother, Eugene, who had graduated from USC at seventeen years of age, became an attorney as well as a key leader in the church. He eventually served as moderator of the entire Covenant Church. One of Albert's sons graduated from Stanford, became a journalist, and won a Pulitzer Prize within two years.

MULTIPLE STAFF

Coming to a large church, I eagerly appreciated the importance of multiple staff to carry on the extensive work in the church. I previously had a part-time music director, but Roland Tabell was full time. A minister of visitation and a couple of part-time youth workers were a delight. I figured that they would all relieve me of the extraordinary burdens of the task. I was naive and had to undergo a steep learning curve. I assumed that multiple staff would allow me to spend most of my time in my pastoral duties and only minimal time in supervision. I believed in treating them kindly, but only meeting when they needed to be corrected. It is an all-too-frequent assumption of ministers who move into a multiple-staff ministry for the first time—one that means poor communication and often poor relationships. If you only meet with the staff member when there is a problem, relationships will eventually suffer.

I then decided to take a course offered by the American Management Association (AMA) on personnel supervision. It was a breakthrough. I learned the MacGregor approach, which assumes that everyone wants to do a good job. Each person must balance relational skills with task orientation. It meant meeting frequently with the staff person, encouraging them, and above all, standing behind them when they are subjected to unfair criticism.

This was followed later with a course in Management by Objectives. The AMA course emphasized that only a few major corporations had successfully adopted this plan because follow-up was seldom implemented. This meant a group process each year for key goals, the first of which was to evaluate the prior year based on achievement of its goals. This needed to be an open-group process. Then suggestions were made without acceptance or rejections. The group would then, by blind poll, set the key objectives for the following year. These goals were then divided among the staff. Each staff member would then develop his or her own objectives for the year. I would negotiate with them on their tasks. That would include their evaluation of their prior year's objectives. They tended to be harder on themselves than I was. These were then shared with the board of the church for their evaluations. This system worked very well and was used for the rest of my professional life, even through years as president of the Covenant.

I also took an American Management Association course entitled Financial Management for Non-financial Managers. Since most conflict between pastors and their trustees occurred at "Ambush at Dollar Pass," honing my skills here was of great help for the rest of my career. It increased my respect for the accountants, but it also relieved me of a sense of incompetence as I realized that even the best accountant can hold no more than three ratios in his consciousness at any one time. Their superiority lay in their skill and knowledge as to where to find them in the mass of numbers in the financial statements.

CHARISMATIC TENSIONS

While there have always been charismatic elements such as speaking in tongues in Covenant churches, schismatic elements had been emerging among nearly a score of church members. We had some of the sectarian sort who insisted that all needed to have the baptism of the Spirit accompanied by supernatural signs. The deacons held separate meetings and took a stand on such views and practices. The sectarians departed, but some in the church who were themselves charismatic did not believe that all needed to be like them. They felt injured by the controversy. Others became overly sensitive of anything that smacked of charismatic tendencies. I preached a series on the Holy Spirit. Within a short time, the issue dissipated, but I am sure that my preaching had little to do with it.

ELIZABETH

The most important event personally was the coming of Elizabeth into my life. She was born and raised in Southern California and met Christ as a teenager. After graduation from California State University in Northridge, she became a credentialed high school teacher. While teaching at Belmont High School in Los Angeles, she and a friend led a Young Life Club in the same school. Her friend, Leigh Thurber, had graduated from Fuller Seminary. She persuaded Elizabeth to pursue a master's degree in Christian Education. She then became the Women's Director at what would become Jews for Jesus under Moishe Rosen. Next she became a women's Bible study teacher at our La Crescenta Covenant Church. During my first year in Pasadena, a matchmaker went to work. Muriel Racine and her dentist husband, John, were pillars of the church. She had introduced a young surgeon, Dr. Paul Johnston, to one of her best friends. Having seen the romance bloom into marriage, she went to work on Elizabeth. I, of course, had hundreds of matchmakers in the church. Almost anyone with an unmarried adult daughter, particularly of any missionary calling, would invite me to Sunday dinner. Awkward as it would often be, I learned to have good conversation and delight in the meal. But it did not seem to be working. Muriel, however, was relentless.

At the time Muriel was attending a weekday women's Bible study class at La Crescenta Covenant Church. Along with Muriel, there were a number of younger women who were a part of my youth pastor days at the Eagle Rock Covenant Church. When conversing at the church while installing its new pastor, these young ladies immediately began to tell me of their wonderful teacher, Elizabeth Taylor. Muriel took charge at the start and brought her one Sunday to hear me preach. She invited both of us to a Valentine's Day dinner following church. Her husband, John, was mortified. The three teenaged children peeked and giggled through the doorway throughout the dinner. I was an hour late because a friend suffering severe cancer had been in church before entering the City of Hope. Feeling awkward, I barely stopped talking through the entire meal. I remember thinking, however, "This is one wonderful person that I want to date." She had to get to her afternoon meeting at Beth Shar Shalom, a Christian Mission to Jews in Hollywood.

I called her within the week. We had a wonderful dinner date at the Old Virginia Steakhouse that weekend. As I dropped her off at her apartment, she made tea for us, and I was strongly attracted to her as I saw the gentle kindness that she displayed. We soon began dating weekly. I went with her to the Beth Shar Shalom—the former residence of Hollywood silent star Mary Pickford. Unfortunately I fell asleep during the afternoon sermon of Moishe Rosen, soon to be founder of Jews for Jesus. Fortunately, I survived the embarrassment.

There were many memorable moments during courtship. Isidore was a devout orthodox Jew who lived with his wife, Ida, just behind the great Jewish temple. Ida had become a believer and would sneak out each Sunday afternoon to Beth Shar Shalom. They invited us both to dinner one evening. And what a dinner it was! They had been to the Holy Land, and soon began to argue vehemently about whether the Messiah was to come by jet plane. He believed it was the first coming of the Messiah, she the second coming, although there was no conflict over the first or second coming—only whether he would arrive in Jerusalem by jet! At that dinner they gave us to two tickets to *The Sound of Music*. The movie was lovely, only we discovered that just a few seats down were seated our church leaders Eugene and Virginia Lowe. As much as I tried to keep our courtship private, no matter where we went in the extremities of Southern California, we were nearly always spotted by some church leaders.

After a number of months I proposed marriage. The proposal took place at beautiful Lacey Park in San Marino. When I tried to give her the ring, she seemed unable to take it. Humbled and stunned, she let me know three days later that she was happy to accept my proposal. When I approached her father to gain his approval in traditional fashion, he gave me his blessing, saying, "Just remember one thing about my daughter: you can lead her almost anywhere you wish, but she does not push worth a darn." Since those words were spoken, I cannot recall a single instance in which he was wrong.

The announcement to the congregation was another matter. It took place at the close of a Sunday evening service. Muriel Racine and Lillian Johnston had prepared a massive reception in the church gymnasium. Her husband, Dr. Paul Johnston, was church chair and uncle to young collegian Rob Johnston, who took the evening service to describe his summer as a short-term missionary to Japan. As the service ended, Rob called on Dr. Johnston to make "an announcement that would be of some interest to the members and friends of the church." He declared, "I am pleased to announce the engagement of our pastor, Paul Larsen, to Miss Elizabeth Taylor!" Total silence. Then one of the little old ladies with the old-fashioned hearing aids furnished by the church whispered to her friend sitting next to her. Both were quite deaf, so the whisper took the form of a loud shout, "He's kidding!" she roared. All broke into cheers and applause and went to the magnificent reception.

At long last the day came on March 19. The church held only a little more than 500 people. Dr. Ray Ortlund at the Lake Avenue Congregational Church just two blocks away offered their large sanctuary. It was a Saturday afternoon wedding in full formal attire. My groomsmen included Paul Brandel and Nils G. Axelson of Chicago, as well as Gordon Bunnell, John Swenson, and Ken Oldenburger from Orangevale. Elizabeth's brothers Don and Merle were the head ushers. Don's son, Graham, at four years old, was the ring bearer. Betty Tabell was the maid of honor. We seated her next to bachelor music minister Roland Tabell at the rehearsal dinner, which led to their marriage and our lifelong friendship as two couples.

The people who gathered numbered 1,280. Our church choir and accompanying orchestral music led the singing, including "Sheep May Safely Graze" from Handel's *Messiah*. Presiding were my brother, the conference superintendent, and Lake Avenue pastor Ray Rotund. The service went off without a hitch, except for one thing. I had become so used to reading the vows at weddings that I knew them by heart. Without waiting for my brother's intonation of "Do you, Paul, take Elizabeth to be your lawful wedded wife?" I blurted out, "I, Paul, take you, Elizabeth, to be my lawful wedded husband." It was on tape—and never forgotten by anyone. Life is a Hoomiliat'n' process!

Then followed a massive reception. It was held in the church's new gymnasium just up Lake Avenue two blocks from the large church. The line extended all the way between the two churches over two blocks and through one stop light. John and Muriel Racine went and played nine holes of golf and joined the reception line before the last person in the line greeted us.

The people of the church were most generous. They gave us all our china and sterling as well as our silver coffee and tea service. We got all of our daily ware, cooking utensils, as well as kitchen, bed, and bath linens. We left joyously and exhausted to catch the plane for a wonderful two-week honeymoon in Hawaii.

Over the next five years, Elizabeth more than won the hearts of the church. She promptly asked Linnea Carlson, wife of my predecessor Arvid Carlson, "How can I be good pastor's wife?" Linnea replied, "Just love them, and they will love you." She was right! As we matured together, she even became in a real sense my spiritual mentor. Prayer and care for the lowly was the byword in all that she did. Our two children, Kristi and Kathleen, were born and received their deserved priority. Among the many things she did was initiate home Bible studies for women—two of which lasted many years beyond our time in Pasadena. I always felt affirmed by the church, but Elizabeth was far more loved and admired than I was.

CRADLE ROLE

I soon discovered a major source of the church's outreach beyond its ethnic enclave. Pastor Carlson had given his full support to the birth of a new movement to reach unchurched mothers of new babies. The program was started by Mrs. Ollie Roth, who had come from Chicago. She gathered a group of women who would get the weekly birth announcements from the Pasadena papers. They would then prepare a layette of products for the newborn—blankets, powders, diapers, and so forth. Then they would visit the homes of the mothers and invite them to a weekly mothers' class. If mothers wished to be enrolled, they were added to the list. Each meeting included simple baby-care teaching and a Bible study. Mrs. Naomi Johnston was a winsome and able teacher. This brought many young mothers to faith in Christ. It became the original Cradle Role program for countless churches throughout the United States. Many of the church's leadership and their families found Christ and a solid church home in which to raise their children.

In her last years, Ollie Roth fell ill with Lou Gehrig's disease, or Lateral Sclerosis. The disease began to deaden the nerves and muscles, leading to a progressive paralysis. In her last days, Ollie could not speak but could only write short notes on a small pad. I have kept those notes. Two days before her death she wrote, "The promises are standing true!" On the last day she feebly scribbled, "Triumphant ending!" followed by a wavy line that rode off the page. In answer to prayers, she did not choke to death, but slipped quietly away in gentle slumber.

YOUTH MINISTRY

A second major outreach was the youth ministries. I knew when I arrived that the church had a strong youth ministry. Arvid Carlson and his youth pastor, John Braun, had developed a unique outreach ministry at the church. It was called Campus Club. Each Tuesday after school, high schoolers would gather at the church gymnasium and youth center. They could play basketball, games, or just study and do their homework. Women of the church would put on a nice supper, which was followed by singing and a message, much in the style of a Young Life club.

Warren Thompson, a salesman for 3M, was a key lay leader of this ministry. He was not a strong speaker, athlete, or even disciplinarian. He would meet with at least three of the young men privately for discipleship over the twenty years he gave his life in that ministry. It was joked that he was the first man in history to wear out a wedding tuxedo as a groomsman, due to the influence he had on so many young men.

I soon had two part-time youth leaders from Fuller Seminary. Gary Copeland led the senior high groups and Jim Larsen the junior groups. Both were Wheaton grads of singular gifts and passion for Christ. President David Hubbard once asked me, "In our faculty discussions we wondered how Pasadena Covenant Church could get Fuller's most outstanding servants to work with their young people; these were followed by Rob Johnston, David Hicks, and Jim Gustafson, young men of the seminary and the church who likewise showed exceptional skill and leadership.

Gary Copeland went on to become a successful pastor at Marin Covenant Church, followed by pastorates in Colorado. In retirement he became active with an organization training pastors in third-world countries. In many ways this has been the most important part of his ministry.

David Hicks, who was raised in Pasadena Covenant Church, did an exceptional job as campus club leader. He went on to pastor in Southern California and then many years as youth minister at the Oakland Covenant Church. He had exceptional gifts for drawing young people into a close walk with Christ and in ministering to the needy.

Rob Johnston was a third-generation son of church leaders. A graduate of Stanford, he served as youth pastor while at Fuller. He married Anna

Eleanor Roosevelt III. I had the wedding during which his cousin, Marc (later a Covenant minister), fainted on the marble stairs, but was held up by the other groomsmen. The wedding was loaded with Roosevelt cousins. He went on for his PhD at Duke and then to teaching at Western Kentucky University. He came back as dean and then provost at North Park University In a second marriage, he wed Cathy Barsotti, who earned her PhD and was key in the founding of the Covenant's Spanish theological school, CHET (Centro Hispano de Estudios Teológicos), and other ministries. Rob became provost at Fuller. He later joined me on the William Carey Heritage Board and was key to establishing India's first accredited evangelical PhD degree in Christian studies. We have been close colleagues over these many years.

David Stoop came as minister of Christian education. With him came his wife, Jan, and their small children. A most effective organizer and wise counselor, he fulfilled numerous pastoral duties. Years later he went to be an editor with Gospel Light Press. He then took his PhD in psychology and became a noted author, editing the NIV's *Recovery Study Bible.*

Jim Gustafson came to us while a student at Fuller Seminary. The nephew of John and Muriel Racine, he was a missionary kid raised in Laos by Christian and Missionary Alliance parents. When coming to the seminary, we asked him to take over the junior high youth ministry. Starting with a dozen junior high students, he gathered nearly thirty youngsters from the neighborhood in just a few weeks. He clearly had the gift of evangelism and a missionary heart. After a time he fell in love with Joan Christenson, the daughter of Mel and Florence Christenson. Mel had been in my father's young men's Bible class for years at First Covenant Minneapolis. I was privileged to marry them. Then a little widow passed away and left her house and savings to the church. The house became the residence of the youth pastors from then on. The money was given to Covenant World Missions to cover the cost of deploying Jim and Joan to northeast Thailand as missionaries in a region previously abandoned by other mission societies. The story of their tremendous work continues in chapter 8 on Covenant Church world missions.

I began to have a weekly breakfast for a half-dozen high school boys at a local restaurant each Thursday morning. So many of these boys became pastors and outstanding laymen. A significant number were boys from unchurched families. Among them were later Covenant pastors Ken and Mark Larson and Dale Tremper. Erik Stone became a medical doctor, and after my retirement I discovered that Scott Morgan had become finance director for the City of Rancho Mirage, California. Randy Thompson became the leader of a movement out of Yale University and ultimately a UCC pastor in Connecticut. Another became a leader of Athletes in Action.

One young man from the church, Dennis Fevergeon, went on to Pasadena College. He gave of himself as high school counselor. He worked part-time as a custodian at the nearby Catholic High School in La Cañada. He shared his excitement about our youth work with a number of Catholic parents at the school. One day a priest showed up at Campus Club with several of their school's mothers. At the priest's request, Dennis was relieved of his janitorial work and made Youth Director of the Catholic Church. When offered the position, he told the priest, "But I am a Protestant!" The priest replied, "Don't worry! Just preach the gospel." The Campus Club continued to grow. It began reaching more than 150 each week. Then they began to organize student-led Bible studies in neighboring high schools. I lyrically declared, "Nothing like this has happened since Martin Luther was excommunicated in the sixteenth century!" Huge numbers of church and unchurched young people became followers of Christ. It was truly a time of awakening.

JONAH'S PLACE

The college students began developing a strong ministry of outreach among the poor. They also wanted to develop camping scholarships. During the summer, our Sunday evening service would often fill even rows in the balcony. The young people came up with a unique idea: Jonah's Place. They fixed the church basement to look the insides of the great whale, including netting and a huge rubber tongue and papier-mâché mouth as the doorway through which everyone entered. After every Sunday evening during summer months, they set up round tables with nautical themes. The college young people then served ice cream, pies, and other desserts while we sang. I would stand on a small platform in the middle and take questions on the sermon's topic that evening. It was always packed with old and young. The food was donated by grocer Bill Pompeian, as well as mothers of the college students. The free will offerings built a substantial scholarship fund for young people to attend conferences such as InterVarsity's renowned missions conference, Urbana.

THE HOUSE OF HELP

The House of Help became a part of our church's ministry when Bengt and Betty Junvik bought and donated an older house across the street from the church. Owner of the Aircraft Forging Die Company, Bengt and his wife had been dedicated to the cause of missions since they were married in our church. The church decided to dedicate this facility for the aid and spiritual assistance of the poor and the destitute. A couple of college students lived upstairs to ensure the presence of round-the-clock assistance to persons and families in crisis. Here a powerful alliance for common ministry developed between the seniors and collegians of our church.

Pulling things together were Kurt Miericke and his wife, Cindy. He was a Chicago Covenanter who had studied at North Park Seminary, but wanted to finish at Fuller. He had done an internship in Grand Rapids, where he had worked with students. The pastor, Clarence Winstedt, however, felt he was even better working with seniors. We then hired him part time to work with our large community of seniors. He immediately went to work developing the House of Help. He also had been working part-time at the Pasadena Welfare Agency. Leaving that, he left his phone number at the House of Help. Hence, every welfare worker's phone had a note by it telling workers to call when there were no other services that the city or county could render in an emergency. We were anxious that we would be overcome. Although we became very busy, we never had to turn anyone away. Elizabeth and I became close friends and colleagues of Kurt and Cindy over the years as he pastored a number of flourishing churches. He became superintendent of the Southeast Conference while I was president. His deep love for people, high social skills, and relentless passion for bringing people to Christ made him a great model for others.

David Stoop joined us minister of Christian education with his wife, Jean. He went on to become a well-known clinical psychologist who helped edit the *NIV Recovery Bible*. While serving as an editor at Gospel Light Press, he published my expositions on the Psalms, entitled *Wise Up and Live*. This sold hundreds of thousands of copies, including Portuguese and Chinese translations.

The star volunteer was Mrs. Edyth Johnson. When her husband passed away, leaving her with several small children, she decided to raise them while she herself ran the family farm. One of her children was Glen Lindell, a most effective pastor and director of evangelism for the church. Now retired, she gave herself unstintingly to help the poor at the House of Help. She did everything from bathing invalids to bringing food. A couple of the deacons began to ask whether we were succumbing to the social gospel and neglecting evangelism. I was asked to come to the board meeting to get corrective instruction. Edyth said, "I will go instead!" I don't quite know what went on, but she came out smiling triumphantly, and twelve deacons left sheepishly and silent, always thereafter affirming the importance of both evangelism and helping the poor.

She eventually came down with terminal cancer. On one occasion I visited her at Huntington Hospital. She asked, "Pastor, am I already in heaven?" My first thought was that she had now begun to move into terminal delusions. Instead, she said, "I see Jesus right beside me, and washing the helpless and caring for the homeless—it is the most beautiful heaven I have ever imagined." I could only pray with her, asking God to forgive my own blindness to the glory of his presence among the sick and the dying.

But volunteers ran short and we decided that we would have to close the House of Help. Arising from her hospital bed, she dismissed herself from the hospital. She then returned, reopened the House of Help, and ran it smoothly for the next few years before God called her home.

CONFERENCE CHAIR

I found myself chair of the California Conference as well as pastor of one of its largest churches by the time I was thirty. Since I had not been through North Park Seminary, my ordination was deferred until 1963. I was promptly elected chair of the Conference executive board. When elected chair by the Conference Annual Meeting in Oakland, California, I responded that I was puzzled about what could have motivated the delegates to name someone so young as its chair. I openly speculated that perhaps their guidance came from the biblical account of the Prodigal Son, and I loosely interpreted the complaint of the elder son, declaring, "Perhaps you delegates claimed this verse, though out of context, thinking, 'Give us a kid that we may make merry!'"

Superintendent Gordon Nelson resigned shortly thereafter, and thus I became acting superintendent for a year. The Conference board assigned Wally Lindskoog, the world's foremost Holstein cattle breeder and operator of one of the nation's six largest turkey hatcheries to join me in meeting with Covenant President Clarence Nelson to find a suitable candidate. President Nelson asked me what qualification we desired in our new superintendent. I gave a rather long list of qualities and skills. As I finished, Wally in typical fashion simply said, "Men, they ain't no such bull!" Wise words I have never forgotten after more than half a century sitting on search committees for churches and institutions.

Rev. Edward Larson was thus nominated and elected at the next Annual Meeting. Meanwhile, the building that housed the Conference offices was demolished by the owner, and I led the search for new offices. I found and led the design and furnishing of the new offices across the street from the Pasadena Civic Auditorium.

At this time the aging Emanuel Hospital in Turlock needed to be replaced. It was my privilege to work with the construction effort and borrow for this most important community facility. Also, our aging Bethany Home for retirees also needed replacement, and I led the conference through another but somewhat controversial project in building the large Covenant Village of Turlock. We later took the lead in seeking funding from a foundation grant in order to build the Arkelion Psychiatric Unit at the hospital. Even more controversy arose over the proposal to acquire adjacent land to the hospital and construct an extended care facility. Paul Brandel optioned the land, but many on the board felt that for the Covenant Church to operate, such a facility was to hone in on free-enterprise principles, denying private investors the opportunity to make a profit. I finally argued that that the premise was wrong. Until the recent century, for nearly two thousand years all hospitals, senior shelters, and orphanages were run by the churches. I didn't understand why it would be helping the poor to give wealthy investors the chance to fill their pockets with even more money. The Covenant Church then proceeded to build the facility as part of the hospital.

The Bay Area churches, together with the Central Valley churches, were finding it difficult to use youth camp facilities in the Sierra Nevadas. A family had been developing a facility in the winter snows that could handle more than fifty young winter ski campers. Still unfinished, it stood on five acres of ground. The owner, who had a semi-finished residence, found himself unable to complete the project. He would give us the whole thing if he could have life occupancy of the cottage. This we did, as volunteers finished the project and churches used the facility well for years.

I also negotiated the donation of a church property on a small lake and worked to build the first unit of what later became one of our largest mountain churches. Further south, costs had run too high on the proposed first units of Simi Valley Covenant Church. I worked with the architect and builders to bring it to completion. Likewise, I was active in searching for donated church property for a church in Laguna Niguel, south of Irvine, in Orange County. It was located on a main expressway.

It was also my privilege to be the host pastor of the Covenant Annual Meeting in Pasadena in 1965. Using the Pasadena Civic Auditorium, I was honored to preside over the retirement of President Clarence Nelson. We were delighted to see Dr. Milton Engebretson as the new president at this meeting. He had been one of my best friends even before that.

THE DES MOINES PETITION, 1965

In 1965, a major crisis erupted throughout the denomination over the question of biblical authority. The Covenant Church's sole confession from the beginning was found in its Constitution: "The Bible is the Word of God and the only perfect rule of Faith, Doctrine, and Conduct." As the nineteenth century came to a close and the twentieth century commenced, Protestantism in particular was engaged in the Battle for the Bible. Earlier, at the end of the eighteenth century, the Enlightenment raised questions about the Bible's trustworthiness and authority. The Covenant Church's statement gave full support to Scripture as the lone trustworthy source in matters of faith and morals. There were some differences regarding the actual implications of this confession from the beginning. It was inevitable that the issues should eventually emerge in questions concerning the teaching of the denomination's North Park Theological Seminary. These controversies had emerged in the 1930s and 1940s, yet they came to a new head in the 1960s. At its 1965 annual Midwinter Conference in Des Moines, Iowa, several hundred ministers heard lectures on the nature of the Bible.

The seminary's New Testament professor Henry Gustafson gave a more liberal exposition of the nature of biblical authority. He argued that the Bible contained many historical, theological, and ethical errors, but was still the vehicle through which God spoke to his people. In the Q&A that followed, Pastor Virgil Wickman of Tacoma, Washington, stood up and in anger declared, "I repudiate you!" Gustafson, in the same abrasive manner, responded: "And I repudiate you! I have vowed that before I die there will not be one Covenant pastor who believes in the verbal plenary inspiration of the Bible." The stunned ministers took a coffee break. A storm was breaking.

That evening a dozen Covenant Church pastors met after the service at the home Iver Erickson, a wealthy layman of the Des Moines church. The meeting was not scheduled to deal with the question of the morning's lecture. It was to discuss the implications of the newly proposed "Covenant Life Curriculum." The subject turned immediately to Gustafson's morning lecture. I was present, as was my brother, David, Paul Fryhling of First Covenant Minneapolis, Wesley Nelson of the faculty, Pastor Ralph Erickson, and nearly a dozen others.

During the afternoon following the lecture, I began to reflect on positive action. The history of a lone dissenter threatening the stature of a faculty member or even arguing for a strong theological statement was not promising. Too often such persons were written off as having a bad spirit or were simply viewed as a divisive crank. Generally, those who were most upset by professor Gustafson's presentation were the least capable of giving a persuasive response. I recalled that in the Northern Presbyterian Church in the 1920s, Presbyterian Clarence McCartney had led a heresy trial over Harry Emerson Fosdick for denying the Virgin Birth of Christ. While Mc-Cartney won, 500 Presbyterian pastors had signed the "Auburn Affirmation"—while they agreed to the Virgin birth, they declared that equally there were other alternatives to Christ's Virgin birth. The General Assembly could not defrock 500 ministers at once. Thus, the normative standards of the Church Confession became nonbinding history. I thought that we might do an Auburn Affirmation in reverse, to ensure that the voice would be heard from a significant number of pastors in good standing. I asked both Secretary Engebretson and President Clarence Nelson if there was a lawful or ethical objection from such a petition to the Covenant Executive Board. They both assured me that it would be both ethical and good order.

As the evening progressed, a petition was drafted. It would not demand a firing, or a strict definition of biblical authority. It outlined a more conservative position emphasizing the historicity of the book of Daniel, the unity of Isaiah, the truth of the miracles, and stances on other such issues. It listed the following reasons for the petition:

> 1) Our unreserved commitment to the orthodox and classical doctrine of the inspiration of Scripture which affirms the integrity of the writers and the complete reliability of the record; 2) Our deep disappointment that the approach to the Bible in our seminary continues to be in opposition to the conservative view of Scripture; 3) Our continuing anxiety that the conservative view of Scripture is not represented on the faculty in the biblical field of our seminary; 4) Our determination that our conservative ministerial students have the benefit of a theologically representative faculty or approval for study elsewhere.[2]

The petition was placed in the church office and had more than 52 signatures by noon. An additional page was purloined by an enraged Covenant Church pastor. There was an angry rebuke in the public meeting. I simply told people privately that the entire matter had been submitted in an orderly fashion by both Clarence Nelson and Milton Engebretson. So we sent the petition to the Covenant Church.

The Covenant Church executive board responded promptly with the appointment of a committee. Karl Olson reports the ensuing action:

> The petition led to some re-examination of the Covenant Church's view of Scriptures and, at the Annual Meeting of 1965,

---

2. Olson, *Into One Body*, 366–67.

to the appointment of a "Committee to Study the Seminary."
The committee, chaired by Rev. Wilbur Westerdahl, served until
1967 when it presented its basic recommendations to the Annual Meeting in Pasadena. These recommendations were:

1. We recommend that the Covenant Annual Meeting affirm the desirability of making North Park Theological Seminary a true model of the Covenant community in action through
the fostering of a spirit of acceptance and respect for divergent
views within the context of our historical commitment.

2. We recommend that a fully trained and qualified teacher
who holds to the more conservative position on Scripture
should be appointed to the biblical field at the seminary.[3]

The Annual Meeting was held in Pasadena in June 1967, at the city's
Civic Auditorium. The report was received with gracious discussion and
was adopted. The decision to appoint a professor of the more conservative
view to the seminary's biblical faculty has had significant impact over the
years that followed. The Covenant Church decisively established that its
seminary was to reflect the faith of the church, not determine or control
that faith.

The committee recommended the call of Donald Madvig, a New Testament scholar from the North American Baptist Seminary in Sioux Falls,
South Dakota. He was a superior scholar with an irenic spirit. After a few
years he was replaced by Klyne Snodgrass, who served until retirement. He
likewise was a recognized scholar holding more conservative views. His
scholarship was recognized throughout New Testament studies generally.
His book, *Stories of Intent,* has received international recognition as the
foremost book on the parables of Jesus.[4] It was one thing for the denomination to make such a decision in balancing its faculty, but it was perhaps
even more significant that the Christian spirit and academic excellence had
been modeled so well. Differences in theological interpretation were to be
tolerated within the historic traditions of the church as long as they could
be argued with integrity and graciously under the authority of the Bible as
the word of God.

FULLER THEOLOGICAL SEMINARY

Fuller Seminary was located within a mile of the church. Pastor Arvid Carlson served as the school's first lecturer on evangelism. Arnold Ehlert was the

3. Olson, *Into One Body,* 372.
4. Snodgrass, *Stories with Intent.*

school's first librarian. Helga Henry, wife of Theology Professor Carl F. H. Henry, was Pasadena Covenant Church's director of Christian education for years before my arrival. The family faithfully attended the church. Harold Nyquist was the business manager. President David Hubbard attended regularly with his family. Missiologist Charles Kraft was a faithful member of the church. His wife, Meg, was a sister to my cousin Jim Sawyer's wife, Rosina. The famed Donald McGavran, perhaps the most noted evangelical missiologist of this period, often attended worship. The same was true of missiologists Alan Tippet, and School of World Missions Dean Arthur Glasser. Homiletics Professor Clarence Roddy attended worship with us frequently. President Carnell's widow attended regularly with her mother-in-law and children.

While the seminary at the time had fewer than 300 students, it today has become the world's largest nondenominational seminary with nearly 4,000 students. At any given time more than a dozen students and their families worshipped regularly with us. Part-time staffers Gary Copeland, Jim Larson, Jim Gustafson, Tim Weber, and Rob Johnston were the best the seminary had. Tom Johnson became president of Sioux Falls College; Dale Tremper became a Methodist pastor; Terry Winter became Canada's most noted televangelist; and Jeff Ebright became a Methodist pastor. George Whitfield became director of evangelism for the United Methodist Church. Jerry and Nancy Reed were active in the church. Bruce Dreon went beyond his role as an InterVarsity staff member to become a partner in a leading development organization for colleges nationwide. Donn Klingberg went on to get his PhD at Fuller, and later came to serve as chaplain of North Park University. Fred Wagner went on to leadership in InterVarsity Christian Fellowship. Walt Wright went on to become president of Regent College of Vancouver, provost at Fuller Seminary, and then director of the Max DePree Center for Leadership at Fuller. Steve Anderson became head of the Covenant Benevolence Institutions on the West Coast. Dick Greenwood and Phil Axelson went on to become Covenant Church ministers. Johnny Nyquist served as director of youth ministries at Trinity Evangelical Divinity School.

During this time I served successively as editor of the seminary yearbook and president of the Alumni Association. During the months of Clarence Roddy's prolonged illness, I taught both his preaching classes, as well as his course in pastoral theology. I had great opportunities for extended formal and informal education at this nearby school. I took postgraduate courses under George Ladd in the Apocrypha and Pseudepigrapha. His Christology course put me right on the doctrine of the Trinity, and made me a competent interlocutor in later doctoral courses at a more liberal seminary.

Being something of a contrarian, I frequently tussled with the high Calvinists, both on the faculty and student body. This sharpened my witness and confirmed my identity as a free church evangelical pietist.

RACIAL JUSTICE

The conflict over race grew intense during the 1960s when I pastored in Pasadena. A significant number of African Americans of the servant class to the wealthy of Pasadena had previously settled in northeast Pasadena. The shortage of defense workers brought many more from the South to fill vacancies of soldiers at war. This community grew extensively over the areas north and west of the church. Some feared the whole area around the church would become a black ghetto. A nationally known Christian leader had previously warned me against ever going to this church at a time of turmoil. Schools increasingly filled with black students. The city council named me to the Human Relations Committee to work on racial relations in the increasingly tense times. I was then named chair of the Human Concerns subcommittee to stand by in the event of crisis in order to ease inflamed tensions.

The riots in Pasadena erupted at the same time as the Watts riots of 1965. Riots at the city's high school sent teachers and students to the hospital. Students engaged in violence were permanently expelled from the school system. I privately went to the president of the Pasadena City College and won an agreement that students who were on probation could finish their high school degrees there. Riots and burnings often cluttered the city streets. I was assigned a squad car and the services of Sergeant Tippett, who was the grandson of a slave. On some days my secretary would say, "Sergeant Tippet has arrived outside to take you to a new trouble spot."

Accompanying me on many of these efforts was Ruby McKnight Williams, chair of the Pasadena chapter of the National Association for the Advancement of Colored People (NAACP). Whether it was action by black or white, Ruby was a powerful and forceful presence. I was then honored to be named to the board of directors of the Pasadena chapter of the NAACP—a rare privilege for a white man. Other leaders became my collaborators. The chair of the Urban League would introduce me to other black leadership with the quip, "Can you believe he's an evangelical?" Even the communists and the Trotskyites affirmed me—a dubious distinction.

The Supreme Court ruling on *Brown v. Board of Education* and the resulting desegregation of the Pasadena schools by busing raised fierce opposition among the white population. I was on the front pages of both the *Los Angeles Times* and the *Pasadena Star News*. Albert Lowe, a faithful worshipper at the church, was chair of the school board. Since he supported implementing the Supreme Court mandate, a massive recall effort ensued. One of those leading the recall effort was a member of our church. I stuck to the gospel, not using it to advance my public posture. Everyone could read about my forthright stand on behalf of racial justice. No one left the church. The recall failed, and the woman from my church told me openly, "I will say that Albert was the only true Christian, those on my side were all rats!"

PRIDE OF PASADENA

Albert Lowe then organized a group of city leaders to explore how the city might overcome its blight and decline. He graciously made me a member. Dr. Eberhardt Rechtin of Caltech was named the chairperson. He was a systems expert who guided the famed Mars landing project. He told us at the first meeting that what he learned in science would be of great benefit toward restoring the city. He said, "Reaching Mars was only 10 percent of the problem; 90 percent was to overcome psychological and interpersonal conflicts." We developed task groups dealing with education, police enforcement, housing, and development of the city as a headquarters center for top businesses. I was unsure of the future when Dr. Rechtin left Pasadena to head all systems management for the U.S. Department of Defense. Looking at the city's transformation over the following years, though, it is clear that Albert and Dr. Rechtin's systems approach was marvelously fulfilled.

AUTO CENTER

At this time the city experienced much white flight. Auto dealerships were beginning to flee to the suburbs, exacerbating unemployment for both blacks and whites alike. A proposal was made to develop an auto mall in the most decaying part of the city. It would bring a number of the best auto dealerships together and open two new bank branches. This would create employment for hundreds of people. It meant the displacement of a couple of hundred poor black people, which raised an outcry. None of the houses to be displaced were owned by either their residents or anyone in Pasadena. A way had to be found to create more than a hundred units of federal leased apartment housing immediately to the east of the center. Properties would be up to code, publicly maintained, and rents fixed in relationship to residents' incomes. I could not advocate this to a private session of the city council, due to the Brown Act. Instead, I went to each member of the city council and won his or her support of the project. When the hearings were held, a large and vocal group of blacks from South Los Angeles fiercely opposed it, and the council dropped the plan. The Pasadena black leadership felt betrayed. Turner Alexander, a successful black activist and business leader spoke to me in tears, "Paul, we have to face the fact that too much black activism is driven not for justice, but to advance the political causes external even to the city."

In 1968, Martin Luther King Jr. was assassinated. I was asked by the city to enrobe and lead a procession of officials down Green Street and preside over King's memorial service. A close personal friend of King's spoke. I chose as my text the words from Joshua 1: "Moses my servant is dead . . . Have I not commanded you? Be strong and courageous. Do not be terrified; do not be discouraged, for the Lord your God will be with you wherever you go" (Josh 1:2, 9). A prominent physician who had left our church met my church chairman at the University Club. Outraged that I was on the front page of the Sunday newspaper, he demanded that I be placed under discipline! No good deed goes unpunished.

THE BATTLE OF CANCER CORNER

The Battle of Cancer Corner became a major struggle in the city. The corner of Orange Grove and Fair Oaks in northwest Pasadena was the trouble spot. Three of the four corners had bars and liquor stores. Mobs would gather there in the evening, spilling into the streets, blocking traffic and terrorizing the black residents. It was so serious that some of these modest homeowners were abandoning their own homes in fear. Further east, Orange Grove had an intersection at Lake Avenue, one block above the church.

No one seemed able to do anything about the crisis. Bill Boone, Pasadena's human relations director, tossed the ball to me, as chair of the Human Concerns Committee, saying, "If we can't resolve this, race relations in the city will hit a new low." Working with key black leadership, we found that the oppressed neighbors refused to file court affidavits alleging criminal behavior because they were threatened with violent reprisals. Without such affidavits the city attorney said no action was possible. The presiding judge of the Superior Court, a good friend, put me in touch with the director of the local Legal Aid Society. With a withered arm and diminutive stature, he helped us draft what is called a pro forma affidavit—written clearly with blanks to fill in dates and simple events and room for the signature. Ruby McKnight Williams gathered more than 100 in a grocery parking lot. They came up with nearly 50 affidavits.

The city still said they had no reason to act. I did find that the California Department of Alcoholic Beverage Control Act did have a provision banning undue concentration of liquor stores. Since there were three on four corners of this intersection, I met with the chief of police and district head of Alcoholic Beverage Control (ABC). Assuming that I was ignorant, they argued that "liquor is legal." The ABC officer acknowledged that this was in the law, but had never been acted on the history of California. At the public hearing of the Human Relations Committee I reported this to the press, saying we would file a writ of mandate in the Superior Court demanding that the State act, and if it did not, to answer before the court. It would be required to provide a satisfactory answer. The city attorney, ABC officer, and the police chief met with me in City Hall. The police chief condescendingly told me, "Rev. Larsen, if we shut down these businesses, the mobs will simply reassemble and attack your church." I admit I lost my temper. I said to the chief, "You have a pre-Civil War view of Southern law, which in essence said, 'If the darkies want to commit mayhem down by the slave quarters at night, they can do it as long as they don' waken ol' massah.'" The police chief exploded. At the sound of all this commotion, all the corridors of the city's massive city hall filled with inquiring questions.

Three days later I received a call from the area head of Alcoholic Beverage Control. He said that they brought in three black undercover agents from Northern California. They made several heroin buys in the liquor store in less than ten minutes. The store owners—who lived in all-white Glendale—immediately surrendered their liquor licenses without protest. One of them actually offered his store free to open an employment center. (The only other center was downtown in the high rent district.) Within months the chief of police resigned, and I hoped I had not been part of his dismissal. So ended the Battle of Cancer Corner. In years after I had left Pasadena, the city's black leadership would occasionally sponsor a reception in my honor at the Wrigley Mansion, headquarters of the famed Tournament of Roses.

THE GREATEST JOY

But out of all the joys of being a pastor, the greatest was to welcome individuals to new life in Christ. Young and old came seeking. Among the many was Federal Judge David Harrison. He was Jewish, and his father had donated the synagogue in an eastern city. A Harvard Law School graduate, he had become an adjutant in the U.S. Army during the Second World War. He served as High Commissioner of Military Justice in Austria and presided over the de-Nazification of the Austrian courts. He then served as a judge at Nuremburg. He was the presiding judge at the trial of German officers who had tortured or murdered U.S. prisoners of war. He met his wife, Melanie, while in Germany. After the war they settled in Glendale, and later he assumed the title of Commissioner for the U.S. Social Service Commission. Melanie was brought to Christ through the church's Cradle Role. David would accompany her and their three children to church and Sunday school every Sunday. Too many people tried hard-sell evangelism on them, and he would simply blush and turn away.

One Sunday I spoke to David as they were leaving the church and said, "David, you are more faithful than most of the old line saints here. Do you think it is time to claim Jesus as your Messiah?" He blushed and said, "I will have Melanie call you." I felt it was a dignified brush-off.

Two weeks later Melanie called and invited Elizabeth and me to their home for an evening dinner. Elizabeth joined Melanie in the kitchen; David began rehearsing experiences as a judge of Nuremburg. I asked him about my question two weeks before. He exclaimed, "Not until Melanie and Elizabeth join us!" We four sat before a bright fire. I asked him, "David, are you now ready to declare Jesus Christ as your Messiah and Savior?" He sat up straight like a judge at the bench, slapped his fist on the armchair, and declared, "Yes, I do here and now!" What an unforgettable moment—to be nearly matched later when I baptized him in the name of the Father, Son, and Holy Spirit. Surely there were many others whom I welcomed, and in their own way no less dramatic.

FAREWELL

As 1970 approached, I began to get persistent calls to the pulpit of the Peninsula Covenant Church in Redwood City, California. It had been started by my brother, David, and was my church home during my Stanford years. After turning down a number of invitations, Elizabeth and I agreed to an interview and met with the pulpit committee. It was a traumatic decision, but I left Pasadena for Redwood City at the start of 1971.

My farewell was moving. Not only did people from the church speak, but others spoke as well. David Hubbard of Fuller, who worshiped with us, gave me one of the most affirming words I have ever heard. Ruby McKnight Williams of the NAACP was most eloquent, declaring, "When I heard Rev. Larsen was leaving Pasadena, I broke down and wept."

On the Monday after my Sunday resignation, I went into a deep depression. Elizabeth, too, felt very pained. I would have given everything to rescind my resignation. We read our breakfast devotional for that morning:

Have I not commanded you? Be strong and courageous. Do not be terrified; do not be discouraged, for the Lord your God is with you wherever you go. (Joshua 1:9 NIV)

In peace I drove to Redwood City on New Year's Day of 1971.

6

Redwood City

I LEFT PASADENA FOR Redwood City early on New Year's Day of 1971. Because our house would not be completed for a couple of months I traveled alone without my family. It was a cold and foggy day with almost no traffic all the way. I checked into a small motel and deposited some of my books in the study at the church. A lay leader and his wife were there the next day to remove holiday decorations. While doing so, he greeted me with, "Here are the first five mistakes you have already made before you even start." Taken aback, I simply stammered, "I assume that when the church called me, it had some confidence that I would be competent as pastoral leader." Rebuffed, he later became a loyal friend.

THE CITY

Redwood City was a municipality of approximately 60,000 residents at the time. Located on the San Francisco Peninsula halfway between San Francisco and San Jose, it lies between San Mateo to the north and Palo Alto to the south. It was originally a redwood logging port on the bay with middle-class suburbs to the north toward San Mateo. It bordered wealthy suburbs like Atherton and Woodside southward toward Palo Alto. The coastal range to the west and the bay to the east moderated the weather. The flatland on the bayside was filled with industrial and lower-class Hispanic communities. Newer housing filled the hills to the west along the great chain of Hetch Hetchy reservoirs on the great San Andreas fault to the west, which bordered Interstate 280, called the world's most beautiful freeway. It drew its population largely from immigrants from San Francisco, who were mostly

69

secular or Roman Catholic. Like San Francisco itself, by 1971, the cities were largely built out, so new housing had become increasingly rare. It did, however, sit at the northern end of Silicon Valley, where the great revolution in computers, technology, and internet development was just beginning. It was located just a few miles north of Stanford University from which these developments were generated.

PENINSULA COVENANT CHURCH

In 1951, a few families from San Francisco had moved down the peninsula and decided to start a church. The church met for the first two years at the Seventh-Day Adventist Church of Burlingame, just north of San Mateo. In 1953, the church bought the attractive little Missouri Lutheran Church on the corner of Jefferson and Clinton in Redwood City. With stained glass, dark ceilings, and a small pipe organ, it seated about 150 people. My brother, David, had moved to our new home in Los Altos, entered Stanford in his junior year, and pastored the new church. I became a part of the church at that time as well, having entered Stanford in 1951. Its two lay leaders were Carl Johansson and Roy Almquist. Carl owned his own insurance agency and Roy was an executive with Standard Oil. He also served as the organist. The church grew quickly, and two years later David graduated with high honors from Stanford and moved south to attend Fuller Seminary.

Following my brother, Wilbur Westerdahl assumed the role of pastor. He was well organized and involved in the community. He gathered a lively group of young couples that soon outgrew the facilities. The church finally decided to purchase ten acres of land on the former Henry Oxnard Estate. Oxnard, a sugar magnate for whom the Southern California city was named, had the property landscaped by William Olmstead, the creator of Golden Gate Park. The church retained the ink-penned linen pen landscape plan. It was a beautiful park overlooking San Francisco Bay. The mansion was used for Sunday school, and an attractive multipurpose fellowship center building that seated about 250 people was erected. Its side walls were of glass on both sides, making it a beautiful setting, but after dark the outside turned black and the interior seemed cold and austere. It was here we worshiped for more than a decade until the main sanctuary was built.

Later Dwight Hervey Small succeeded Westerdahl. A former Presbyterian minister, he was a disciplined biblical expositor and pastoral counselor. During his time as pastor, a large one-and-a-half-story educational building was built, together with a small office suite. The electronics boom dramatically took off, raising the price of property significantly.

The counterculture that arose in the late 1960s affected local church visions, and in 1971, Peninsula Covenant was particularly unsettled. Its theology and ethical standards were not in dispute, but the nature of the church was. Sunday worship remained as it was, with attendance running about 400. The church had raised more than $400,000 to construct its first sanctuary. Donald Powers Smith was the architect. The younger set, however, grew restless with the current worship forms and the emphasis on an elegant sanctuary building. The goal to build a megachurch came under stiff scrutiny. Even the flourishing church growth movement came under fire as an accoutrement of corporate America and its marketing proclivities. Successful business leaders were the power of the church's vision. The new concern wanted to emphasize reaching the poor. In the midst of the restlessness, Pastor Small took an appointment at Westmont College, teaching marriage and family courses. With the pulpit vacant, I at first resisted many phone calls. Finally, Elizabeth and I went up for a weekend. As a result, I accepted the call, starting in January 1971.

ARRIVAL

On that cold New Year's Day in 1971, I left my family and drove all the way to Redwood City. I lived in a motel room until our home was completed. Then Elizabeth, Kristi, and Kathy arrived with the moving van. Arrangements for the house were made by realtor Rudi Helin; he and his wife, Janet, were to become two of our closest friends. The house was being finished by the next-door neighbor, Par Ring, a Swedish Pentecostal, and his Swedish Covenant wife, Dagne. It had a beautiful view overlooking the bay, and was only one block from the Roy Cloud Elementary School and less than two miles downhill to the church.

ELIZABETH, KRISTI, AND KATHLEEN

Elizabeth kept busy as a mother of young children, but before long she was also active in church life. Feeling that she had not been involved outside of the church, she opened her home to her neighbors in the community for a bi-weekly Bible study in our home. She allowed only one woman from church to attend since she wanted to prevent insider church conversation. She selected ten neighborhood women. She called them each week. She prayed for and phoned each one weekly. She set a goal of all of them becoming true Christians within two years. Those goals were met by God's grace.

Numerous people visited the church, but only one in five ever became a member. Elizabeth joined Associate Pastor John Strong to initiate a successful follow-up program. A Newcomers Class of four sessions would be offered continually. Three teams were formed, each leading a new four-week class. The first team would take four weeks to contact and befriend all visitors. The team would lead the actual four-week sessions and then shepherd the new converts and/or new members into the life of the church. The second team would be contacting visitors and newcomers after the previous course had begun. While the second moved on to leading these people through the class, the third team would begin contacting visitors regarding the next cohort. Thus the three-team cycle proceeded without interruption. These were the four classes:

Week One: What does it mean to be a Christian?

Week Two: What do Christians believe?

Week Three: Whence is the Covenant Church?

Week Four: What does it mean to be a member of Peninsula Covenant?

The three teams met for an hour for prayer and encouragement each Sunday before the early 9:30 a.m. service. The results were amazing. Instead of one in five visitors eventually joining the church, three out of five actually became members. By God's grace nearly half of these made their first life commitment to Christ.

So Elizabeth and I teamed together in both parenting and Christian service. Yet we also ministered to one another. Her gentle and winsome manner could soon melt the anxieties and angers in my life. She has indeed been a partner more than equal to her task!

FINDING THE PROCESS

A number of leaders told me to declare the vision, and they would follow. I had already begun to question within myself the much-sought-after desire for a visionary leader. That may be all right for a pioneer starting a new church or movement. But a twenty-year-old church had its own culture. I declined to give my vision. Instead we would work together to develop a common mission. An army must find common unity if it is to battle successfully.

Some of those in leadership were initially frustrated that I did not come as a visionary leader. I told them that the vision and mission would be developed as we worked to find unity in our leadership—both staff and lay leaders. I later found that even the strongest proponents of this style of leadership saw that too often a new leader's coming in with a vision before he or she has understood the dynamics and tradition of an ongoing organization or church, particularly in a church, often ends up in conflict. A new leader with "visionary leadership" often can bring serious division. Unity must be developed first.

It was a slow process to build this unity at Peninsula Covenant Church inasmuch as the church was already somewhat divided by the rapid cultural changes of the 1960s. I finally decided to take a course on Strategic Management through the American Management Association. I bridled a bit at first, because mission and purpose statements seemed to amount to trite expressions of some innocuous truisms. Then I saw that it was not the mission statements as much of the process of bringing people together in a common task. The process also involved an inclusive group in a context where each person could deliver their thoughts without correction or put down. People tend to support what they help to create, thus the process transcends the product. I assumed this would be a tedious process, but later learned that even some of the largest corporations never implemented a process of continuing evaluation, and thus 80 percent of even big businesses failed in the process. But I swallowed the bait and was hooked. Our strategic management process, first of all, brought staff and board members to a day and half meeting at our Community Center for a joint scoring of the prior year's goals and objectives. Friday evening was a time of scoring the outcomes of each of the prior year's goals. Strangely, this exercise turned out to be more affirming than disappointing. It gave opportunity for strengthening and reinforcing the highest goals.

We were, of course, swamped with goals, strategies, and objectives. Here I tried to bring some order. My problem was that I had too many thoughts. Sitting at my desk the thought occurred to me that I might be able to combine these in a simple acrostic that each person could understand. Thus I created "Paul's Pyramid," consisting of often-used mission statements, goals, and objectives. It would be easy to recall as a tool to develop goals for each ensuing year:

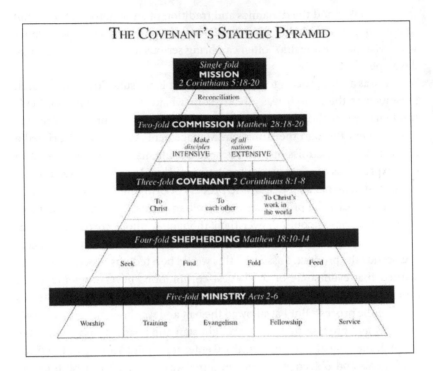

THE COVENANT'S STATEGIC PYRAMID

Single fold
MISSION
2 Corinthians 5:18-20

Reconciliation

Two-fold **COMMISSION** *Matthew 28:18-20*

| *Make disciples* INTENSIVE | *of all nations* EXTENSIVE |

Three-fold **COVENANT** *2 Corinthians 8:1-8*

| To Christ | To each other | To Christ's work in the world |

Four-fold **SHEPHERDING** *Matthew 18:10-14*

| Seek | Find | Fold | Feed |

Five-fold **MINISTRY** *Acts 2-6*

| Worship | Training | Evangelism | Fellowship | Service |

Defining the mission of the Christian church is the top of pyramid. The next level is the Great Commission and its equal commitment to both quality and quantity. Then the threefold covenant is followed by the steps in evangelism and discipleship. At the bottom are the five elements of the traditional elements of Christian education. The pyramid is a memory device combining all of them. I used it throughout my entire ministry as well as my time as President of the Covenant Church.

PREACHING THROUGH PROVERBS

My preaching was primarily expository through successive biblical books. One of these took us through the book of Proverbs. Perhaps the highest calling is the privilege to preach the word of God. The most sacred trust, however, is the care of souls. The everyday care of counseling, encouragement, weddings, and funerals constitute daily life for the pastor. Exposition and pastoral care are necessarily linked. Week by week we often experienced occasions of vibrant hope.

P— was an attractive young woman who became a faithful member of the choir. Sitting across my desk during an appointment, she broke down weeping. She declared that she had grown up in a very strict Christian home. She took up a major in modern dance at UC Berkeley. Running out of funds, she began dancing at a San Francisco theater. This led her into high-class prostitution. Disowned by her parents, she tried desperately to find a new life. She was bright and quickly became an executive secretary for a top executive of a world-renowned corporation, also in San Francisco. On the way down the elevator at work one day, another senior executive entered the elevator and greeted her by name. Horrified, she recognized him as a former client. Filled with fright and revulsion she fled the office and never went back. I prayed with her and then encouraged her to finish the last semester at Berkeley while continuing to serve in the choir. She then took a job as a legal secretary in San Jose. A year later she called and told me how she had not only been forgiven but was flourishing in her walk with Christ. She then surprised me by saying that she had just become engaged to a prominent and honorable attorney. "Jesus saves! Jesus saves."

Preaching and Publishing

The expository preaching through Proverbs led to the publication of these sermons. *Wise Up and Live* was published by Regal Books. This sold more than one hundred thousand copies in English, through more than eleven printings. It was also published in Portuguese and Chinese. The foreword was written by David Alan Hubbard, President of Fuller Seminary. I was his pastor during my Pasadena days.

CHURCH BUILDINGS

The arrival of the counterculture in the 1960s saw the revolt of the younger generation against traditional middle-class values. Anti-war, anti-establishment radicalism, and drugs also had their effects upon even the most evangelical churches. Peninsula was no exception. The thought of building an elegant sanctuary in a world of poverty became increasingly divisive. The projected sanctuary seating 600 would necessitate razing historic Covenant House and its swimming pool. The largest specimen of the monkey pod tree in the park of the old Oxnard Estate not only made it beautiful but also untouchable. Despite the ten acres, the steep hillside made enough parking impossible unless we planned for underground parking below the sanctuary. Hundreds of thousands of dollars had been pledged, but it all came to a halt during the controversy.

Swim and Tennis Club

I had no idea how to unite the polarized groups. I attempted to suggest that we should try to do both—build an outreach facility and the sanctuary—except that would double the cost. We nonetheless hired noted architect Al Hoover to come up with a solution. One day I received a phone call from the owner of the three-and-a-half-acre Redwood City Swim and Tennis Club, who told me he adjoined our property. It had become insolvent and he would sell it for two hundred thousand dollars. Sitting on more than four acres of land across the steep ravine from the church, on a clear day its commanding view of the East Bay even included the splendid First Covenant Church of Oakland. The facility consisted of a 10,000-square-foot clubhouse, an Olympic sized pool, and five tennis courts. There were lockers and steam rooms, as well as a large Jacuzzi. A small building housed a snack bar. In an attempt stave off bankruptcy, the upstairs was remodeled by a successful chain of pre-schools, which also added a magnificent playground along the creek at the bottom of the canyon. It had a multiyear lease from the preschool.

The owner told me that our properties adjoined in the bottom of the canyon where a year-around stream flowed. Mr. Hoover made a study and came up with the proposal that we acquire the facility and build a hundred-yard-long, twelve-foot-wide wooden footbridge to join the facilities. The proposed sanctuary would be moved to a viewpoint over the whole San Francisco Bay from the site's high point on the southeast. When priced out, the entire project would not only provide the parking on both sites, but the total cost would be hundreds of thousands of dollars less than trying to build all on our original site. Needless to say, the decision was controversial, but the congregation took the option. The result was a most unusual church campus. Within the year the preschool went bankrupt and abandoned the lease—freeing the entire facility for church use.

The Sanctuary

The Worship Center was to seat 800, with seating for 500 in the greater nave and 300 in the lesser nave. It would be basically a glass and redwood structure. It was thus one of the last large redwood structures to be built, and the diminishing redwood trees were depleted in California's forest. It was triangular in shape, rising to some thirty feet at the chancel peak. A large space was left over the choir loft to house a potential pipe organ. Thus, large expanses of glass filled two sides with a massive twenty-by-twenty-five-foot window overlook. Its bright, red-cushioned pews gave a ruby glow toward automobiles driving uphill past the church on Farm Hill Boulevard. The ten-story carillon tower made the church a visible landmark even to planes beginning their descent to San Francisco's airport twenty miles away.

The Pipe Organ

The newer forms of church music had raised serious concerns about the ancient pipe organs in a world of younger worshippers. Yet I felt that we needed to be both contemporary and traditional. I asked the architect to include space for such an organ. A wood and purple screen would allow the use of an electronic organ. I opined that perhaps there might be a wealthy widow from Woodside who loved only cats and pipe organs. Perhaps she might pay the enormous and prohibitive cost as a gift, I said, with a wink of the eye.

Instead, God sent Paul Sahlin, personnel director of the C & H Sugar Company, to our fellowship. He loved pipe organs and built a thirty-rank organ in his own home. Church chair Carl Johanson got excited when Paul announced that he had found a 1914 pipe organ carefully stored at a church in Oakland. Carl bought it as a gift and Paul went to work. With volunteers, the massive instrument was built over the next few years. It ultimately had eighty ranks, making it the largest church organ in northern California, surpassing the Catholic and Episcopalian cathedrals in San Francisco. During much of the time that followed, David Parsons played the organ beautifully; he had been the organist in the Princeton University Chapel even while a student. He was also organist at the historic Round Church at Cambridge University while he was completing his PhD at that famed school. Replacement of the organ would have been in excess of $1 million dollars. Our new building was also used as the Bay Area gathering place for people who loved the era of silent movies. On occasion we would have Gaylord Carter, the original music writer and performer of the famous movie *King of Kings* and others of the great silent movies. This brought many to our worship center who would have never come for worship.

The Community Center

As we sought to transform the swim and tennis club into the Community Center, in a few years it needed significant remodeling and expansion. Fred Strathdee, an architect in our church, created the design, which Alan Miller, a major building contractor in the church, together with creative genius Dick Martin, our superintendent of buildings and grounds, turned into reality. Most significant was the erection of a huge gymnasium with a full-size basketball court. It also served as a recreation hall and dining hall with a large adjacent kitchen. The gym itself would have a giant tempered-glass wall overlooking the pool, tennis courts, and East Bay. The two lower floors accommodated youth offices and classrooms. We also added a large exercise room, again all glass, with a full Nautilus fitness center. At another end of the building, a reception room and three offices for psychological and spiritual counseling were built. The development of the ministries of these facilities would be developed in a year-long massive research paper as part of my doctoral program.

SAN ANSELMO DOCTORATE[1]

Within a year of my arrival at Redwood City, I decided I needed to continue to grow academically and spiritually. Yet I could not get this education through a seminary or university with a residency requirement. I discovered that San Francisco Theological Seminary at San Anselmo had a five-year doctoral program. This nearly century-old Presbyterian Seminary—part of the Graduate Theological Union, which had ties to UC-Berkeley—was located just north of San Francisco, less than two hours away. The five-year program included three summer sessions and would be more akin to a medical residency in applied theology. Each year would involve research and development of some aspect of parish ministry. The fifth year entailed a doctoral dissertation. The degree was a revival of an earlier European degree and was called a Doctor of the Science of Theology or STD. The Association of Theological Schools accredited it as an equivalent of the traditional PhD. The summer sessions were held on weekdays, allowing me to attend to pastoral duties over each long weekend. The church graciously offered to cover the tuition of my program.

Year One: Psychology and Religion in the Life of the Church as a Healing Community

The first summer session was comprised of a small group under the tutelage of psychologist Glenn Whitlock. He introduced us to research methods, personal and institutional planning, and exercises in holistic growth. He

---

1. Larsen, "Expository Preaching."

then advised me on my topic, entitled "Psychology and Religion in the Life of the Church as a Healing Community."

I first began a study of the ways that leading thinkers had related the cultures of psychology and religion. I took as my matrix H. Richard Niebuhr's classic book, *Christ and Culture*, utilizing his five types of cultural interaction. I then took a well-known spokesman to characterize each of the five types. I chose the fifth type, "Christ transforming Culture" as the model I would use to establish my own perspective. While theologian Paul Tillich was no orthodox Christian, his analysis of the sources of neurosis had a powerful influence on contemporary secular theory. I then synthesized this view with my own theology of reconciliation, predominantly based on 2 Corinthians 5.

Meanwhile, I visited a number of prominent churches that had developed professional counseling ministries, such as Hollywood Presbyterian Church and Garden Grove Community Church. Dr. Russ Llewelyn, a clinical psychologist and member of the church, began practicing counseling at the church, then Dr. Marvin Branstrom, already a church member was added. Each served on a part-time basis. Later Karl Miller, a marriage and family counselor, came full time. The Covenant Counseling Center became so large that it took a suite of offices at a nearby shopping center. This center has been of great service not only to the congregation and members of the Community Center, but also to people from the community at large.

Among the many moving accounts of the Counseling Center is that of psychiatrist Dr. Ron Chen. He had escaped communist China by coming to medical school in the U.S. He then took his psychiatric residency at the famed Menninger Foundation at Topeka, Kansas. Following that he took a post-doctoral residency under noted anthropologist Margaret Meade. Later he became Director of Mental Hygiene for the state of Michigan. Deciding to pursue private practice, he moved to Redwood City with his family and joined the Community Center. He then declined an offer from then-governor Jerry Brown to become California State Director of Mental Hygiene. We became friends and we had lunch one day at the Sequoia Club. His father and two brothers were Christian evangelists who remained under intense persecution in China. He secretly sent funds each year to keep them from starvation as the Communists would not give them funds. Following the opening of China, he visited the family. His grateful father then told him he must take the ultimate step of becoming a Christian. Ron then asked me to receive him for true Christian conversion and baptism. His public baptism was a great day. He was the first psychiatrist to serve part time on the Covenant Counseling Center staff.

The nearly one-hundred-page study from that first year profoundly affected my theology and practice in the years that followed. It has been invaluable even through my years as president and into retirement.

Year Two: Developing the Community Center

The second year-long project was to develop a plan for the missional use of the Community Center. Dr. Bob Lee, Margaret Dollar Professor of Social Ethics at San Anselmo, guided my studies. A leading authority on religion and leisure, he helped me discover the historic roots of church involvement in training and athletics. The early Sunday schools of nineteenth-century England even taught both reading and Bible studies on Sunday afternoons to the slum-dwelling children in England ,and included physical activities as well. The YMCA spread worldwide due to its use of athletics and training in Christian discipleship—especially during its early days. Both basketball and volleyball were games devised by the early YMCA to create a healthy body and strong Christian character. As immigrants flooded the American shores in the latter nineteenth century, the churches sought to bring Christian evangelism and cultural adaptation to the teaming millions. They built schools and hospitals as well as programs in literacy and basic business skills. The early Swedish Covenanters did likewise with the establishment of North Park College and Swedish Covenant Hospital, as well as an orphanage and the Covenant Home of Mercy. From the beginning, the Covenant Church was involved in spiritual and social ministry.

But what about a swim and tennis club? It would be an outstanding facility for the church's families and young people, but operations would be incredibly costly. Longtime members of the swim and tennis club were outraged at the possibility of losing the use of the facility. Could we operate the facility as a missional outreach to the community, especially in the Peninsula's upscale affluence?

My studies led to the book of Acts. In Acts 19:9–10, Paul and his companions moved to the school of Tyrannus and rented a hall and preached Christ. I was intrigued by a comment by R. B. Rakham in his classic commentary on Acts. The school of Tyrannus was in fact the public baths where aristocrats would bathe and relax at the close of each day. They would further relax by listening to wandering teachers who regularly retained one of the rooms for lectures. Paul rented one of these. Acts tells us that since Ephesus was the capitol of the Roman province of Asia, leaders from the whole province would visit the baths regularly. Thus Paul was able to spread the good news throughout the province of Asia. Voila! So we would use our Community Center.

We then opened the center daily at 7 a.m. except for Sunday, when we opened at noon. Families paid a monthly fee if they were not church members. Soon several hundred persons and families joined. This covered our expenses and helped cover capital costs as well as charitable outreach ministries.

Ed Holt, a former youth pastor, was our first director, who was followed by Donn Anderson, a former station director at American West Airlines. Their work was incomparable. Bill Rapp became our tennis director. Even Sandy Maier, then Wembley star, and his brother joined and brought us real competition. Ron Chlasta, a swimming star from our Glenn Ellen Covenant Church, came to direct our aquatic and fitness program. During this time we added a huge full-sized gym with glass walls overlooking the entire bay. Our swim teams became very competitive. Even the Men's Olympic Water Polo team practiced at our center until the American president canceled U.S. participation in the Russian Olympic Games. Each November we held the annual face off between America's top two swim champions. Businesses and individuals sponsored the event and raised large contributions to provide family Christmas dinners for poor families in the area. One year the magazine *U.S. News World Report* produced a large picture and accompanying story of the nation's two top swimmers.

But was there spiritual fruit? Indeed there has been much fruit. With a united Christian staff and dedicated church volunteers, the stories abound. I remember Helen Potter, whom others privately called the queen bee. She was the club's social arbiter and an inveterate tennis player. She had no church connection, but gradually became a friend. Then she became the center's receptionist. Frequent church attendance led her to faith in Christ. Then her husband came to faith. Though later stricken with cancer, to her dying day she lived with joy in Christ.

Jim Fuller, my neighbor across the street, had a similar story. A stockbroker, he confronted me angrily at our takeover of the center. Raised a nominal Lutheran, he and his wife had become involved with an upper-class cult movement led by law professor Harry Rathbune of Stanford University. The leader developed his movement of several thousand by basing it on the psychology of the unconscious of Swiss psychiatrist Carl Jung.

Reasonably gracious despite his initial outrage at the church's acquisition of the center, he nonetheless continued to debate our differences of faith. I saw him at church one Easter Sunday, and he asked to have lunch with me at the Sequoia Club that week. At lunch he simply stated that he just decided to abandon Professor Rathbun and surrender to Jesus Christ. What joy! Somewhat inflated, I asked him what in my Easter sermon helped him to faith. He sneered, "Nothing, the worst sermon I've ever heard!" He then said that a few weeks previous, he, his wife, and children had been helplessly bedridden for nearly a week. "All I got from a group of believers were phone calls asking us to stay away until we were all well. Your wife, Elizabeth, began appearing on our doorstep with chicken soup and other goodies. It was then we decided to profess Christ." Later Jim became vice president of the New York Stock Exchange. While there he served as chair of the Wall Street Committee to reelect President Reagan.

As my wife stopped by the center one morning, a young man of somewhat grungy appearance swung into the parking lot and asked what this place was all about. He had come from Southern California to help a cousin who was building a house nearby. He slept there because it was free and he could keep watch during construction. Seeing Elizabeth, he asked, "Is there any way I can use the shower, as I have no running water?" Elizabeth said yes and invited him to church. *Will Milne* was very bright and passed all his junior college courses without attending classes. In desperation, his mother sent him to his cousin so that at least he would learn to work. He began to attend church, but argued with me regularly. If I referred to Lincoln's Second Inaugural, he would correct me by saying that the quote came from his Cooper Union Address. If I quoted from Marx's *Communist Manifesto*, he would tell me it came from *Das Capital*. Soon he came to see me weekly. I told him I had hundreds of people I needed to care for and didn't have time for such debates. He countered, "But you are a pastor, aren't you? It's your duty to teach me!" I then agreed, but insisted he read heavy theology and history each week. It was a marvel to see him grow. He went to stay at the home of Ken and Shirley Lincoln. He continued to work in construction and eventually went out on his own. Today he annually builds several mammoth mansions in nearby Woodside and Atherton—each home running between ten and fifteen million dollars. He fell in love with my secretary Marge Dillman's daughter, Karen. He then toiled to put her through college. Together they are raising their four children in their massive home overlooking upper Green Lake. We communicate and visit from time to time. He is a model husband and father, while winning the gold medal for his age bracket in the 2012 Veteran World Championships in Fencing in Austria. Some have wondered whether Will was in some sense the son I never had.

Some have facetiously asked, "Paul, you don't have an athletic bone in your body. How did you ever get involved with a swim and tennis club?" I glibly respond, "Because I am the only pastor whom God could trust with such an enticement." One summer the Swedish Ministers Chorus put on a concert in our church. During a Q&A session the next morning, a pastor asked, "Do you think Peninsula Covenant will become a new model for American churches?" I replied, "Heavens no! When I see all the millions sunk into this facility and a world so filled with pain and poverty, I don't know whether to brag or repent!"

Year Three: Strengthening Lay Ministry

The third year I devoted to a study of lay training. My advisor was Dr. Clifford Erickson, a member of our church. He was president of the College of San Mateo with its three large campuses. He had previously headed all of Chicago's junior colleges. I studied the biblical and historical development of training and empowering lay persons. I had already experienced some of the perennial struggle between the clergy and the laity. For many centuries the church had been crippled because of the control of the church by a caste of priests, pastors, presbyters, and bishops. Yet St. Peter had written that all the people are kings and priests. The Reformed Protestant churches rejected the power of monarchical bishops. They taught that God ruled the church through its elders. Luther, however, understood that God rules the church through laity who then choose their leaders. The rise of an educated clergy gave the pastors the power of superior knowledge. This centralization of power inevitably led to resentment by the less trained. I wondered if there would be more unity and missional effectiveness if the clergy would see their laity as people with whom to share the power by passing the fire to the ordinary Christian through training.

I saw in my congregation many godly men and women who had graduate degrees and expertise in business, education, and politics. Yet many had no disciplined Christian training since childhood. Could adults who were well-trained in their vocations also learn about their faith and practice their faith on a more adult level? Thus, the church supported an effort to establish a lay academy. We looked at successful programs developed in other noted churches, and took particular note of the ministry of the Garden Grove Community Church in Southern California.

The result was the effort to enroll all church members in the process of growing and development. The training took place in four stages as the individual disciple progressed.

Level One: Introduction to Christ and the Church. The first course concerned basic Christian faith and the meaning of the new birth. The second course first introduced the mission of the church, then the history of the Evangelical Covenant Church, and then the history of Peninsula Covenant Church, with both the privileges and responsibilities of such membership.

This turned out to be the most productive way to both evangelize and disciple new believers that we had developed.

Level Two: Basic Bible and theology. Growing Christians need more than a third-grade understanding of the faith. Most churches no longer have the two-year confirmation course for junior highers that had long been a part of the Covenant Church tradition. Now many adults have no prior training in the essential truths of Christianity. Since the congregation and lay leadership have ultimate authority in a local church, how can shared ignorance do anything but endanger the church? We began this level with a Wednesday evening, two-year class in Bible and theology. I utilized the highly successful Bethel Bible Study series as the foundation. Nearly thirty of our leaders successfully completed that course. One of this level's goals ensured that everyone elected to the governing boards needed to complete this course prior to their election.

Level Three: Empowering for Lay Ministry. Here we helped each person discover his or her interests and gifts. One could be mentored in teaching, counseling, care-giving, crisis intervention, music, and worship. The development of these gifts would be ongoing.

Level Four: Lay Pastor. Such a position would amount to lay ordination. Years of spiritual growth, interpersonal skills, as well as tested leadership roles would receive special recognition. I even suggested that such standing would best be granted by the conference in which the church was located.

As time went on, laypeople from neighboring churches began taking courses. Two neighboring Baptist churches had lay leaders attending. The same was true for two nearby Presbyterian churches. Soon members of Lutheran churches came as well. And surprise, there soon came a few from Catholic churches!

While I gave overall leadership, this was by no means a solo operation. The entire staff and leadership furthered and implemented the development of the academy. I give special mention to Bruce Finfrock, our Christian education minister, for giving the real organizational administrative leadership to the academy. When, some years later, he took another position in Southern California, he was pleased to report that 75 percent of the entire church membership participated in some form of lay ministry, thanks to Bruce and the Grace of God. This formal program constituted but a part of the education and Sunday school work of the church.

On Sunday mornings I began noticing a bright young couple coming into our 9:30 a.m. worship. Dr. Joseph Welch and his wife, Carol, had lately moved in nearby. He had been recently named as the chair of the Department of Micro-Neurosurgery at Stanford University Medical School. I soon found out that they were both committed atheists. Being of broad intellectual concerns, though, they regretted that the public schools had been stripped of all biblical teaching and stories. So they did research and decided that Peninsula had the best children's Sunday school on the Peninsula. They would simply drop them off for the school and pick them up afterward.

Wanting to avoid two trips, they decided to sit through our morning worship while waiting for Sunday school to end. One Sunday he asked me to meet him for lunch. I invited him to the Sequoia Club. It was a Sunday in Advent and I was preaching on the virgin birth of Christ. He felt like he had a hole in his head to sit through such a silly fable. "I was an atheist and a scientist," he said. "I don't know what happened, but as the service closed, I suddenly believed in the incarnation, virgin birth, and resurrection. I went home troubled because Carol and I had firm commitments to atheism. At dinner I stammered out my sudden conversion." Carol gasped and said, "I was trying to figure out how to tell you that, at that very point, I also became a believer in Christ." They were faithful worshippers in our church until the travel distance to a new home made the weekly journey too formidable.

Year Four: Enhancing Worship

The rise of the counterculture in the 1960s and 1970s created great conflict in nearly every denomination. These worship wars sprang up everywhere from Roman Catholic all the way to the Pentecostal congregations. The Covenant Church, with its middling ways, was no exception. North Park Seminary Dean Glenn Anderson agreed to be my supervisor.

I began an extensive study of worship from the Old and New Testaments and then over the course of church history. This then moved to contemporary theology and practice. Union Seminary's Professor Paul Hoon struck an important caution in confusing worship and art. If seen as art, authentic worship is sidelined in its real purpose. He clearly laid down the line: worship can be artful when using "artful" as an adjective or adverb, but never when "art" is simply a noun. Worship must not become merely classical or popular entertainment.

My studies showed that music is a central part of corporate worship. More than anything else, it is a way for Christians to share their personal experiences of Christ with a common voice. This requires a familiar melody and message for the hymns. Too many professional musicians overlook this. The introduction of new music to broaden the sharing of the common moving stories of redemption and salvation must also be done prudently.

I then engaged in an extended series on the life of David as seen through the Psalms and history. Arranging the traditionally purported Psalms according to the great events in the life of David, I was able to enrich the expositions using Robert Prothero's out-of-print study, *The Psalms in Human Life*. We could then integrate the Psalms into the order of worship and the music.

Our outstanding minister of music, Jonathan Brown, not only had his outstanding high school choirs compete at the annual California State High School Choral Competition, he also gained a Master of Arts in Sacred Music from the University of Southern California. His skill and flexibility crossed the full range of Gospel and contemporary forms. Our organist, David Parsons, had served as organist at Princeton University and while studying at Trinity Evangelical Divinity School. While writing his PhD dissertation on Puritan music at Cambridge University, he also served as organist at the historic Round Church. He gained access to the massive music library at Stanford and to different settings of the Davidic Psalms. I felt that at last I had been able to achieve an appropriate synthesis of preaching and music in Christian worship.

But did this really reach the contemporary audience of Peninsula Covenant Church? This required feedback. We then recruited a random group of some thirty respondents from the congregation representing diverse ages, genders, and education levels. They would respond each Sunday for twelve weeks on the same evaluation form. Music was then varied from classical, Gospel, and contemporary forms. Examining the scorings clearly showed that 10 percent of the responders on either the traditional or contemporary ends were purists. They felt quite negatively about music from the opposite end of the spectrum. But 80 percent of the responders wanted a blend of both. This left an indelible impression on me.

The tensions arising from emerging peoples and cultures are inevitable. The real test is not just in the differences in the broad spectrum; it is more often between good music and bad music. Charles Wesley wrote more than 5,000 hymns in the eighteenth century, but only a few of his greatest survive to this day. I am sure the mass of contemporary music will undergo the same refinement. Thank God!

The differences in musical taste are based most often on personal experiences. The attempts to umpire musical preferences seem to be largely cultural. At a reception following a great presentation of Bach's St. Matthew's Passion, I came across two men in heated debate about church music. One side stressed that only traditional and classic music could be used in public worship. The other side argued that only contemporary music could reach the coming generation. The traditionalists felt that the hymn "Blessed

Assurance" would be classic. The other side declared that Simon and Gar-
funkel's "Bridge over Troubled Waters" was truly contemporary.

Let us pray that civil debate may resolve any ongoing tensions before
rekindling worship wars!

Years Five and Six: The Exposition of Ephesians

For my dissertation project I selected preaching as my topic. In most ways
I had always utilized the expository method of preaching. Nearly two thousand years separate the last book written in the Bible and the closing years
of the twentieth century. Add a thousand years in the writing of the Old
Testament. How indeed can anything that old enlighten, renew, and transform middle-class Americans in their current cultural situation? I needed
this project to explore the effects of such exposition on my own congregation. Dr. Harland Hogue of the Pacific School of Religion and the Graduate
Theological Union was approved as my project supervisor. His counsel and
advice were incomparable.

I selected the book of Ephesians as my topic. My thesis was "The Exposition of Ephesians in a Suburban Middle Class Context." I roughly divided
the six chapters of the book into sermons, making twelve sermons in all.
Then I created an evaluation form that included criticisms and affirmations
for each sermon. But I also had to ask how it changed their outlook and lifestyle. This was most critical because it could begin to test behavioral change.
In addition, my research had to show doctoral-level competence in Bible,
history, theology, communications theory, and statistics. That was heavy!
Moreover, could we in any way credibly measure behavioral change?

The challenge, Dr. Hogue cautioned me, was that most modern scholarship had denied that St. Paul could have written the letter. "You will have
a tough time getting past the examining committee—so be prepared!" I
discovered, however, that Marcus Barth and other more recent scholars had
reaffirmed Pauline authorship. One side argued that Ephesians reflects a
Christianity altered by the intrusion of Hellenistic mystery and myth. The
other side showed that all of these references were also found in the Old Testament, reflecting on the book as a product of Palestinian Judaism. I argued
the latter extensively and got through my exam without a challenge.

This led to my conclusion that the book was a paradigmatic way in
which to move from one major culture to another without altering the biblical message. That is, all supposedly Hellenistic stories and metaphors were
also found in the Old Testament. To this day Ephesians provides my model
for cross-cultural translation.

But what difference did it make in hearts, minds, and behavior of the hearers? The randomly selected hearers ranged in age, gender, and education levels. This resulted in more than twenty thousand scorings. Computer science expert Don Noren graciously helped me through this onerous task.

What were the results? The findings were valuable:

1. The responses helped me to change and alter my preaching style.

2. The changes of outlook, viewpoint, and lifestyle became apparent as we progressed.

3. This disclosed a rising curve in understanding and outlook.

4. The study clearly showed that evaluation and note-taking had a profound impact.

5. Learning to listen is a vital part of Christian maturity. As a part of the seventh- and eighth-grade confirmation instruction, students were required to submit notes on each Sunday morning sermon.

6. The preaching of the word of God is weakened by both poor preaching and poor listening skills.

How long the changes in behavior lasted after the series ended is perhaps impossible to know. We rest, however, on the word of God:

> So is my word that goes out from my mouth:
> It will not return to me empty,
> But will accomplish what I desire
> and achieve the purpose for which I sent it. (Isa 55:11)

It took two years to complete this project. In June 1978, at San Anselmo's Commencement, the Seminary awarded me the degree of Doctor of the Science of Theology. I was surprised when the dean read aloud a full-page, four-paragraph excerpt from Dr. Hogue's commendation of my thesis.

My dissertation was 450 pages long. The faculty then voted that no dissertation could henceforth be more than 250 pages. Win some, lose some!

THE KAINOS HOME FOR THE MENTALLY DISABLED

This was never my idea. It was the vision of two schoolteachers, Dorothy and Jim Philbrick. Active members of our church, they lived under the heartbreak of their son, Jim, who had severe learning disabilities. He was now an adult, and there were no facilities on the Peninsula to care for and house him. He did have public disability assistance, but he could only find affordable housing on skid row in San Jose.

They were tormented by the fact that this would be his destiny when they could no longer care for him. On numerous occasions she would confront me with the need to care for so many of these disabled children when their parents were either deceased or too old to care for them. Dorothy Philbrick pled with me to help the church begin the project. I had other priorities.

After one rather intense confrontation I said to her, "Dorothy, I believe that when God wants something, he generally burdens the heart of the ones he wants to use. He has not laid that burden on me. Do not keep demanding that I take leadership. Do not come back to me unless you have five people who are willing to meet every Wednesday evening who are prepared to pray, seek guidance, and personally sacrifice for this mission." Two weeks later she appeared with five dedicated women.

Meeting and praying regularly, they first proposed using the church hall one night a month for a square dance to include all developmentally disabled adults. Since rhythm and dance tended to help with these disabilities, the church heartily approved. A realtor on the team found an acre of land next to the Community Center, but they had no funds to buy it. One Sunday evening she appeared at sharing time during evening worship. She and Jim had prayerfully decided to take a huge second mortgage on their large home to make the down payment on the property. Bob Pierce, a member of the church announced that his Thursday evening poker game with a gang of wealthy friends would play and raise the money to build the home for a score of residents. That group and other community donors covered the entire construction costs. Kainos was incorporated. Finding disability funds from the state, the residents, under professional supervision, would handle maintenance of our fourteen-acre church property. Some nonchurch members of the center angrily objected to "having these people around" while they were indulging their sports activities. I dismissed the complaints, saying that it was very important for professional middle-class people to constantly be exposed to the less fortunate. If such presence was too objectionable, we would deem such objectors no longer eligible for membership in the center. Fortunately, none left. Whether in worship or recreation, "the least of these," Christ's children, always enriched us with their presence.

Kainos needed a skilled agriculturalist with a heart for these people to guide their work and teach them elementary gardening. Paul DeNeui had just graduated from Cal Poly in agriculture. He came with his wife, Gretchen, to assume the position. They joined our church and soon became active. Paul chaired all campus Bible studies under InterVarsity at Cal Poly.

Joining our King's Runners Bible study on Tuesday mornings, he quickly showed himself the most gifted inductive Bible study leader I had ever seen. He moved on to seminary and from there both he and Gretchen led an outstanding work in a new area of our Thailand mission field. After gaining his PhD from Fuller Seminary, he has held the chair of Missions at North Park and become a major writer on Buddhism in Asia.

COLLEAGUES

The dedicated lay leaders of Peninsula Covenant Church are too numerous to account for here. I regret I cannot mention all of the staff members who made me look far better than I really was. One long-term colleague, though, is Bob Gillikin. I met Bob and Betty in the second year of my pastorate in Orangevale. An associate pastor of the large Arcade Baptist Church, he led a weekly early morning meeting of several local pastors. Bob had been among the original founders of International Christian Leadership (ICL) under Abraham Wrede. In this group was Senator Mark Hatfield of Oregon. Throughout the rest of his life he continued to lead these key Bible studies that included members of the prestigious Hoover Institute at Stanford. In Orangevale I learned about small group Bible study and prayer. After a few years he came to Peninsula Covenant Church as associate pastor. A gifted counselor, evangelist, and administrator, he was far better than I in these tasks, even while caring faithfully during the prolonged and disabling illness of his wife, Betty.

COVENANT AFFIRMATIONS

My responsibilities to our larger fellowship led to my two terms as a member of the Covenant Executive Board, during which I served as vice president of the Covenant Church. I was liaison to the Board of Church Growth and Evangelism during that time. President Engebretson named me to a committee to draft a series of doctrinal affirmations as the Covenant Church was emerging from its Lutheran Pietist Petition. It had been sheltered under the Unaltered Augsburg Confession of the Lutherans. It had, however, decided to place its trust in the Bible as God's word, rather than a brief doctrinal confession. Despite our lack of a formal creed, we nonetheless kept the Covenant Church clearly within the historic Christian faith. As the church developed broader contact with twentieth-century churches, there was some fear that the lack of a confession was an open door to any modernist or liberal viewpoint. Hence the committee was charged to develop a series of Covenant Church Affirmations in the interest of expressing our own self-identity as well as informing churches and people who journeyed with us in the mission of the kingdom.

In addition to myself and the president, the committee included Professor Donald Frisk of the seminary, Edward Larsen, Dick Sandquist, A. Eldon Palmquist, and Jim Hawkinson.

I developed the basic format and outline with the approval of the committee. Each member then wrote a concise and clear statement on one of the Affirmations. The committee members represented the center of Covenant Church tradition, well balanced on both center left and center right. It took a couple of years of earnest endeavor to finally get the precise wording on which we could unanimously agree. Thus emerged the short booklet *Covenant Church Affirmations*.[2]

There were legitimate apprehensions that this would turn us into a rigid confessional body. Yet every one of the great Protestant confessions had eventually weakened and lost its binding character. As a committee we earnestly sought to avoid this retreat into rigid confessionalism. In other words, the Affirmations were descriptive rather normative. Newcomers could then sense the basis of both our faith and heart in a way that would help prevent misunderstandings. The Affirmations have well stood the test of time. Minor additions since have only clarified and strengthened the document.

THE MISSION OF A COVENANT[3]

In 1985, the Covenant Church was to celebrate its 100th birthday. In anticipation of that event, President Engebretson asked three of us each to write a book in honor of the occasion. Mine was to be a forecast of the Covenant Church's future. Karl Ohlsson would write an additional book on Covenant Church history. And Zenos Hawkinson would produce a pictorial coffee table book. It took nearly three years to complete on my schedule. Yet the book in fact appeared in time for the Covenant Church's Centennial celebration. I entitled it *The Mission of a Covenant*. As I studied and wrote the book, I found myself articulating my own theological perspectives in a more systematic way.

Chapter 1: *The People of a Covenant* is basically rooted in a study of the sociology of religion. Under the influence of such teachers as Robert Bella of Harvard and Berkeley, I accepted the neo-Kantian premise that all

2. Covenant Committee on Doctrine, *Covenant Church Affirmations*.

3. Larsen, *Mission of a Covenant Church*.

identity in society is based on a common set of beliefs and practices that is inevitably religious. I then related the concept to the covenantal process. The chapter then sought to show how this identity formation is central to Covenant Church identity.

Chapter 2: *The Theology of a Covenant* is a study in the centrality of the biblical understanding of holy covenant. While this theology is mostly understood as arising from the Reformed or Calvinist traditions rather than our Lutheran traditions, I came to discover that it is at the heart of the Old and New Testament. Here, Lutheran scholar George Mendenhall of Johns Hopkins and Presbyterian theologian Delbert Hillers demonstrated theories that the Old Testament notions of covenant arose from the earlier suzerainty treaties of the Middle East. Even Martin Buber, one of the preeminent theologians of twentieth-century Judaism, described the covenant as the governing concept of Israel's faith.[4] The centrality of covenantal thought emerged, as did post-doctoral studies under Charles McCoy of the Pacific School of Religion. My studies further confirmed that Covenant Church theologies clearly appeared in the early pietism of Spener, Frankel, and other progenitors of Lutheran pietism. This holy covenantal process openly embraces so many of the basic doctrines of evangelical faith, which I briefly indicated in this chapter.

Chapter 3: *The Community of a Covenant* describes how the covenantal process clearly functions within the Covenant Church. Here I became openly revisionist. The early pioneers of the Covenant Church made scant use of that term in their writing, preaching, and teaching. In Sweden and America, the early leaders used the term "covenant" in a secular manner— simply meaning "association" or "society." This was clearly the case. I argued that such a use of "covenant" was "incidental, but not accidental."[5] Here I argued that the covenantal process lies at the heart of the biblical narrative. As students and expositors of the Scriptures, the leaders absorbed the fundamental thoughts and actions embedded in the fundamentally covenantal structure of Scripture.

Chapter 4: *The World of a Covenant* demonstrates this covenantal approach in both personal and social ethics. I particularly wanted to show how the sanctity of marriage underlies the stability of marriage and the sexual relationships within it. I also tried to urge pastors to use this theology to reinforce the ethics and practice of the emerging generations. I then turned to ethics of social justice. Here again I referred to Robert Bella's theory that social reform arises not from Enlightenment ideals, but in popular

4. Buber, *Prophetic Faith*, 27.
5. Larsen, "Convergence of Covenantalism and Interiority," 21, 22.

evangelical revivalism. I also attempted to address an approach to peace and world order.

Chapter 5: *The Mission of a Covenant* then turned to a strategy of revitalization of the Covenant Church and its mission. I attempted to show that both optimism and pessimism were a part of the biblical record itself. I used the metaphor of building a swift ship designed for stormy seas. Christ would be the keel. The key rib is the word of God. To it is added the rib of community. I warned against the "Mainline Morass"—that is, the enculturation to a broadening acculturated mainline church. I further cautioned against the "Sectarian Furies." In reaction to liberalism, much energy can be generated by furious doctrinal sectarian rage. But we are also tempted to become a Covenant Church becalmed—having passed the vitality of its origins, the Covenant Church might simply slip into calm nostalgia, sleeping in sweet dreams of earlier days as it fades away under hospice care. I proposed rather that we look for the "Zephyrs of the Spirit" that would drive us out of the calms into renewed mission. Here we first come to the rising tide of spirituality and spiritual formation. The second is the zephyr of evangelization. It is universally acknowledged that rapid church planting not only spurs vitality, but also ensures against divisive fractures. The third is the zephyr of cross-cultural missions. Such cross-cultural approaches to missions have kept the Covenant Church together despite the stormy shocks of world culture this past century. But we needed to turn to the cross-cultural populations of America; the Covenant Church needed to reflect the face of America, not just its third-generation Scandinavian face. One of the key proposals was for a school to train both U.S. and Latin American Spanish speakers.

I concluded by reasserting the primal mission of Christian communities: to be reconcilers to Christ as well as to the peoples of the world.

THE COVENANT CHURCH'S 1985 CENTENNIAL

The celebration of the Covenant Church's centennial took place in Minneapolis during the church's Annual Meeting in 1985. Plenary sessions were held in the Minneapolis Municipal Auditorium. I remembered finding my place as vice president sitting next to the president's wife, Rhoda Engebretson. On Saturday afternoon, an outdoor celebration was held at our historic Minnehaha Academy. I had been asked to engage in an open dialogue on the Covenant Church's future with noted Christian philosopher Dr. Paul Leroy Holmer. The leading Kierkegaardian scholar, he was raised in the Covenant Church. Now in retirement, he was an active member of the Salem Covenant Church of New Brighton, Minnesota. Some assumed that fire might ignite an exciting contrast of competing visions. Instead, we remarkably shared a complementary vision of the Covenant Church's future. This did, in fact, set off a deepening friendship with the great Christian philosopher until the day he died.

Unknown to me, the Covenant Church's centennial marked a significant change in my life as a pastor. I looked back with satisfaction on my seventeen years of patrol leadership at Peninsula Covenant Church. Despite my obvious weaknesses, I could celebrate the fact that by God's grace I had fought a good fight. Perhaps it would not be arrogant to hope that these years had allowed me to be a small pea under the devil's mattress!

7

Chicago—Covenant Church Leadership and Strategy

In September of 1986, President Milton B. Engebretson retired after sixteen years as president of the Covenant Church. He was surely God's man who led us passionately in Christward dimensions, struggling to maintain "the spirit of unity in the bond of peace" (Eph 4:3). His deeply passionate faith, disciplined work habits, and incomparable organizational and interpersonal skills led the Covenant Church through those years. In late fall of 1985, I received a letter from the Presidential Nominating Committee stating that my name had been submitted as a candidate for the next president, along with the other pastoral leaders.

I had not given this much thought. St. Paul had declared that anyone desiring to be an overseer desires a good thing.[1] I was honored by the request. I had found, however, that my people had taken sixteen years to see through me and could trust me. I had a vision of new steps both in the church and the community. It was a time of fulfillment.

On the other hand, I had been engaged in many of the theological battles in the denomination as a whole. I knew that I was a polarizing figure and was occasionally regarded as arrogant and polemical. I asked myself if I would wish to get into the stress of leadership with my personal baggage and history. So I faced the dilemma as two questions came to me. One was, "Every pastorate has its ups and downs, what makes you so sure that further pastoral work in Redwood City would be storm-free sailing?" The other question was, "What makes you so sure that your leadership as president

1. 2 Tim 3:1.

95

will be so controversial and stressful?" I decided to answer the lengthy questionnaire and wrote intensively throughout our Christmas holiday.

The committee invited me for an interview early in the year. I flew to Chicago with my younger daughter, Kathleen. We were hoping to get her interested in North Park in a couple of years. As the day closed, I received a phone call in our hotel room from Trustee Chair Marshall Dahlstrom. Going to the committee room, I was declared to be the candidate for the next Covenant Church president. I then told Marshall that I had a stipulation in my response. I said, "I know the necessity of time away from Elizabeth that this will entail. You may either pay me what a public corporation would pay me for a job of this size or agree that any time I travel, Elizabeth may accompany me at Covenant Church expense. I will not spend the next years romancing the walls of Holiday Inn." Marshall immediately granted the latter. I congratulated him saying, "Now I know you can add two plus two." As it turned out, nearly half of the time I was away from home. But Elizabeth joined for half of that time. What a fine bargain it became!

ELECTION AS PRESIDENT

Needless to say my election was controversial. My outspoken theological advocacy for the more conservative evangelical cause stirred much anxiety. As I mentioned, my quick tongue and sometimes arrogant demeanor also factored into the concern. The more moderate on the left decided to nominate Arthur A. R. Nelson, pastor of the Winnetka Church, as an alternate candidate. He had a distinguished career as a pastor and Covenant Church leader. Both Clarence Nelson and Milton Engebretson had alternate candidates in some of their elections. Those supporting Art demanded a debate between the two of us, both in the Annual Ministerium and in the Annual Meeting. This was unprecedented. The debates went well. It has been said that I am fairly quick in debate. *The Chicago Tribune* covered the election. I was overwhelmingly elected.

MOVE TO CHICAGO

I was elected in June and assumed office in September 1986. The intervening months brought many difficult farewells along with much encouragement in our new venture. It was a difficult time because the housing market was in a slump and sales were slow. The girls were still in school. Elizabeth and Kristi could join me in Chicago in January, but Kathy would stay with a church family from January through May. We, of course, made several trips house hunting and communicating. Elizabeth finally drew the line at eleven miles as my maximum commute. I always stayed at my brother's home in Lincolnshire while we looked for a house. We finally bought a townhouse in Northfield by the Eldens Expressway, less than thirty minutes to the office. We did not buy a large house since the Covenant Church had always provided its presidents with a membership in Chicago's Union League Club. Paul and Bernice Brandel purchased a membership for us at Wilmette's Michigan Shores Club. There we could entertain larger groups than we could in our home. The home was in a small development of townhouses carefully constructed in eighteenth-century Christopher Wren style. It was two stories above a garage level, which also included a room to be used as my library. Being a Churchill fan, I was delighted in that it resembled Number 10 Downing Street, the residence of the English Prime Minister. It was located on the North Shore bicycle path going through many miles of lovely wooded parkland. It was ideal.

Elizabeth and Kristi joined me in January, as did Kathy in May. This was a time of adjustment for all of us. We joined the nearby Winnetka Covenant Church. Everyone was gracious—but many were uncertain about me. I felt quite insecure in the new environment. I had always thought that I had a good idea about the duties and structure of the Chicago headquarters. I had even served as vice president. Like most of those living on the outer perimeters, I occasionally felt disdain for the leadership at the center. "Chicago Headquarters" occasionally had a sardonic tint. What I discovered was a group of self-sacrificing, passionate servants of Christ. If the battle cry of the "outlanders" was "Throw the bums out!" I quickly discovered from that distance I was now "the bum at city hall."

Since the founding Covenant Church President Carl A. Björk, I have been the only Covenant president to emerge directly from the pastorate. I soon discovered that I could not even find the men's room. My brother, David, was now teaching at Trinity Evangelical Divinity School and graciously supplied much encouragement, support, and wisdom.

My predecessor, Milton Engebretson, was a constant companion. For the next ten years until he passed away, we had a two-hour lunch each week whenever we were both in town. His experience, wisdom, and encouragement came with wise counsel. No one but he and I knew what foolishness and mistakes he helped me avoid. My own father loved me deeply, but was not an affirming person. In this sense Milton became a surrogate father to me. I would sometimes assert that I was of greater stature than he—I was the dwarf that stood on his shoulders.

I knew I needed coaching in leading the many institutions, persons, and finances of the entire Covenant Church. Ken Block, a member of the

Winnetka Covenant Church where we attended, was the managing partner of A.T. Kearney, a top national management consulting firm. He also served on the board of four corporations among the top 400 firms. We began to meet monthly for breakfast. His wisdom and support were invaluable. One of the first and most important words he gave me was, "Learn how to manage your time, or you will never be able to manage the Covenant Church." Those words I have never forgotten, but have too often neglected them.

My pastor at the Winnetka Church was Bob Dvorak. Wise, caring, and always available, he helped us through some of the deepest grief and loss we had during the twelve years I served until my retirement. He came one vote short of becoming the Chaplain of the United States House of Representatives. His music in any venue added so much to worship and community.

Last, but not least, was my administrative secretary, Karen Farmer. Her husband, Pat, was a senior financial officer at Swedish Covenant Church Hospital next door. She had been Milton's administrative assistant for many years prior to my coming and was with me until my retirement. She kept close order on all business, including calendar and correspondence. Early on she researched all the resolutions over the past years both granting and limiting my authority as president. She knew how to keep silent over confidential material. I believe she knew how to keep silent in at least seven languages. She would occasionally irritate me as I would rush out of the door to catch a plane or a meeting. She would say, "But not before you write the four letters and answer these four phone calls." I was her boss—until I remembered that every leader soon comes to grief if he or she is not prompt in answering mail and phone calls. She had the courage to spare me.

ADMINISTRATORS

The Covenant Church's by-laws provided a Council of Administrators to direct the operations of the national church. I was designated chair and chief executive. They were, in a sense, the church's gift to me as well as the entire church. These formed the leadership team with which I would work over the next twelve years. The chief leader often serves under many titles: I was the President, Chairman of the Board, and Chief Executive Officer for the entire Covenant Church. But a leader must have more than just legal authority; in the church so much leadership takes place by example and encouragement rather than legal power. It was best to see my office as that of Team Leader. Each administrator was hopefully far more informed and competent in their area of leadership than I could hope to be. My task was to help them unite in common mission and purpose. That eventuality came more as the result of the grace of God than my own skills. I had a superb team of leaders on the Council of Administrators. Here is an account of these senior leaders:

Vice-president *Tim Ek*. Ek was the other general officer of the Covenant Church during my entire time as president. We were elected at the same time. He was to serve as Corporate Secretary and Director of Stewardship. In many ways we complemented each other. His warm and outgoing personality certainly surpassed mine, compensating for some of what I lacked. He had countless friendships and ties across the entire Covenant Church. He developed a team of lay stewardship consultants in each conference, working with churches to increase their giving. He completed a doctoral degree at Fuller Seminary on Stewardship Development for the Covenant Church. In no small measure I attribute our capacity to grow our budget to the gifts God had given him.

Nils Axelson had headed all of the Covenant Church's benevolence work through our retirement homes and hospitals. Coming to take this role in his mid-twenties, he led the development of Swedish Covenant Church Hospital, Emanuel Hospital, and all of the retirement communities. Joining with Covenant Church Philanthropist Paul Brandel, he assembled a very large conglomerate. Ultimately he helped establish a dozen of the finest retirement communities in the nation. A devout and inveterate reader, he was really almost a universal man. He seldom spoke just above a whisper. I remarked once to former North Park President Karl A. Olsson, "Nils seldom speaks before thinking." Karl replied, "And sometimes he does not speak after thinking!" We worked together from my early years at Orangevale. In fact, he was a groomsman at my wedding!

Ray Dahlberg was Executive Secretary of World Missions. I had known his parents, who wintered each year in Pasadena and were active in our church there. He had been a successful pastor and conference superintendent. Always cheerful and optimistic, he never showed anger or bombast. He said on several occasions, "I learned to survive with five older sisters!" Most people did not know that he was a math major at Northwestern University. Rather than contradicting other analyses, he would simply ask a few questions from various pages of the monthly financial report. He was a compassionate leader. He and I traveled the world together during those entire years and steered the International Federation of Free Evangelical Churches in totally new directions. He was recognized by the national church leaders in our mission fields. In Africa, official naming was done after watching the conduct of a leader over time. In Lingala his title became *Tata Bobeto*, "the father of kindness." He truly was.

A longtime friend from the time of his pastorate in California, *Jim Hawkinson* represented the best of the traditional Covenant Church spirit. Always ready with an anecdote of Covenant Church history, he was like his father, Eric, the long-term dean of the seminary, a preacher of surpassing passion and eloquence. While coming from a different tradition than mine, he always worked in harmony with me and was cautious but open in dialogue with me. He was an excellent editor and author of several books. He shared openly with me of the deep and painful things in his life.

David Horner was named president of North Park in the first few months of my tenure. David, his wife, Sue, and two children had come to Peninsula Covenant Church while I was pastor there. He had come to pursue a joint PhD and MBA in higher education at Stanford, which had the premier school for the training of college and university presidents. As I assumed office, the presidency of North Park became vacant. He had been the principal higher education consultant for the massive management firm of Pete Marwick and Mitchell. From there he had moved while still in his twenties to become president of Barrington College. Merging the school with Gordon College, he was ready for further things. Dewey Sands, pastor of the Barrington Covenant Church, nominated him for president of North Park. I felt I should not nominate him as he was too close a friend—so I remained silent until after the interview. Nominating committee chairperson Paul Ziemer went through each nominee and asked each committee member, "If he were the only candidate, would you vote yes?" Amazingly, Horner was the only candidate who received unanimous support. He wrote the first journal article on the use of strategic management for higher education while still only a candidate for his doctorate. The school was in acute financial crisis at the time of his call. He turned it around and moved it to full university status while making invaluable contributions to the entire Covenant Church. His good humor, excellent speaking skills—he had been a boy preacher for the Plymouth Brethren—and mastery of financial skills made him a wonder. He always worked closely with me in finding teachers of religion and philosophy throughout the university and seminary. He was wildly innovative and one of the three members of my informal Dream Team. He and I worked with Lorraine and Harold Anderson in the funding and construction of the Anderson Chapel.

David Johnson was our Chief Operating Officer. Exceptionally quick and bright, he designed and built our first automated electronic accounting system. He also served as president of National Covenant Church Properties, as well as Director of Pensions. At one point, he rescued our Bond Counsel with certain financial protocols that they could not solve even with all their highly expertise. He presided over a rapid growth both in the assets of National Covenant Church Properties and the Covenant Church Pension plan.

Doris Johnson was our initial Director of Covenant Church Women Ministries. A professionally trained social worker, she had been raised as the daughter of missionaries to China. As a young girl, she had witnessed the beheading of a number of prisoners from her own window. She was married to Arnold Johnson, a Covenant Church minister who had been disabled by blindness. Her compassionate heart for the needy was written over both her walk and her talk.

Evelyn Johnson became executive director of Christian Education and Discipleship as I assumed the office of president. A gifted schoolteacher, she had served various roles in the Midwest Conference, including acting superintendent. A former math teacher, she managed every financial detail of planning and reporting over which she had control. She was an excellent supervisor of personal and team building. Lyle Schaller, the foremost authority on Protestant churches, named her as his chief resource in childhood education. Her unique skills made her a second member of our Dream Team. Evelyn and her husband, Phil, became close friends, and have continued to be over the many years since my retirement.

Leroy Johnson served as the longtime Chief Development Officer. After graduating from seminary, he went into estate planning and then became the head of all such planning for the Covenant Church. With a sharp mind surpassed only by his generous and outgoing nature, he built up the confidence of Covenant Churchers across the nation. Recruiting retired businessmen, he set up a network of estate planners across the country to assist him in this important task. Pioneering with the use of Revocable Trusts, we became the largest manager of these trusts in Illinois. Sensing the need for separate incorporation, he led in the creation of America's first nonprofit trust company. Hundreds of millions of dollars have ultimately come through this ingenious approach. Leroy always brought calm words to all of our council meetings. When our trustholders passed away, we euphemistically talked about "the maturing of the trust." I would also ask Leroy in passing, "Are there now even more new trusts that have matured?" He would reply, adding that "since you and Elizabeth now have such a trust, you are also now a maturing trust!"

Bob Larson, a longtime Covenant Church leader, had a PhD in urban planning. He founded National Covenant Church Properties, a Covenant Church bank that borrowed from covenanters to aid in acquiring and constructing Covenant churches. It has grown to be the second largest of such in-house banking institutions among all denominations, and has reached hundreds of millions in assets. Becoming executive secretary of Church

Growth and Evangelism, Bob rigorously studied principles of church growth and evangelism. He organized the Southeast Conference and later the Midsouth Conference. With his knowledge of planning, he became an expert in acquiring strategic locations for new churches. He worked closely with each of the superintendents in their respective conferences. No one has traveled more diligently or extensively than Bob. Early in my time as president he would follow me onto a Northwest Airlines jet to Minneapolis. I was pleased with my apparent public persona when the stewardess welcomed us aboard with, "Welcome, Dr. Larsen." It felt good until I realized that Bob's frequent flying was known by flight crews across the nation. He had progressive and brilliant ideas, and I am honored to say that I agreed with them.

Donald Njaa, the Executive Secretary of the Office of Ministry, led the organization of the roster of licensed and ordained Covenant Church Ministers. With now more than a thousand ministers, the task was daunting. He undertook the computerization of all of the records. He was the chief investigator on questions concerning clergy misconduct. He worked closely with the superintendents in this matter. Because of legal questions, he also worked with our external attorneys regarding policy and disciplinary actions. Don was even-tempered but decisive. He neither hesitated to confront erring clergy, nor lagged in going to bat for them in the presence of false charges. He earned the respect or the entire ministerium. Always well organized, he gave much honor and dignity to the office. Though coming out of different theological corners in the Covenant Church, we always stood together in the core values and conviction.

LATER ADDITIONS

Roland Carlson was a longtime friend and Covenant Church lay leader. He had risen to be a senior vice president of Harris Trust. He had served on many boards and committees. He mentored a large number of young Covenant Church lay leaders. When Nils Axelson retired as president of Covenant Benevolence Ministries, Roland took early retirement and assumed Nils's role. For many years he cared for his blind and disabled wife while raising his children. He was a model of sacrificial servanthood. A hardheaded leader, he and I had our clashes, but Covenant Benevolence Ministries flourished under his leadership.

Deirdre Banks succeeded Doris Johnson as head of Covenant Women. She is a native Australian nurse who went to Nepal to lead a leprosarium. Returning to Australia, she then headed a Bible college and became known as an effective public speaker. Later, America's Bible Study Fellowship called her to succeed retiring founder Audrey Wetherell Johnson. From there she became the Missions Pastor of our Oakland, California Covenant church. She gave strong leadership to the women's ministries, and the Covenant Church was beginning to adjust to the new role of women in both church and society.

John Hunt, the son of Covenant Church Pastor Stanley Hunt, was a practicing attorney. He went to work for the Covenant Church serving as an attorney with the Department of Church Growth and Evangelism. When transferring from legal practice in the state of Michigan, he passed the Illinois Bar Exam in the 97th percentile. With the emergence of legal issues for churches and clergy, the Executive Board named him General Counsel and Secretary of the Covenant Church. An avid student of Covenant Church history since his days as a student at North Park, he later took special training in legal mediation and settlements. He joined the ongoing discussions of the Covenant Church founders and their decisions. In these debates each side would like to be true to the fathers. As John joined the discussion, he came to the conclusion that in many of the early discussions and decisions, the language became ambiguous. He helped me to conclude that there were many differences among the early leaders, but their passion for the unity of the Covenant Church overrode the differences. To this day, the same spirit rules the Covenant Church. John helped us in massive litigation over clergy misconduct. In the crisis of hospital finance, he helped negotiate our entrance into the Northwest Health Care system. Jim Serritella, our external counsel, served the same role for the Chicago Archdiocese. Serritella told me that John's work was then used in dealing with the same issues in Catholic hospitals entering larger, secular systems. John was also quiet, but more than anyone else, he would be kind but frank with me when he felt I was crossing the line either with staff or in a legal capacity.

Dean Lundgren was a lifelong Covenanter from Connecticut. He graduated from Brown University and took his master's degree from Carnegie Mellon. After a year as a Rockefeller Brothers Fellow at Andover Newton Seminary, he earned his PhD in finance from Harvard University. He worked his way up to a senior vice-presidency at Cigna—the mammoth insurance conglomerate. National Covenant Church Properties, our in-house church-planting bank now exceeded hundreds of millions in deposits. David Johnson had managed both the denomination's finances and the bank. Concerned that regulators would see too much internal connection between the church and the bank, David decided to become president of the bank. Meanwhile, Dean had served on both the North Park Board and the Covenant Church Executive Board. North Park President David Horner and I challenged Dean to become the next Covenant Church Chief Financial

Officer and to proceed to direct and develop an MBA degree in Nonprofit Management at the university. To do so, he would have to take a 40 percent pay cut. Happily he accepted and moved to Chicago with his wife, Jill, and four young sons. His service has been exemplary. He quickly developed that master's program. In the first two years as CFO, he reorganized the Covenant Church's finances and saved more than his salary in each of those two years. Even-tempered and positive, he never used his expertise and power to bully anyone. Always the conciliator, he would annually get the estimates of income and general priorities. He would then meet with each department and negotiate with each of them. I never experienced conflicts with the departments over priorities. His doctoral work at Harvard involved asset management. I eventually relinquished the chair of Covenant Church Trust to Dean, who took over as chair. His skill in asset management brought significant increases in both church income and trust distributions to heirs.

CHANGING LEADERSHIP

Jim Persson was a successful church planter who then took over church planting in the Pacific Southwest Conference. When Bob Larson took an early retirement part way through my time in office, Jim was chosen as Executive Secretary of Church Growth and Evangelism. Some superintendents wondered whether—although he was a superb church planter—his humble and gentle approach displayed sufficient strength to lead the department. I simply replied, "Did you ever see anything that Jim attempted to do fail?" Bombast is not the key to leadership—as I have sometimes forgotten. The loving, gentle spirit proved a most powerful tool in his new leadership.

He brought in *Gary Walter* to take the Church Planting division of the department. A graduate in rhetoric from Berkeley, I noticed his extremely fine leadership qualities as he co-led the 5,000-student CHIC triennial in Fort Collins, Colorado. I had seen him as chair of the Interchurch Relations Committee of the Covenant Church. he and his wife Nancy joined us as we journeyed as couples to the Annual Meeting of IFFEC in East Germany. Included were Elizabeth and myself, Ray and Nancy Dahlberg, and David and Sue Horner. Under his leadership, the rate of church planting soon experienced a great expansion reflected in not only a significant increase in churches planted, but also missions giving from the same new churches. The rate of church planting more than doubled.

Paul Peterson was the son of a Covenant Church pastor who began his career as a schoolteacher. He began bringing students to visit hospitals as a part of vocational education studies. He was hired by a hospital and soon proved an effective administrator. Then he became assistant administrator of the noted Eisenhower Hospital in Rancho Mirage, California. Nils Axelson persuaded him to become director of our retirement center in San Diego. In the significant expansion of our benevolence ministries, he then asked Paul to assume the task of being president of Covenant Church Retirement Centers—by then one of the largest providers of full-care retirement communities across the nation. Paul took the position with gusto, and he did an exceptional job of bringing the organization to a fully funded and amortized basis. He later showed the most effectiveness of all our institutional heads in introducing training in Covenant Church faith and values throughout all levels of management. When the president of the Eisenhower Medical Center retired, the board asked Paul to replace him. Paul was reluctant. The Eisenhower Board sent two of its premier board members on a charter flight to Chicago to persuade him. He chose to stay with the Covenant Church Retirement Centers. The names of those board members? Dolores Hope and Betty Ford!

Thus was I given a splendid team of leaders. In each of their areas they possessed much greater ability than I. Early in my leadership I had vowed to use only leaders who were superior to me in their particular expertise and skills. If God could grace me with enough wisdom and skill to build this team, I believed significant advances would be made in all areas. I do believe that this is in fact what happened.

BUILDING THE TEAM

It is one thing to have a group of godly and gifted individuals at the head of each major department, institution, or division. Their forming a team is quite another thing. In too many instances, organizations leave such leaders as standing stovepipes with no significant interaction or joint cooperative processes. Each element needs to develop matrices, or joint committees and task forces, at relevant areas between major segments. All of the individuals just introduced served under what the by-laws describe as the Council of Administrators, which I would chair. All matters moving up to the Executive Board or the Annual Meeting must first be approved by the council.

This group would meet each month. When I came, the meetings took all day. But I believed that we could produce the same results with less time on small details and a bent for action. Despite protests, this worked well— the council had to be action oriented. I insisted that reports must be just one page, or at the most two. Financial reports or important lengthier documents had to be presented with a summary. We also used a consent agenda in which perfunctory business was presented in the agenda and adopted with one motion. Any member of the council could call down any item when he or she felt there needed to be more discussion or amendment. This procedure was new to the Covenant Church, but very common in government and corporate deliberations. After opening prayer and devotions, each member of the council would briefly share departmental or personal needs for prayer. Some thought this would make the meetings too long. I believed, however, that much business is stalled by hidden stress and agendas. As a result, the decisions came to be reached much more rapidly. As in other areas of leadership, I now wish I had done less talking and more listening.

Most important was the annual fall planning retreat. It was limited to one afternoon, one full day, and an additional half day. It meant two nights away and allowing two half-days for going and coming. We would go to some quiet place such as a church retreat or even a discounted hotel. I insisted that there be no current business—the last monthly meeting would have cleared the immediate agendas. After arriving at the site and having lunch, we would have just one hour-and-a-half session. We would look at last year's Annual Plan and score achievements on a 5-point scale—each person rating each provision or section. This gave us a good sense of how well the plan for the last year had worked. These were scored on huge chart papers taped to the walls of the meeting room. Each person would receive five dots to place anywhere on the goals, leaving a numerical score for the achievements of each goal. It generally was an affirming experience. By three o'clock we would take a break for recreation or reflection. This would be followed by dinner together at a nearby restaurant.

The second session, the next morning, would begin with more large sheets also taped to the wall and a free-for-all on suggested goals and objectives for each element and department. The afternoon session would combine and clarify the key objectives together The objectives would then be scored by each person with the dot system, which would put goals and objectives for the ensuing year in ranked priorities. Responsibilities for the high-scoring priorities would be assigned the following day. The results of this simple process would then be given to the Executive Board for action.

INDIVIDUAL OBJECTIVES

Each individual would later develop his or her own annual plan. First that involved asking what they had done the past year to strengthen areas suggested for growth. Invariably they would be harder on themselves than the rest of us would. The council would then rate the individual's performance based on their job description. Then they would be asked which objectives and practices they would no longer pursue in the new year, followed by the question of how they would handle new assignments. All this would be submitted to me on no more than two pages. By way of evaluation, the chair of each board or division would meet with me and briefly make affirmations and suggestions for growth. The ratings would then be used by the Executive Board to determine new salaries. The system worked well.

STRATEGIC PLANNING

Every few years in the past, Covenant Church leaders from across the nation would gather to make recommendations and set priorities. That practice served to introduce comprehensive Strategic Plan Development in a formal sense. David Horner openly wondered whether such a thing would be possible for the whole denomination. As a doctoral student he wrote the first strategic planning process for higher education. But with David coming up with creative ideas, Evelyn Johnson organizing and laying out the steps, and Dean Lundgren keeping the ledger on the process to make sure all segments of the church would be involved, I insisted we do it. This, again, was my Dream Team. That did not place them in a special role, but we all recognized how this successful team could lead the whole church forward. We got priorities from conferences, boards, pastors, and delegates. Every suggestion was tabulated. And after a few years the plan emerged. We now had a comprehensive strategic plan. Then Dean Lundgren would check with each department for regular reports on progress. By the grace of God it worked! Looking back we can feel gratified by how much God enabled us to accomplish.

CONFERENCE SUPERINTENDENTS

The Covenant Church has regional administrative units called conferences. Their boundaries are set by the national church, which must also approve the call for each superintendent as well as by-law changes. As such they are regional mid-judicatories. Discussions with other denominational heads show unanimous agreement that their role as both supporting the national body and assisting local churches is sometimes quite difficult. As president, I would meet with the Superintendents' Council collectively several times a year and would consult with each superintendent regularly regarding actions and policies.

The superintendent is the person in the middle. Or, as someone has said, "An expert is some person from a long distance away who is called in at the last moment to share the blame." He is to be pastor to the pastors, counselor to the congregations, and mediator of disputes. In addition, he or she hears the concerns of the pastor and must balance them with the welfare of the congregation. He or she has to lead in raising the budget and to act as an agent of the denomination in the event of ministerial misconduct. The superintendent has the task of representing the national body to the churches and at the same time bringing the needs of the conference churches before the national Covenant Church leadership.

In the matter of gender and racial equality, he or she is really the front line. My first attempt to bring a woman forward as superintendent was flat-out rejected by one of the conference annual meetings. Thankfully, we now have two outstanding women as superintendents. The work of a go-between like this is too often a thankless task. Perhaps it is like the proverbial soldier in the Civil War with relatives on both sides of the struggle. He tried to solve the problem by wearing a Confederate tunic and Union pants. When they picked up his body on the battlefield, there were Union bullet holes in is tunic and Confederate bullet holes in his pants. One of the hardest tasks is to be a pastor who keeps the confidences of pastors, but also has to ensure the pastor's conduct meets biblical standards. A meeting of denominational heads unanimously agreed that it is virtually impossible to be both a pastor's pastor and a disciplinary officer. In civil society a defense lawyer cannot serve as a prosecutor and advocate in the same case. Even as president I had to inform a pastor seeking help that in some instances I could not keep confidential serious misconduct. These issues remain a difficulty for virtually all denominations.

Nevertheless, the superintendents that I have known have been sacrificial, godly servants of the Lord. The rapid growth of the Covenant Church in the last twenty-five years is due in no small measure to the faithfulness of its superintendents.

THE ORDERED MINISTRY

From the beginning the Covenant Church has clearly adopted a pattern of central ordination by the Annual Meeting. It also required training at its seminary at North Park. Earlier it had been afflicted by wandering teachers and sectarian preachers. The ordered ministry had the purpose of ensuring an educated clergy who have been deemed worthy to be trusted with the care of souls. Ordinands were nominated by conference ministerial associations.

Discipline was then organized on a central plan. But prior to ordination, ministers were first licensed, given a time of internship, and evaluated in terms of their Christlike character and faithfulness to the gospel.

Donald Njaa effectively served as Executive Secretary to the Board of Ordered Ministry. He brought all of our ministerial records into a computerized center, trained board members, and helped find assistance for troubled pastors and spouses. He also was the cop on the beat, the Covenant Church's chief disciplinary officer. He was soft-spoken, but unafraid to face issues of misconduct. We frequently shared lunch together.

Our biggest crisis came in a matter of ministerial conduct in the Northwest Conference. The church, the conference, and the denomination were ultimately involved. Don and I immediately reacted when we received a phone call from the conference superintendent. I asked Don to catch the next plane to Minneapolis—which he did. This was the first word either of us had received of the misconduct. The charges were for extreme misconduct over a period of time. It brought us into court. I gave an 80-page deposition by Jeff Anderson, the noted attorney for the plaintiffs.

The sordid claims had to be endured. Despite the fact that the lawyers tried calling lists of Covenant Church ministers for evidence that we knew of and covered up the wrongdoing, they found no cover-up. With nearly a score of plaintiffs, I met with the their parents in Minneapolis. The pastor had resigned his credentials. I said I had no reason to disbelieve the claims, but I had no authority to make findings of fact since we had no hearings because of the resignation of the pastor from the ministerium. I did assure them we would provide counseling and assistance to any who felt victimized. I submitted an affidavit about the governance of the Evangelical Covenant Church and its by-laws. This affidavit was later used in a successful appeal by the Assemblies of God churches of a southern state.

The press in the Twin Cities and all newspapers carried daily news of the charges and the trial. Thankfully, our general counsel, John Hunt, together with external counsel Jim Seritella, steered us through these deep waters. In the end Saddam Hussein's invasion of Kuwait drove the matters from the headlines and daily TV news. The matter was settled with no admission of liability on the part of the Covenant Church.

What followed was intense training of our pastors and superintendents in establishing clear protocols to protect every person, and especially every child, that came under our care. It was over, but oh, to this day the suffering and pain continues to afflict the young people who were victims of such criminal and evil conduct. Other disciplinary matters were resolved in an orderly fashion.

We also reviewed ordination requirements, seeing that so many of those seeking ordination were settled in distant cities with families and could not move. Working with Rob Johnston and David Horner, we opened pathways for students to meet ordination requirements from other seminaries, but with distance learning and participation in short courses at Midwinter Conferences and Annual Meetings. With this flexibility, the church was ready to embrace a more rapid expansion in both numbers and spirituality.

Another important activity was to help the Covenant Church accept the equality of women in church leadership. It has been an ongoing process. So have the same issues of ministerial misconduct and its accompanying liabilities. The board and leadership worked hard to make it a reality that the church is always a safe place for women and children. It also became clear that most of the misconduct toward women and children came from laymen who held prominent church positions or who had powerful relatives in the church leadership. The question must continue to be: Is this Covenant Church pastor a reliable teacher of doctrine and conduct? And as a consequent corollary: Is this minister's living in congruence with his or her teaching on doctrine and conduct?

CHURCH GROWTH AND EVANGELISM

The Department of Church Growth and Evangelism lies at the very heart of the Covenant Church's national mission. Formerly known as the Department of Home Mission, the name was changed under executive secretary Robert Larson. Studying the church growth movement in world missions of Donald McGavran, Jim Persson adapted it to church planting and growth in North America. He then saw the need to find new strategies of evangelism for the pastors and lay people of local churches. Thus came a major strategic adjustment. He also set in motion and led the formation of the Southeast Conference and later the Midsouth Conference, initiating rapid church planting in these regions new to the Covenant Church.

Coming into office in the fall of 1986, I was committed to the principles McGavran had espoused. Jim and I became friends, as he had often attended the Pasadena Covenant Church when I pastored there. I often asked him which of McGavran's principles and strategies might not work as well in North America. He simply demurred, saying that he felt no calling in this area. One empirically established principle was that the rate of church planting had a direct effect on the rate of denominational growth, as clearly demonstrated by American denominational statistics. The faster the rate of church planting, the faster the denomination or mission grew numerically.

A second corollary is that rapidly growing churches and church bodies are less susceptible to conflict and schism. This corrected the assumption that to deploy more resources to church planting would curtail the help the denomination could give to the existing churches. It was known that the successful strategies of church planting actually stimulate the commitment and involvement of existing churches. I have observed that a sizable portion of a church's growth occurs in its first ten years of life. It is as if congregations tend to pass the age of childbearing around ten years. If a stable older church decides to help in planting new churches, a rejuvenated spirit appears, a sort of second childhood. A rule of thumb was then developed for a church to maintain a healthy rate of growth: The suggested rate of growth was an annual addition of 10 percent of the church membership. A church of 200 members needs to take in at least twenty new members one year, twenty-two the next year, twenty-four the next, and so on, in order to remain growing and vital.

We must beware of stereotypes though. Many factors play a role in church growth. Among them is location in growing areas of suburban migration or ethnic dispersion. Then the qualities of pastoral leadership can help determine growth in terms of the pastor's own gifting. The same can be said of a congregation's early lay leadership. A declining population will be a more difficult place to plant a church or gain new converts. Various strengths and weaknesses in pastoral leadership certainly can affect growth rates. The same is true of key lay leadership where their networks into the community are widely connected. Then, most importantly, the unpredictable zephyrs of the Holy Spirit move with great power for no discernible reason to bring both spiritual renewal and rapid growth.

More recently, McGavran's church growth principles have came under further critique. He was undoubtedly correct in arguing that most tribes and individuals would like to become Christians without crossing boundaries of language and cultural solidarity. As a teenager I found in hunting pheasants with my father that it is much quicker and easier to run on top of the furrows of a plowed field than to run across them. This is why Bible translation is so important. Studying the cultures and traditions of a given society allows new ways to discover common ground. But some have pointed out that this may work internally within a given culture or tribe, but it does little to reach across cultural divides that isolate one community from another.

I was brought up sharply regarding the homogeneity principle by Lutheran theologian Loren Halverson. He said the homogeneity principle was precisely what reinforced the development of apartheid in South Africa and the rise of segregation in America. This also affected church planting strategies across America. Michael Emerson pointed out in his book, *Divided by*

Faith,[2] that the strategy was wrongly used to enhance ethnic and racial separation. In rural America the farm was a two-dimensional matter. The early farmers were fairly homogeneous except for the Native Americans who were kept on separate reservations by treaty. But increasing populations in towns and cities added third dimensions. As towns and cities grew, different cultures occupied the same space. In fact, as cities grew they became high-rise cultures of many cultures, almost always arranged on economic lines.

But these multiple cultures are very often stacked in a hierarchical nature by their size and relative affluence. Thus, those on the bottom would be the poor, and those on top would be the more well to do. Thus, the Christian church in the more urban communities remains segregated by language, race, and economic stratification. The same stratification occurs in terms of the average age of each level.

In this sense, the strategic use of the homogeneity principle in evangelism and missions can be turned into segregated communities dominated by the more affluent. I discovered this when I was one of the main speakers at the Covenant Church Quadrennial at the YMCA camp in Estes Park, Colorado. Having persuasively proclaimed evangelization by the homogeneity principle, my corresponding theologian, Dr. Loren Halverson of the Evangelical Lutheran Church, simply stated that I had just delivered a splendid defense of South African apartheid ideology. Each tribe should have its separate and equal homeland. I confess that I have never quite recovered from that devastating reproach. America's churches, especially its evangelical churches, were surprisingly apartheid in reaching their own kind.

While working through culture to advance homogeneity is a missiological strategy, it is not an ecclesial strategy. The whole gospel involves homogeneous strategies in evangelism, but is not to be an ecclesial strategy. Much of Acts and Galatians represent Paul's struggle to bring Jews and gentiles into one body. Thus, a maturing church must become multicultural to reach toward the fullness of Christ. Jew and gentile require different evangelistic approaches, but their growth in the body of Christ must eventuate in a true evangelical cosmopolitanism in which not only do black, white, and other groups exist side by side, but they must also enrich each other. Thus it is necessary to emphasize ecclesiology as well as missiology in church growth strategy. Such strategy requires a homogeneous extension with a cosmopolitan approach to Christian maturing. I used to remind people that North Park Church in Chicago, with its more formal preaching and liturgy, would not flourish under the powerful African American preaching and singing of African American pastor Willie Jameson. Nor would the

2. Emerson and Smith, *Divided by Faith*.

eloquent preaching of Glenn Wiberg be entirely welcomed by the African Americans at Jameson's Oakdale Covenant Church.

Thus the principle of homogeneity as a mission strategy is both biblically and sociologically sound—particularly when joined by a cross-cultural mission's strategy of the great missionary movements of the last 100 years. But if it is used to buttress insularity and solidarity, it turns sour. Though evangelicals could cross denominational and confessional barriers in worldwide evangelization, they were unable to do so ecclesiologically and sacramentally. As a result evangelism in America has virtually collapsed into missiology. Yet there is much action and discussion to move forward ecclesiologically as well.

CHURCH PLANTING

My core premise was that the Covenant Church could not really progress and renew itself without significantly increasing its rate of church planting. This axiomatic approach has been established by virtually all studies in national and global mission strategies. We were planting at a rate of between four and six churches annually. Our growth had almost stopped. If the Covenant Church was to flourish, it needed to double the rate at which churches were planted.

When in charge of church planting, Gary Walter described two approaches to church planting. One he called "reptilian"—a description of the thousands of eggs that a reptile would leave abandoned on the beaches. Only a few would survive. This model resembled the Assembly of God churches or the rapid church-planting techniques sometimes used in the house church movement. A high rate of church planting can also create a high rate of church infant mortality. On the other hand, there is the "mammalian" model. With a low birthrate and an extended time of parental nurture, it has a relatively low mortality rate. Both types of procreation seem to have survived well in the natural world. But in the church-planting world, a low birth rate could lead easily to decline or even extinction.

The Covenant Church had so embraced the mammalian principle that its growth rate was too small, and the aided infant churches often became dependent and thus stunted. New at his job, Gary Walter soon discovered a group of three Baptist General Conference pastors who held large annual conferences on church planting. He began attending and becoming acquainted with the Johnson brothers and Dave Olson. Jim Persson, I, and Gary began working with them. They had been extraordinarily successful at church planting themselves. Ultimately we hired Dave Olson to assist us with church planting. Over the years he served in both the Pacific Southwest Conference and the Northwest Conference, and ultimately served as the Director of Church Planting. An inveterate researcher, he compiled the growth statistics of North American Protestant churches. He soon discovered that sociologists had noticed that the Covenant Church, the Free Church, and the Baptist General Conference were virtually identical sociologically, if not always theologically. These sociologists lumped the three of us together and called us "the Three Sisters." Our common Swedish heritage had held some constants even as the three denominations became less ethnic and more diverse.

Another discovery was that successful church planters were a species of their own. Often lacking in gifts for larger church leadership, they seemed to flourish in reaching out and gathering people into community. So we sent potential planters to a seminar for testing and interviews. Those who scored well were then put in the pool for church planting. The results have been striking. It immediately cut our mortality of church planting starts by more than half.

It was becoming apparent that our church planting was becoming too centralized. While centralization brought more expertise, it led to declining motivation on the part of Conferences and local churches. We decided to concentrate on developing a thirst for local churches to partner in planting new churches. Organizing this thrust, known as "Churches Planting Churches," vice President Tim Ek and Conference Superintendent Glenn Palmberg developed the plan for local churches in cooperation with both conference and denominational leadership.

Leadership would look for a church planting opportunity somewhere in their wider neighborhood. Churches could partner with other churches. Members of local churches and their leaders would join together in prayer, planning, action, volunteering, and financial sacrifice. This again accelerated the rate of church planting. Together with new ethnic churches and joining churches, the Covenant Church became one of the more rapidly growing denominations. In my years as president, Sunday attendance grew by more than 40 percent. Together with increased church planting in the years that followed, the Covenant Church has doubled. Such growth has moved the Covenant Church from among the smaller denominations to place us among the mid-sized denominations.

The side benefits are numerous. Chief Financial Officer Dean Lundgren continued to show that most of the income growth in the Covenant Church was coming from the new churches. Likewise, some of the older churches were reinvigorated as their membership noted the effective outreach programs of the new churches. This resulted in the renewal and strengthening of a number of otherwise static churches.

GROWTH BY JOINING

In addition to our increasing church plants, a significant part of the Covenant Church's growth came as existing churches joined us. Heretofore the Covenant Church had become allergic to independent churches, which were inherently anti-denominationalist or who tried to survive the left-wing march of the mainline into modernism. I now discovered that the Covenant Church was being approached by a number of previously affiliated churches that had left mainline denominations over doctrinal decline and independent churches who saw that the New Testament taught that local churches needed affiliation with other congregations.

One of the first of these was Trinity Church of Greensborough, North Carolina. Its founding pastor, Roy Putnam, was a graduate of Duke Divinity School. He was a deep admirer of our eminent pastor Paul Rees. The bishop of his conference practiced itineration by moving conservative pastors to liberal churches and liberal pastors to more conservative churches. In doing this to Trinity, the bishop named a Unitarian to its pulpit. The congregation rebelled and called Roy back as the pastor of the now-independent church. Finding out that Roy was interested in affiliation with the Covenant Church, I began negotiations for the church to join us. Over the summer, however, Roy died of cancer. A period of intense instability followed. Len Putnam, Roy's son, called me one week and said they were unsure there would even be a preacher that Sunday. He asked me to come down and preach. For once my schedule was clear, and I went. They had gotten into a series of disputes as to who might be called as pastor, with some leaders threatening to leave the church if their candidate was not called. I pleaded with them to call an experienced pastor to serve as interim. Jerry Stenberg had just retired as superintendent of the Canada Conference. There was scarcely a crisis situation he had not encountered during his many years of leadership. He was called as interim pastor and remained for a couple of years. He knew how to bring the congregation together and ultimately helped it become part of the Covenant Church. The church has since flourished under the pastoral leadership of Marc Putnam, Roy's son. Its expanded ministries and dramatically beautiful facilities represented a breakthrough for the Covenant Church in the Carolinas.

A number of congregational churches (United Church of Christ) had also grown restive under that denomination's stand on homosexuality. They joined us. Some of them were more than 100 old. The same thing occurred at the new Covenant church in Tulsa, Oklahoma—only in this instance, Bill Clark, of a large Methodist church, started a church with the blessing and support of that large congregation. From the beginning, retired superintendent Ed Larson of the Pacific Southwest Conference joined with him in building now one of our strongest new churches. The outright hostility of Oklahoma's mainline superintendent led a number of new churches to be founded or to join the Covenant Church. The state has become one of the Covenant Church's fastest-growing areas. Craig Groeschel helped plant a church in Edmonds, Oklahoma, that soon became one of the largest churches in America and has many different satellites in a number of states. It was recently voted one of the nation's most innovative churches. Their television ministry led them to an internet ministry using many versions of the Bible, which they make available online at no charge. YouVersion has reached more than one hundred million people.

The Newsong Church of Southern California had been an independent church whose pastor, David Gibbons, established a rapidly growing Asian (Korean) congregation. Soon in the thousands, it also became interracial and multiethnic. It then planted other related congregations throughout Orange County. These new congregations were clearly evangelical and passionate about the gospel. Bringing new forms of worship and music, they have enriched us greatly.

Dr. Peter Cha brought his Korean/Chinese congregation into the Covenant Church. Second-generation Chinese and Korean professionals found themselves in a common place in the Chicago suburbs. But the Koreans were Calvinist and the Chinese were products of Wesleyan believer Baptist traditions. They felt the Covenant Church fit them well. Other mixed Asian congregations have continued to join, and others have been planted since that time. Their leaders have emerged in conferences and Covenant Church ministries around the nation.

EVANGELISM AND PRAYER

> Prayer Without Evangelism Is Passivity
> Evangelism Without Prayer Is Manipulation

The key to effective evangelization is to use the two legs necessary to spreading the gospel to the ends of the earth. It is especially easy when a whole culture or society is seething with religious and spiritual fervor. But as churches are formed and strong communities with strong inner ties become more and more isolated from the broader culture, strong friendship ties with the larger society inevitably diminish. As Christians mature, they have fewer and fewer non-Christian friends. Yet more than 80 percent of those who find Christ find him through another Christian or close relative. Christ is most readily found through a trusting relationship rather than through just a powerful evangelist or persuasive apologist. These latter are of importance—but only secondary importance. Eighty percent of all reported conversions through the Billy Graham ministries also reflect that these same 80 percent come because of prior contacts with trusted friends.

Since the 1960s the countercultural revolt against traditional culture has increased the tension between the Christian and non-Christian worlds. With rapid secularization since then, hostility toward Christianity has dramatically increased due to conflict over abortion, homosexuality, and gay marriage. The internet has brought atheism and relativism even to the farmers of Swede Bend, Iowa. Tolerance and syncretism have made Christian witness and evangelism seem to many in the postmodern culture to be little more than a form of bigotry and intolerance.

After more than a century of life, the Covenant Church appeared to be going with other denominations—mainline and evangelical—in the decline of widespread evangelization in American culture. We needed to be led by the Spirit to find what would be, in marketing terms, a product champion. Such a leader needed to be a gifted and godly person with a heart burning with the passion for souls. He or she needed to be excellent as a recruiter and motivator for evangelists throughout the country. This leader needed to be able to summon the whole church to this task. The search was long and at times discouraging. Young Lon Allison had grown up in a non-Christian home in San Francisco's East Bay. He had come to Christ through a high school Young Life Club. Its leader was also the youth pastor at the Walnut Creek Covenant Church where Jim Persson was the senior pastor. Jim mentored him in an extraordinary way, eventually making him youth director. Gifted in acting and music, Lon planted a contemporary church in a nearby community under Jim's mentorship. In a rented theater, the Sunday attendance soon surpassed 1,000, and a large percentage of these new attendees were new converts. When interviewing him and his wife, we expressed concerns about his holding such a demanding job, with much travel, and its impact on family life. His wife, Marie, simply stated, "I felt from the beginning that Lon was more of an evangelist than a pastor." What a difference they have both made.

Lon began by recruiting volunteer prayer teams and evangelism teams with a healthy mixture of both laypersons and clergy. He trained them at repeated sessions. They would go to spend weekends at churches upon invitation. The participants covered their own expenses. The teams were enthusiastic and electric. At one point Lon told me that he had eleven teams out in various churches on the following Sunday. He had decided to spend the Sunday with his family instead of another trip. He seemed to be able to handle family and career responsibilities better than almost anyone I have ever met.

Conference leadership became central. The superintendent of the Pacific Southwest Conference led the superintendents in advancing the causes of prayer and evangelism. They all agreed to follow a conference-wide, year-long program in each church to promote both prayer and evangelism. It used the "Bringing My World to Christ" program that we had developed in Redwood City.

Too often the churches attempted to make everyone into a personal evangelist. Yet the gift of evangelism is only given to some, but all are commanded to witness by word and deed. Since more than 80 percent of new converts come primarily through trusted friends or relatives, gentle witness through friendship and caring so often opens the door. Assuming that virtually all Christians have four or five such close friends and relations in their circle of nearness, they must understand that they can be much more effective in bringing them to Christ than anyone else, whether clergy or expert in evangelism. At the beginning of the year, each person would make a list of three to five persons that they would pray and care for throughout the following year. Each person would bring forward the list of such persons to the altar following the dedication service. These would be recorded. Team leaders would contact these people in the congregation from time to time. Special harvest events would allow the gospel to be shared in some nonchurch venue, whether through a round of golf, in a business profession setting, or at some special event. At the end of the year, the new believers could be counted. Some of these prayers went on for years, but with remarkable results.

At each Conference Annual Meeting, the names from all the churches would be brought forward in a ceremony and laid on the altar. Then at the close of one evening session at the national Covenant Church Annual Meeting, each superintendent would bring forward these names—often with a flower representing each new conversion. It became a central highlight for many years, even after my retirement. Results were gratifying. The Evangelical Covenant Church was recording one new believer for every fourteen members. The conservative Presbyterian Church of America reported one in every twenty-two members. The Southern Baptists were recording one for every sixty members. Numbers do not tell everything, but they are helpful and do indicate a renewal of prayerful passion in welcoming others to Christ.

As in the Gospels and Acts, the accounts of new believers invigorate the church. "There is more joy in heaven over the conversion of one sinner than over many righteous" (Luke 15:7). At a gathering of church leaders in Minneapolis, a church chairperson from one of the churches approached me with the following story about a man in his congregation:

> On the Sunday of commitment by church members, the chairperson felt guilty because he hadn't been able to name one person to pray for. Embarrassed, he saw a stranger sitting at the other end of the pew. Feeling guilty, he met the man and invited him to dinner at a restaurant. The man related the following story: "I was away from home on a business trip and had just learned that my marriage was broken. Alone in my motel, I was determined to take my own life. I then remembered the one person whom I always admired. He was compassionate and full of unflinching integrity. I remembered that he was faithful in church. It was a Covenant church. In desperation I looked for such a church in the phonebook and found this one. Can you help me find Christ?"

That day a man came to new life in Christ. Such life stories are always an empowering experience in a local church.

At another church, a woman was starting the list of loved ones outside of Christ when she burst into tears and hastened out of the sanctuary. The pastor's wife followed her, seeking to be of comfort. The woman spoke through her tears saying, "When I was listening I remembered my loved ones outside of Christ. I knew how desperate I was that they find Christ. It dawned on me that I, too, was not yet a child of God." What a glorious welcome the pastor's wife was able to extend to this new follower of Jesus! Such accounts have significantly strengthened the Covenant Church's vitality in the early days of the twenty-first century.

This emphasis throughout the Covenant Church soon came to be noticed outside our fellowship. At the founding of Mission America near Wheaton College, the head of the Billy Graham Association for North America, Sterling Houston, told me that the association was impressed with Lon's leadership and had come to believe that this would be the best strategy for personal evangelism in the twenty-first century. At the same meeting, Dr. Larry Lee Lewis, president of the Home Missions Board of the Southern Baptist Convention, clearly stated that his organization would make "Bringing My World to Christ" one of the recommended strategies for the entire

Southern Baptist Convention. Insignificant though we may be numerically, God's work among us is known across the land.

CHRISTIAN EDUCATION AND DISCIPLESHIP

The Department of Christian Education and Discipleship encompasses the equipping and training of leaders and teachers in the conferences and local churches. From its earliest days the Covenant Church has published and/ or recommended Sunday school and Confirmation materials. Phillip Jacob Spener, the founder of Pietism, had reinstituted the training of children in confirmation from the second half of the seventeenth century.

Coming to head this department, at the same time as I assumed the presidency, was Evelyn Johnson. She was serving as moderator of the Covenant Church Annual Meeting during my election in 1986. So we started out together. Even beyond my three terms (twelve years) in office, close collaborative efforts and friendship continued steadfastly between us two couples—Evelyn, Phil, Elizabeth, and I—until Phil's passing in 2014.

Originally, Evelyn was trained as a schoolteacher. In children's ministry work she developed tremendous skills. Directing Christian education for the Midwest Conference, she became acting superintendent of that conference when "Red" Swanson retired. Her tremendous skill as an administrator soon became apparent. A former math teacher, relevant finances were always at her fingertips. She had mastered planning and process, developing Christian education for American military families stationed in Korea. She mastered group process as well as long-term planning skills. She also developed skill in gaining feedback from participants on all levels. She then showed great skills in conflict management for both churches and pastors.

Her work in the education of children grew to widely recognized significance. Her book on the subject was included in the extensive series of leadership in church life in America. Lyle Schaller, widely recognized over the years as the nation's foremost authority on church leadership, openly affirmed her as his chief source of knowledge in children's ministries.

Resource Center

The Covenant Church's Resource Center had been developed under the outstanding leadership of Millie Lundgren. It was further strengthened as Evelyn supported her continuing development and leadership, providing both curriculum and training materials to churches and conferences. As a result, several denominations outside the Covenant Church regarded the center as one of those providing the most extensive such services.

Leadership Development

Leadership and organizational development skills were increasingly seen as necessary for both lay and pastoral leaders. Lay leaders increasingly needed such skills to actively lead their congregations; otherwise power and control could be too deeply centralized under pastoral control. Too many pastors were themselves ill equipped to understand this, even among seminary graduates. Evelyn went at this matter with great gusto and energy. She brought Alan Forsman into her department for this task. Trained in Christian education, he developed exceptional management skills. Teaming with Evelyn, they began to develop means of training in human resource development, strategic planning, and conflict management. Teamed together, Evelyn and Alan did much to strengthen leadership in our conference centers and camps. This enabled the twenty-four conference and camping centers to improve their focus, finances, and programming. Thus, the Covenant Church came to have the largest and most advanced camping ministry among similar denominations. This team was also important in helping the Covenant Church's own central departments. Even more, they became vital to the national Covenant Church leadership. While remaining a critical employee of the Covenant Church, Alan then became a partner in the vast management firm of Arthur Anderson. At one point he was giving significant assistance to such large corporations as Pepsi. To Christian organizations outside the Covenant Church such as the Billy Graham Center at Wheaton and Truthseekers International, he became an independent consultant, working with Evelyn. To this day, they continue to make contributions to these disciplines and practices.

YOUTH MINISTRY

Youth ministry has been one of the Covenant Church's strong suits over the years. Our vast camping system and open cooperation with InterVarsity, Campus Crusade, Youth for Christ, and Young Life organizations have found support and have significant influence all the way down to the local level. Every three years Covenant Church High Congress has been held on a major university campus. Often more than 5,000 teenagers gather for music, worship, Bible study, and sports. Nationally known youth leaders have come from many organizations to strengthen a ministry of evangelism and discipleship of young people. The returning young people have had a profound impact in their churches.

Elizabeth and I attended every triennial gathering. She was involved in the twenty-four-hour prayer intercession for the entire week of the conference. I decided to conceal my office and was only "Paul" to the thousands. I avoided meals and time with my older cronies and congress staff. I ministered at the dining tables and counseled young people in the massive altar calls after each evening's message.

Kyle Small

One evening during one of the conferences, I was praying with individuals at the altar. I almost stepped on a hefty young athlete who was lying unconscious on his back, ignored and stepped over by several students. I knelt to awaken him while summoning help from nearby students. He gradually awakened but could not stand. Together with a couple of husky football players we helped him into a seat. A true unbeliever, I asked if he had ever had such a seizure before. He said no. Was he charismatic or Pentecostal? Again, "No, I am a Methodist. I have never heard any of that—I am a Methodist!" I simply said, "Perhaps God has spoken to you!" I then had the privilege to welcome him to Christ. To summarize his story: He had come to CHIC with a friend, who happened to be the son of a pastor in Omaha. His church contacts had been minimal. He was interested in girls and was running a nightly poker game on the floor of one of the high-rise dorms housing students. On that night he had gone with his friend to the evening meeting. When his friend went forward at the concluding invitation he was repelled, but then he was seized by a strong compulsion without any known reason to move to the altar. When he got there, he suddenly had a strong experience of bright light. He felt himself weaken and he collapsed. Together with counseling by Melva Wickman, a pastor's wife and well-known Bible teacher, we counseled him throughout the rest of the camp.

His name was Kyle Small. He remained in touch with Melva and me over the next years. Working through college, he was repeatedly a summer camp counselor at our Midwest conference center. I even had him to lunch in Omaha where I was meeting with the conference board in electing a new superintendent. Finishing seminary, he was ordained and married the daughter of one of our pastors. He finished a PhD through Luther Seminary in St. Paul. He and his wife have jointly pastored two churches, and he now serves as associate dean at Western Seminary in Michigan. Joining me later on a mission to India, he now serves on our board of the William Carey Foundation of India.

Youth Ministry at North Park

North Park decided to offer youth ministry as an undergraduate degree. Evelyn negotiated what would be a new innovation, creating a joint position teaching at North Park and serving as the youth administrator for the Covenant Church. This was one of the first breakthroughs in the use of matrix management in the Covenant Church. It not only saved money, but also strengthened the whole denominational youth ministry. For too long the central administration had been like two silos that related only at the top.

Doug Stevens had done an outstanding job as youth pastor at my church in Redwood City. From there he directed the youth ministry degree at Barrington College in Rhode Island. He assumed the dual role with great effectiveness until assuming the pastorate at our Walnut Creek congregation in California.

Ray Johnston had been youth pastor at the Marin Covenant Church just north of San Francisco. The entire organization of Young Life in Marin County was near collapse. Seeing Ray's dramatic expansion of youth ministry in our Marin church, they asked him to serve on the county committee. His leadership soon reinvigorated the whole county movement. His winsomeness made him the volunteer director for the county. Because he served as a leader for all the high school clubs, many students came to make Marin Covenant Church their church home.

Evelyn, with my assistance—in the Lord's providence—persuaded him to take the dual position in Chicago. The youth ministry so flourished that Ray and the Covenant Church gained a national reputation for their youth work. At one point, the vice president of Youth for Christ said that at the meetings among all the evangelical youth ministries in the country, the consensus emerged that the Covenant Church was at the top in both theory and practice. Returning to California some time later, Ray led in the planting of the mammoth Bayside Covenant Church east of San Francisco. Under his successor from Redwood City, Chuck Wysong continued the development of this work.

I remember the remarks of one of teachers while doing my doctorate at San Anselmo. Through a couple of courses, I had gotten to know Robert Bella, who taught at Harvard and then at Berkeley. He was highly recognized as a top scholar in religious and secular sociology, known especially for his bestselling book, *Habits of the Heart*.[3] He said in class, "Evangelicals are now growing rapidly while the mainline is declining." No evangelical himself, he declared that those evangelicals had not been successful in evangelism. The mainline churches had lost their young people; the evangelicals had retained theirs. Thanks be to God for his blessing the Covenant Church's youth work!

3. Bellah et al., *Habits of the Heart*.

8

Chicago—Missions Abroad and Beyond the Covenant Church

WORLD MISSION

FROM ITS SECOND YEAR since its founding in 1885, the Covenant Church has been committed to a global vision of evangelization. Beginning with the commissioning of Swedish Covenant Church Axel Carlson at the Covenant Church Annual Meeting in Rockford, Illinois in 1886, the Covenant Church launched its world missions to Alaska and reached into the Russian Far East during the early days of the Russian Revolution. Peter Matson launched the work in China, which became the mission to Taiwan after China's communist expulsion of missionaries. The Covenant Church's reach extended into the heart of the Congo with Dr. Titus Johnson in 1937, and then into Ecuador in the postwar years, as did the mission to Japan. During the 1960s, Jim Gustafson launched the mission to Thailand with funds from a widow at the church in Pasadena. As I assumed the presidency in 1986, virtually half of the Covenant Church's coordinated budget was allocated to our global missions. As a result, the number of believers in our mission fields, particularly due to the African revival, soon reached nearly a million followers of Jesus.

AFRICA

In 1987, during my first full year in office, the Congo mission celebrated its fiftieth anniversary. Struggling through the Great Depression in the 1930s, the Covenant Church had been unable to pay its Alaska missionaries for several years. When young medical missionary Wallace Thornbloom applied to be sent to the Congo in 1937, the mission board at first declined. "How can we send you to Africa while we are in default in paying our missionaries in Alaska?" Wallace replied, "Well, the Methodists have offered to send me." The result: the Covenant Church sent Wallace Thornbloom forthwith to Africa. He went to the Ubangi-Mongala region, the most primitive part of Africa—a territory about the size of Ohio. Work was not abandoned during the Second World War despite the great Atlantic submarine warfare that shut down virtually all shipping. Following the war, the Covenant Church vastly expanded its missions. It set up more than three hospitals, a nursing school, a Bible school, a seminary, and two trade schools. There were also 100 clinics and more than 60,000 in the church schools—together with 1,100 churchless. A huge revival throughout the field energized all this growth. This was one of the great stories that awakened the attention of missionary scholars throughout the world.

Covenant Church World Missions Secretary Ray Dahlberg and I eagerly flew to the fiftieth anniversary celebration. When we arrived in the Congo by missionary plane, thousands of chanting Africans danced and sang. They hailed me with their traditional hymn "To the Great White Chief." I was startled, and looked behind me to welcome the chief, only to suddenly to discover that I was the great white chief! From there we went to the Karawa Station, the largest mission station in all of French Equatorial Africa, which had our largest hospital, nursing school, and a school for missionary children.

On the celebration day, more 16,000 Africans gathered by foot at this our head station. The parade lasted several hours, with floats and bands from each district. The traditional African procession began singing the all-African hymn "God Save Africa," sung solemnly with much weeping. Seated in the front row for the ceremonies were present and former missionaries being honored.

One honoree was longtime Covenant Church missionary Vannette Thorsell. Now in retirement from teaching, she had spent her last years at Gbado. There she lived with her pet black panther and chimp. She rode alone over the dirt roads throughout the state on her motorcycle. She became nicknamed "Moving Van." Short, with heavy glasses, few realized she was summa cum laude from UC-Berkeley.

As I was seated in the front row, when she was presented I was puzzled to hear a massive rustling behind me. Looking back, I saw all 16,000 standing to honor her. "Why was she so singularly honored?" I asked. The reply was, "she taught them to read." I later noted a long line of men standing in a line while she talked with them two at a time, and then brought her arm down with a dismissive gesture. Puzzled, I was told, "She is recognized as a high judge in the setting of the bridal price between the bride's father and the groom!" I cannot think of any of us who have been so singularly honored as Vannette.

So also was Kay Sundstrand, a missionary nurse who had worked with Dr. Paul Carlson—the doctor who Simba rebels seized in 1964 and later murdered in the infamous Stanleyville Massacre.

Nor can I forget Dr. Theodora Nordlund, our longtime medical doctor. During the revolution, all our personnel left for the Central African Republic. When the time for evacuation had reached its last possible moment, "Dr. Teddy" failed to show and was left behind. *Time* noted in one issue that she was the last Western physician to exit the Congo at that time. Years later I asked her, "Dr. Teddy did you or did you not deliberately stay behind because you could not leave your sick patients?" She looked sternly at me and remained in total silence.

Another one of the physicians was Louis Lanwah, a Canadian doctor and foremost leprosy specialist. In a subsequent evacuation, he too had to leave the Karawa Station. Along with his wife and children, a little black orphaned girl accompanied them. He told me that her mother had been brought to Karawa hospital dying from a murderous beating by her husband. He could not save her, but managed to bring the little girl to birth as the mother was dying.

There was no one to take the little baby. Contrary to mission policy, the family welcomed her as one of theirs. Taken by French soldiers to the NATO base in Turkey by military jet, she was then flown with the family to the NATO base in Belgium. From there the family took a commercial jet to New York. There's the rub. There are two things you must never bring across a national border—a gun or an undocumented child. Louis did not know what to do as he approached the twelve immigration stations at the airport. He randomly took the family to one of the agents who asked where the traveling papers were for the little orphan. Louis had none. Then the agent said that he had spent some years in the Congo. Did the little girl speak Lingala? That was the trade language on our mission field, and the little girl could explain herself to the agent who passed her through by a wave of the hand.

In the extremities of danger and pain, the Holy Spirit continues to perform miracles such as this. It is little wonder that the Covenant Church's sacrifices for world mission have been a great source of renewal and awakening here in the U.S. and Canada.

CHINA AND TAIWAN

In 1889, when the Covenant Church was only four years old, it took over the mission work of the Swedish Covenant Church in Alaska. The following year the Covenant Church ordained and commissioned Mr. and Mrs. Karl Wallen for missionary work in China. They settled in and began work in Southern Hupei province. Northern Hupei was to be the area of the Norwegian Lutheran Mission. The Swedish Covenant Church joined us also in the north. Later our missionaries also joined with the Swedish Covenant Church in starting a seminary in Kinchow. Social and political struggles made the work difficult. In 1927, the Covenant Church had to withdraw nineteen missionaries due to a communist rebellion. There were as many as twenty missionaries at the high point in 1925. In 1931, four missionaries were kidnapped for a time. At the collapse of the mission in 1946, there were more than 6,000 believers. There were hundreds of churches, a hospital, and many schools. In 1948, Dr. Alec Berg, a member of the Estonian Royal House, together with missionaries Esther Nordland and Martha Anderson, were murdered by Maoist bandits. They were our first martyrs. This was the beginning of the end.

Marcus Chen, a brilliant Chinese Covenant Church physician, trained at Wheaton and Chicago Medical College, became the chaplain to Marshall Feng, the Christian warlord. In his struggle with Chiang Kai-shek, he formed an alliance with Mao Tse-tung in the victory of the Communist revolution. Mao rewarded Chen with the position of Minister of Religious Affairs in the new Communist government. He then was dismissed. All of this was an embarrassment to the Covenant Church. One note should be made, however. Marcus Chen was the official interpreter of Foreign Minister Chou En Lai of China, and a Swedish Covenant Church missionary was the interpreter for UN Secretary General Dag Hammarskjöld in the final negotiations ending the Korean War.

Now we know that in this case what looked like a mission's failure in China was actually a seed planted that germinated in communist soil and grew into one of the greatest Christian movements in all of history. Missiologists tell us that Christians now comprise at least 15 percent of the population of Southern Hupei.

Several missionaries then sought to plant churches in Taiwan. The work was slow and discouraging, but the missionaries carried on. Two veterans, Norman and Martha Dwight, began a little theological school at the back of their residence. Covenant Church women funded the first library. This grew to include other students from similar missions. It became China Evangelical Seminary, with splendid facilities, and is looked upon as Taiwan's foremost theological school. Covenant Churcher Dr. Paul Way became the president while pastoring a key church in the main city. Strategically, the Covenant churches recruited the most gifted and godly students for church planting. The Covenant Church then became the fastest growing of the Christian churches of Formosa. These were hardly third-world primitives. When I preached in Dr. Way's church in Taiwan, he pointed out the little widow who came early to pray every Sunday. He said her late husband left her four massive supertankers. Funds from these soon enabled aggressive outreach for missions not only in Taiwan but also throughout the world.

As the Dwights came to retirement, the association of all evangelical missionaries in Taiwan honored them both as "having done more to advance the cause of Christ than any other missionaries since World War II." The other missionaries were similarly effective, and they gave witness that perseverance in almost impossible times can bring a great harvest.

Among the pastors was Nathan Chang. He built a megachurch in the center of Taipei. The eight-story high-rise building was being completed as I visited him there. A creative and widely aggressive evangelist, he came up with a solution to get Bibles into communist China. He went to the Chinese communist government and asked for a license to import the most advanced high-speed automated German Heidelberg printing press then available. He proposed to print one million Bibles using all Chinese materials and workers. When this was achieved, he donated the press to the government. He then began much work in training Mainland Chinese in factory methods. He built factories on the mainland and trained Christian workers to return to their homeland to further their Christian witness and labor. How is it that the most hopeless become the most hopeful?

JAPAN

With the collapse of the China mission following the Communist revolution in 1949, the Covenant Church transferred missionaries to both Japan and Formosa. The earliest were the Bob Vermes family, who came to Japan in 1949. In 1950, the Covenant Church sent the William Rigmarks and the Melbourne Metcalfs. The work expanded slowly, and a seminary was established in Meguro, Tokyo, which became an accredited four-year seminary. The legal openness to Christian missions of the U.S. Occupation government did not result in any cultural openness. The faithful witness and discipleship did produce an excellent though small group of Japanese churches. But the Covenant Church and virtually all other Western mission groups found the work of converting Shinto/Buddhists held captive by centuries of entrenchment painfully slow and hard.

Language studies became a most effective way of producing individual conversions. But other marvelous stories can be told as well. One of the missionaries took an abandoned woman off the streets. She had been found tubercular and thus cast out by her husband. The missionary nurtured her and taught her the Bible. In the small town in which she lived, she began teaching a small group of women in the things of Christ. Eventually, the local pastor left the church. There was no one to preach or lead worship. Contrary to Japanese and much Christian culture, women could not be pastors. But this dear woman decided to preach on Sundays. Then men began to come. Soon there was a higher ratio of men to women than in any of our other churches. This infuriated the pastors of other churches. A wealthy widow from Tokyo had an estate across from the church. Although she was Buddhist, she attended worship faithfully. The church building had become so dilapidated that it needed to be replaced. There were no funds. The Buddhist widow built and donated a beautiful new church building for the congregation. God loves to bless the "wrong" people!

In a meeting with noted missiologist Donald McGavran, who often worshipped with us in Pasadena, he described the unique situation in Japan. He noted the exceeding tightness of family structures in Japan. But because the churches were far apart and scattered, in most cases young men and women were unable to find a Christian spouse and would inevitably marry outside the faith. This meant the loss of most young couples to the faith. He suggested that the churches of Japan institute the Office of Matchmaker—persons designated to find Christian partners to single Christian young people. This has been done in many cultures, even among Christians in many places throughout history. He felt that strong churches and evangelism would languish without stable Christian families undergirding the life of every congregation.

Meanwhile, I discovered that the Evangelical Free Church, the German Frei evangelischer Gemeinde, the Swedish Missionsforbundet, and the Covenant Church each had missions operating in Japan, the Free Church being the largest. They were hardly in competition, for each of them operated in different geographical areas. All four denominations were members of our International Federation of Free Evangelicals. They were basically in communion except for their missions. One of my continuing efforts was to develop a Japanese federation that included all four of these missions, while allowing them to still operate independently. This would create a federation of nearly 100 churches. Only the future will tell.

We need always to go where the openness to the gospel is the greatest. But McGavran exhorted us to continue our witness in the hard places. So it was in Taiwan, Alaska, Africa, and virtually all of our earlier seemingly difficult places.

THAILAND AND LAOS

The move toward mission work in Thailand began in the 1960s in Pasadena. When *Jim Gustafson*, born and raised in Laos by Christian and Missionary Alliance missionary parents, came to Fuller to prepare himself to go to Thailand as a missionary, he worked as our part-time junior high school youth director. At first Jim wanted to take his MDiv at Fuller and then take a PhD in Buddhist philosophy in order to teach at a Thai university. He could then reach Thais for Christ as a prominent Buddhist philosopher. I told him that philosophers were seldom good evangelists and that he should follow Donald McGavran's pattern of reaching the lower classes through people movements. Jim at first rejected this strongly. But his first class from McGavran led him to abandon that effort when he saw that evangelizing the masses was the fastest and most effective way to reach the Thai people.

I was privileged to conduct his wedding with Joan Christianson, a daughter of the church. About that time a childless widow left to the church a home, which became a residence for youth pastors, and $70,000, which went to pay for the first two terms that Jim and Joan served in Thailand. Set free by the Covenant Church in northeast Thailand among the landless Buddhist Thais, Jim led in the planting of more than 300 churches in a region previously abandoned by other mission societies. He soon began a radically contextualized form of evangelism and discipleship. Employing the singing of the Thai culture and Thai instruments, the movement grew rapidly. Only the tenant rice farmers were desperately poor, so Jim set up small cooperatives that involved digging ponds, filling them with fish (tilapia), and raising pigs whose offal fed the fish. These unique fish and pig cooperatives made the work self-sustaining.

The success of the pig farming increased with a half-million-dollar grant from the Danish government for the especially elongated Danish pigs. The ponds began raising vast numbers of tilapia fed by the pigs' offal. Each cooperative consisted of seven families, each tending the pigs and fish one day a week. Citrus trees came to that part of Thailand and were planted on the banks of the ponds, providing citrus fruit for the first time. All this began to improve the nutrition of the poor peasant Thai population. In addition, 10 percent of the income went to strengthen the newly formed church centers. The process grew rapidly, and soon there were over 300 such little cooperatives in northeast Thailand. It then spread to other parts of the nation. Next, the savings provided enough money for the cooperatives to own their own land. This unique movement drew the attention of the State Department of the U.S., who declared it to be perhaps the only such enduring agricultural project in Southeast Asia. Noted missiologist Ralph Winter told me personally that Jim's leadership in Thailand had developed the most successful missionary movement in postwar Southeast Asia. Jim later finished a PhD at the University of Wisconsin and served a term as Secretary of World Missions. He continues to lead magnificent development work in Thailand.

Jim was radically innovative. This sometimes created problems. We had received a grant for a huge supply of seed rice from Covenant Church World Relief to raise the produce to feed the pigs. It was stored in a warehouse of the mission. But crop failures had produced hunger and starvation. Jim opened the warehouse and gave the seed rice to feed the hungry. This raised some ire about misuse of designated funds. I, however, wrote Jim congratulating him on having the heart and wisdom to break the rules and so silenced his critics.

Others joined Jim and Joan in Thailand. Paul and Gretchen DeNeui had come to Redwood City to assist our Kainos ministry among developmentally disabled adults. Paul was a graduate of Cal Poly and taught gardening skills to the residents. He longed for missions service Gretchen was the daughter of missionaries to India. It was a joy to see them, among others, join the Gustafsons in Thailand. Later he earned a PhD from Fuller Seminary and became professor of missions at North Park University and a leading writer on Buddhist missions.

Across the Mekong River from northeast Thailand lay communist Laos, where Jim had been raised. Hostile to Western capitalism, they were nonetheless intrigued by Jim's cooperatives. Peter Dutton had attended the Laos mission school while Jim was there—although he was much younger. Remarkably, Peter and his family settled among nomadic peoples. Afraid of insurrection, the communists forced them to settle in permanent communities. But with no skills, their lack of sanitation and drinking water led to their possible extinction. So Peter and his team taught them to take water upstream for their animals and to cultivate gardens. This raised the ire of an American employee of the UN. He warned the regional communist leaders that this was a capitalist plot to overthrow the government. The local secretary of the Communist Party asked him what the UN had done to help these poor tribals. He then ordered them out of the territory and let the mission proceed in peace. It is remarkable that a Laotian community in California that affiliated with the Covenant Church was made up of refugees from the exact same spot as our mission work in Laos—although they never knew it.

LATIN AMERICA

Ecuador

Covenant Church missions in Latin America began after World War II. Covenant Churcher Reuben Larson and Clarence Jones began a powerful short-wave radio station in Quito, Ecuador. Its location enabled it to reach all parts of Latin America. Its call letters meant "Heralding Christ Jesus' Blessings." In Ecuador, they found that radio was not enough. They needed missionaries on the ground to plant churches and train leaders. They asked the Christian and Missionary Alliance and then the Covenant Church to send missionaries. So began our mission to Ecuador. At one point we had nearly twenty missionaries there. Our secondary school, Collegio Theodore W. Anderson, became a multistoried, block-long school building, housing what had become the nation's most prestigious secondary school. The South Side Church in Quito grew to well over 1,000 believers.

Colombia

The next South American nation the Covenant Church went to was Ecuador's neighbor, Colombia. Starting from the city of Medellín and then proceeding to Bogotá, the work began well. The drug violence in that nation has made our mission both vital and perilous. Medellín was at that time the capital of the drug cartels. Missionary Baxter Swenson was stopped on the street and his car seized by Escobar's thugs. When in Medellín we met with church leaders at their headquarters. At noon we walked to lunch through the historic city square, replete with statues of generals and a cathedral. As we entered the park, the church leaders formed a human shield all around Ray Dahlberg and me. They resumed regular walking to the restaurant. Returning, they again made a human shield around us in the central plaza. While at the headquarters in the afternoon, a pastor came asking us to pray for him and his family as they prepared to flee that evening to safety in nearby Ecuador. Their son had been in an altercation with the son of one of the drug lords. School intervention led to the discipline of the drug lord's son. They had just received word that the entire family had been marked for assassination. We prayed for them as we left. It was said that on the streets of that city you could hire an assassin for as little as thirty-five U.S. dollars.

Warned to go out only in the daytime, we were especially cautioned about being in the slums on the steep hillside above the main city center. But on Sunday as we kept visiting churches and their leaders, it grew dark. When darkness fell we were told that it would be highly offensive if we did not visit a church high up in the slums. At one point we had to stop and climb a stairway toward the church. Suddenly there was an explosion and the lights went out. Our guide called out, "Hit the ground, they've got us!" Fortunately, it was only a blown electrical circuit that had exploded. At the entrance to the small church, the pastor's wife met us and shared God's work. She then said that drug dealers had tried to hide automatic weapons in the foliage outside the front of the church that week. Fearlessly she demanded that they leave with their weapons. Surprisingly they did. We then descended the long staircase to the road where we awaited an automobile to pick us up. We were then told that the prior Sunday on the place we were standing, several people were shot and killed. We were relieved when we saw a line of motorcycles winding through the streets toward us from above. They were police with a rider holding a submachine gun pointed skyward as they snaked past us. The snaking, we were told was to mitigate the possibility of accurate sighting by terrorists. Our fears returned as they disappeared down the street. It was good to get back to our lodgings.

It was much the same in the capital city of Bogotá. We stayed in a hotel built to resemble an Inca palace. Its entrance was sandbagged against assault. In the morning Ray and I lingered in the central courtyard before breakfast. But approaching the entrance of the dining room we saw an expensively dressed gentleman and a soldier before and after him, each with a submachine gun. All three of them were constantly searching the roof lines of the surrounding building. Ray and I returned to our room, deciding on a midmorning breakfast later. We went to the residence of the Marc Westlunds, but even there found a guard booth outside with an armed guard standing by.

But God was at work in the struggle and chaos. Dr. Metcalf, an anesthesiologist from Youngstown, Ohio, had a secretary whose college-age son had, together with his girlfriend, entered the drug world and had been caught selling drugs in San Francisco. Fleeing to Colombia, he was arrested for drug dealing and imprisoned, leaving his pregnant girlfriend outside with no support. When Dr. Metcalf heard of the mother's concern, he contacted missionary Jerry Reed. Jerry and Nancy began caring for her and visiting him in prison. The young man was Gwynn Lewis and his companion, Pooka. Jerry eventually led them both to Christ. There was little chance the U.S. embassy could get him released, and the prison sentences were very harsh and long. By an act of grace, Gwynn was released. Jerry married the two, who left with their baby for the United States. Gwynn went on to graduate from both North Park College and Seminary. As they were being commissioned as career missionaries to Ecuador, they announced that Gwynn would be going straightway to Youngstown, where he, as a newly ordained minister would preside over the remarriage of his long-divorced father and mother. Their dramatic story was later made into a movie by the Billy Graham organization.

God was at work. Jerry had begun a Covenant church in that very prison where other addicts had come to Christ. The government was so impressed that the church was given a ranch outside the city that had been seized from Pablo Escobar, the notorious drug king. They turned it into a drug rehabilitation center. Manning the center were former drug cartel assassins. The story also gained national attention in U.S. newspapers.

God has continued to do many marvelous things in that land, which is now quieter. More recently, the national church elected an attorney to be its president. She is now the first woman to hold such a high office in any Covenant Church body in the U.S. or abroad.

Mexico

Covenant Church missions in Mexico began initially about forty years ago through the Home Missions Department. Andy and Marie Rojas began mission work in the border town of La Villa, Texas, where Mexican nationals did field work near the Swedish American farming community of Lyford. Here the Covenant Church helped Marie and Andy plant a strong Hispanic church. After the twentieth-century Mexican revolution, all Catholic and Protestant missionaries were expelled from that nation. Migrant workers, although undocumented, would often sneak across the border. The Rojas's began winning and discipling them in their home. Some, after an extended period, were sent home, and they planted more than twenty congregations. One of the migrants was Agapito Villafañe, a *bandido jefe* (bandit chief) from the state of Oaxaca, 1,000 miles to the south. He was a full-blooded Zapoteca native. It is said he had nine notches in the handle of his pistol, symbolizing the number of men he had killed. After months of training in Andy and Marie's home, he returned to his people and planted more than twenty-eight tribal churches.

A series of churches in and around Mexico City also began in earnest. One small congregation in Cuernavaca established a large number of small church plants in that area. Pulling this together was no small task for the

Department of World Missions, which had taken over the mission from the Department of Home Mission in the late 1970s.

CIPE—THE INTERNATIONAL CONFEDERATION OF EVANGELICAL COVENANT CHURCHES

A work began to establish clusters of Spanish-speaking Covenant churches, particularly around Chicago and Los Angeles. Many of these new believers came from other parts of Latin America. In my time, a number of these new believers had returned to their native lands and sought to establish Covenant churches. Under the leadership of the Reeds and the Marks's, the works in Ecuador, Mexico, and Colombia were organized into the Confraternidad del Pacto Evangélico (CIPE). The new organization began by welcoming a group of churches from Chile as its first additions. The Chilean body then began planting churches in Argentina and Paraguay. The Covenant Church was not in charge, but simply one of the national bodies. They compiled their own Book of Worship and they joined the International Federation of Free Evangelical Churches.

IFFEC—THE INTERNATIONAL FEDERATION OF FREE EVANGELICAL CHURCHES

Covenant Church World Missions made its entrance into Europe through its membership in the International Federation of Free Evangelical Churches.[1] The Federation began as a result of an awakening in Switzerland as the result of the work of Robert Haldane, a Scottish Free Church missionary, during the 1830s. Thus, churches were born in Bern, St. Gallen, and Geneva. Their leader was Steven Schlatter (father of the famous New Testament scholar Adolph Schlatter). He separated from the Baptists when he declared that immersion was not required for membership in the church. Several churches were soon born in France and northern Italy. In the 1840s, the French church wrote to the American churches, requesting them to repudiate the institution of slavery. Germans also became a part of the federation. Then Free churches in Belgium and Holland also joined these churches. In 1860, the full International Federation was formed. Later the Russian churches born under Ivan Prochonow led in the formation of the Free Evangelical Churches of Russia. Instrumental was the influential Lord Radstock of England, who held small group meetings among the aristocracy in Helsinki and

---

1. Persson, *Free and United*

St. Petersburg. The present leaders of the church now claim that both Leo Tolstoy and Fyodor Dostoyevsky were frequent attendees. Meanwhile, the Scandinavian countries all experienced the birth of Free church bodies.

The movement was largely among the young peoples' groups. The Second World War brought the organization to an unfortunate cessation. But the federation was reawakened and formally established in Bern, Switzerland in 1948. Today there are thirty-one national member federations,[2] with mission work in over fifty nations.

During these years, my predecessor, Milton Engebretson, brought skilled organizational and spiritual leadership to the Federation. The Federation holds a General Assembly every four years. Between the four-year intervals a theological conference is held two years after each General Assembly. The executive committee meets together annually for planning and development. I served on this executive all the years of my presidency, holding most positions, including president. At retirement in 1998, I was general secretary and continued in that role two years after.

These meetings every two years built strong ties of fellowship and mission within the federation. Burdened with the weakness of free evangelical churches in Europe, Covenant Church World Missions began partnership with mission work on the continent. The Covenant Church sent church planters to assist in Belgium, the Netherlands, France, Germany, Czechoslovakia, and Spain. Raymond Dahlberg (the world missions secretary) and I could thus meet with our missionaries in a conference every two years. Together Ray and I drafted the proposal to make World Missions a standing committee of the federation.

Later during my tenure, with my recommendation, the federation created a standing Theology Committee to pursue the communication and advancement of over twenty seminaries and Bible schools among the national member federations. North Park president Jay Phelan was exceptional in the implementation of this committee's planning a theology conference every four years in the place of the executive committee's previous theology conference. This brought more reflection and expertise. These consultations began with their first meeting in Prague. This even progressed to offering joint summer sessions at different locations.

Czech Republic

I had a great opportunity to itinerate among the Czech churches with noted theologian Jan Urban. A graduate of Princeton Seminary, its president, John

2. See https://iffec.org/.

Mackay, had asked him to take a chair at the seminary. Instead he chose to return to Prague, where he was immediately imprisoned by the Communist government. The churches in Bohemia and Moravia were often filled to standing room during my itineration. Arriving in Prague, I was immediately taken to a meeting of the Prague area Czech Brethren. Their diminutive president Ludovit Kubovy had come directly from a command summons to Prague Palace by the Communist premier. All church bodies' leaders were there. The premier threatened drastic penalties if they gave any support to the thousands of university students imprisoned by the government for their presence at a mass protest rally at Wenceslas Square. President Kubovy then asked the premier, "Do you know why the Bohemian king refused to punish Jan Militch for denouncing him as 'the Anti-Christ' from his pulpit?" Receiving a negative answer, he replied, "Because the king said that to lay a hand on one of God's servants is to bring down God's wrath. So, Sir, shall you be remembered if you let these students go free!" I was stunned to hear that all the students were set free the following morning.

Bulgaria

I was invited by Kristo Kulichev, president of the Bulgarian churches, to preach and travel across the country. The churches were founded by missionaries from Park Street Church in Boston during the mid-1840s. Kristo had been arrested and exiled during the Communist era. All their churches were seized and led by Communist-appointed pastors. The church properties were still under state ownership even after the fall of Communism. The federation asked me to assist in the process of gaining the return of the property. Helpful to me were Catholic Cardinals William Keeler and Joseph Bernardin, who secured a private audience with the pope and his authorities on Eastern Europe. I spent three days as their guest in the Vatican, where I was assured that Kulichev was a true Christian hero. Later, I was able to bring him to our Annual Meeting and nominate him for an honorary doctorate at North Park. Later the Bulgarian parliament declared him "Hero of the Bulgarian People."

Romania

Romania was not officially a member of the federation but attended all of our meetings. They had never been a part of the Protestant movement. Instead, more than fifty years previously, an Orthodox priest experienced a dramatic conversion. Ostracized by the Orthodox, he led in the founding of Biserica

Evangelica, the country's largest movement in the southern territories. Being very legalistic, the president felt that church growth and youth work in the United States were the result of compromise. At the fiftieth anniversary of the federation in Bern, Switzerland, I had said that we did not have to make the young people good before they accept Christ. He then pleaded with me to come to them and teach them evangelism. I replied that I would be able to help them organize and plan for church planting and evangelization, but only Jerry Reed could teach them about personal evangelism. Thus, Jerry and I had a preaching circuit throughout Romania. Sometimes the audience reached or even surpassed 1,000 people. Meeting with their executive committee just before my departure, I challenged them to send missionaries abroad. Claiming that they were too poor and persecuted to dare such a venture, they then relented and said that they might send my young interpreter to a romance-speaking country in Latin America as their first missionary. His name was Narcis Dragomir, a recent graduate in Petroleum at the University of Ploesti. They agreed. Narcis then came to Baja, California. He met a spring break student volunteer. She was a Mennonite Brethren college student from Kingsburg, California. They subsequently married. They then returned to Baja, California where they had children and have planted both a church and school. We remain in touch to this day.

Belgium

I also was invited for a preaching mission by our Belgian federation. This small group of churches had begun to show signs of awakening, with evangelism and church planting. I was privileged to be a speaker at their Annual Meeting and encampment and then at other churches. They had been injured by American missionaries who had come without sensitivity and had divided the churches. I prayed and hoped that the rift would be healed.

Switzerland

If Switzerland is the origin of the federation, it is in Switzerland that I experienced some of the most adventure. I remember preaching to a large church in St. Gallen. This state was like a donut with the picturesque state of Appenzellen filling the hole. The church was right next to the state line. Appenzellen was "Heidi country," with tiny people who wore strange clothes. I saw women from there in church, and they dressed like nuns. Appenzellen was the only state that denied women the right to vote. The music was led by a woman wearing a sweater and slacks. I had luncheon at the 400-year-old wooden home of the associate pastor in the little state. Its ceiling was only a little more than five feet high. When I saw the clash of cultures, I asked the pastor, "How do the two cultures get along?" He replied, "Not easily!"

I was also able to minister briefly in French-speaking Switzerland. It was at a little mountain town founded by the Piaget family, built by the famous Swiss watchmaker of that name. The town was dominated by the watch factory. The little Free Evangelical Church was filled to capacity, as it was the Piaget family church. The family continues to give massive sums to the cause of world missions to this day. The current family head of the firm worshipped with us, and we dined with members of the family. I came to know François Piaget with his ties to the federation. A couple of years later, I asked him if the famous educator Piaget was part of the family. He then remarked that the world-famous child education authority was a true Christian. I also learned that the famous nineteenth-century New Testament scholar Frederic Gödet was also a part of this small French-speaking federation.

The Bicentennial

Perhaps the most inspiring experience in the federation was the celebration of the 2,000-year anniversary of Jesus' birth. We decided to celebrate it on the isle of Patmos where the apostle John wrote the book of Revelation. We began in Turkey, where two splendid buses took more than eighty of us on a multiday tour of the seven churches of the book of Revelation. We then met in a brand-new, small tourist hotel right on the beach of the Aegean Sea near Ephesus. As president, I helped organize the theological papers and lectures on each of the seven churches of the book of Revelation. Three papers were presented on each church. One was the historical background of each city. Then followed an exegetical paper of the relevant passage in Revelation. The third paper contextualized the message for the present age. Each paper was translated into four languages: English, German, French, and Spanish. I was most fortunate to get them published as a single volume. We then left for the island of Patmos by ferry. There we entered the traditional cave of St. John and then shared the Lord's Supper by the sea. From there we took the overnight boat to Athens where we worshipped, and then went to the Greek church's beautiful marble retreat center overlooking the Aegean from the opposite shore. Two days later we flew to Copenhagen and spent the evening together in the historic Tivoli Gardens. We Americans flew back to Chicago the next day.

NORTH PARK UNIVERSITY

All revivals and awakenings move promptly to establish education as a major goal. This was no less true for nineteenth-century Swedish immigrants. Centered in Chicago, they led the new young immigrants and their children into living in the American culture. North Park University was born in 1895, the same year that marked the birth of both the University of Chicago and Stanford University. It was a training school for new immigrants in learning English and mastering basic skills like bookkeeping and business, as well as offering Christian education. Unlike outstanding Christian colleges such as Wheaton, Bethel, Gordon, and Westmont, it was open to both Christians and non-Christians. It was meant to serve the whole Swedish immigrant community. Its courses in Bible and religion would be an important tool in evangelism even as the school prepared young people to establish themselves in the new land. An academy was established for secondary education, then a Bible school was established, and then, following World War I, a junior college. In the 1940s, the seminary was opened for ministerial students.

The land donated along Foster Avenue had originally been deeded with the promise of a much larger piece of property surrounding it. The development failed, and the school from the beginning was strapped financially. The first buildings were financed largely through Alaskan Gold claims, but even these proved more of a headache than a blessing. The Great Depression and the modernist-fundamentalist controversies created additional struggles. The fact that the school, unlike most evangelical institutions, promoted enrollment of even non-Christian students in hope of reaching them for Christ, and the building of the nation, gave the school a more distinctive mission. Through the faithfulness of Covenant Churchers everywhere, the school continued to survive and flourish.

During the long years of Karl A. Olsson's presidency (1959–1970) the school grew and became a fully accredited four-year college. Likewise, North Park Seminary gained full accreditation. Assuming the Covenant Church presidency in 1986, though, I found the school in a deep financial crisis. The deferred maintenance that had been keeping finances in balance was beginning to take its toll. Moreover, the school had used up its line of credit for continued operation. National Covenant Church Properties, while a Covenant Church affiliate, had a higher duty to its Covenant Church investors than to church solvency. It declined to advance more credit. Covenant Church general reserves were quite low. But North Park was unable to make its payroll. I recommended to the trustees of the church that we drain a large segment of our reserves to protect the school. Thanks be to God for faithful donors who could save a central mission of the church in its time of difficulty.

Adding to the uncertainty of the situation was the fact that North Park was in an interim period while it sought a new school president. I was, of course, a member of the nominating committee. It was chaired by Dr. Paul Ziemer, dean of Health Sciences at Purdue University. Among those nominated was Dr. David Horner, president of Barrington College. He and his wife, Sue, along with their children, had come to our church in Redwood City while he was doing his doctoral work at Stanford. He was in a special program at the university that offered a PhD jointly with an MBA in business. It was the most preeminent of any such program anywhere. We soon found that this boy preacher from the Plymouth Brethren became a celebrity among grad students at Stanford. We met together often and became close friends. He had left school to become the managing partner for the western states of one of the big five national accounting firms. He soon left to become president of Barrington College in Providence, Rhode Island. He was nominated by Pastor Dewey Sands of the Providence Covenant Church, where the family attended. I did not feel it appropriate for myself to nominate him since it might be perceived as cronyism. After all the interviews, Dr. Ziemer polled the large committee with the question, "If Dr. Horner were the only candidate, would you vote for him?" It was unanimous—something that no other nominee achieved. The faculty interview again brought unanimous support.

Looking at the deficits, David decided he had to make drastic personnel cuts in order to balance the books. They came quickly and decisively. The next morning I was deluged by phone calls from outraged relatives and churches at the termination of their relatives and close friends. I told David, "I am glad you never gave me their names, because I wouldn't have had the courage to terminate so many friends of theirs who were powerful members of the Covenant churches." But David offered to pay for vocational counseling for each of them. A year later all were invited back together. Virtually all said that they had now found better jobs more suited to their skills and fulfillment.

David's next step was to lay out a five-year plan to broaden the curriculum. Board member Ken Block, managing director of A.T. Carney—a leading management consulting firm—reluctantly agreed. He said, "Ordinarily you don't solve financial deficits by increasing expenses—but I'll go along with it." And David did bring the school into balance. He was a joy to work with.

As David Johnson moved from covenant financial officer to full-time presidency of National Covenant Church Properties, we asked Senior

Aetna Vice President Dean Lundgren to take a huge financial cut. He would become our chief financial officer and, with his PhD from Harvard Business School, head our new master's degree graduate program in nonprofit management. Our other Covenant Church institutions reached into their reserves and together created a million-dollar endowed chair. We named it for the head of our outstanding hospital and retirement homes under the Covenant Church Board of Benevolence, Nils G. Axelson. Now offering a master's graduate degree as part of the college, we were delighted to change the school's name to North Park University.

The college had a unique Scandinavian Studies program that was playing the significant academic role of providing research and exchange opportunities about the history and influences of Swedish immigrant populations and culture. Given the fact that there had been almost no Swedish immigration since 1914, our experience needed to serve as a resource to the newer immigrants. David and I then proposed the establishment of Korean, African American, and Hispanic Centers. This opened the way for more diversity at the college today, with the highest enrollment of non-Caucasian students of any similar college.

Shortly after my arrival the restoration of Old Main was completed. The state made it an historical monument, and the governor of Illinois participated in the inauguration. The library, built after World War II, was becoming so overloaded with books that it was important to build a replacement. Bernice and Paul Brandel had a large farm, which was sold and given to North Park for the Brandel Library. With this foundation gift of several million dollars, the Covenant Church national fund drive provided the additional $20-million-dollar cost of a magnificent and splendid new library.

The school also lacked a formal chapel. A. Harold and Lorraine Anderson, who were also significant givers to the Covenant Church over the years, offered to fund this project. It turned out to be a beautiful new chapel used for many events. My former church had a partially installed pipe organ in its new gymnasium and sports complex. Both were built by Paul Sahlen, a sugar company executive. The church offered to donate it to North Park. Paul Sahlen's close relatives, the Ray Magnuson family, donated the fund to enlarge and rebuild it into a first-class, sixty-rank organ. The acoustics were perfect. Music critics said it was one of the finest concert facilities on the north side of Chicago.

More than that, however, was the decision to remain in Chicago itself. Students at North Park University would learn how to function as Christians in modern-city living. The whole world was going urban, and Protestants were successful in the farm countries and small towns, but increasingly weak in the cities. We went against the tide, involving the students in working among the poor of the cities. Coeds spent nonclass time holding crack babies and teaching illiterate prisoners in the county jails to read and write. So also did the male students. Thus, a good academic education at North Park would assist the student to mount the golden escalator to money and prestige, but it would also train them to be servants to the least, the last, and the lost. It is now clear that North Park has a higher percentage of students who volunteer skill and time to serve the urban poor; higher than most colleges. Praise be to God!

NORTH PARK SEMINARY

Training pastors was the principal reason for the birth of North Park Seminary. Our first president, Karl August Björk, did not consider such training necessary—it could even be harmful. But other leaders prevailed. The earliest seminary education was at Chicago Theological Seminary. Because the Congregationalists felt that Swedish immigrants would be welcome within their umbrella, they helped build churches for us in the East and established a Swedish Department at Chicago Theological Seminary. They even appointed a Swedish Covenant Church pastor, Fridolf Risberg, as a professor. Later, the Covenant Church withdrew and founded North Park Seminary. Its culture differed from that of Chicago Theological Seminary. The denial of the deity of Christ by some Chicago faculty had isolated Fridolf Risberg. Despite the generosity of the Congregationalists, they were far removed from the times of revival. The movement had become middle and upper class. The seminary was now in the full throes of modernism, with faculty members clearly denying the deity of Christ, the resurrection, and miracles. It was strange to have Fridolf Risberg in one class leading a prayer meeting and revival, while in the next class professor Shirley Jackson Case was denying the Trinity, the virgin birth, and the necessity of the new birth. David Nyvall and Axel Millender withdrew, and North Park Seminary became a real seminary.

Because the North Park faculty and David Nyvall wanted to keep the school abreast of academic studies, it was no Bible school. The college already included that component. As the twentieth century bloomed, the modernist-fundamentalist controversies created tension even within the Covenant Church. Since the school and the Covenant Church had no historic confession, misunderstandings were inevitably arising. Yet because of its close connection to and oversight by the Covenant Church as a whole, the school escaped the most radical polarizations of the modernist-fundamentalist controversy.

The coming of professor Don Madvig and then New Testament professor Klyne Snodgrass made it clear that biblical studies would remain within the broad evangelical framework. Later, internationally known New Testament professor David Scholer joined the faculty, as well as accomplished Old Testament scholar Robert Hubbard. During these years, the combined biblical faculty in both the college and seminary became as strong as at any biblical studies program among evangelical schools.

In searching for the Milton B. Engebretson Professor of Evangelism, the school settled on veteran missionary Jerry Reed. Having served with his wife, Nancy, in Ecuador, Colombia, and in Mexico, they were constantly involved in church planting and evangelism. Jerry developed a simple method of discipling new converts and then helping them to reach their friends for Christ. This simple program became used throughout many nations. Around Mexico City, they traced a new believer through more than twelve generations of converts. In one place nearly a dozen small churches were established through the planting of one small church. We strongly felt that every Covenant Church pastor should be practicing and involved in such personal evangelism. As I often told incoming first-year students, "if you have not led at least one person to Christ by the time you are through here, you will find yourself chronically unhappy as a Covenant Church pastor." The Mexican missions staff felt that I had robbed their field of two of their most gifted and effective missionaries. I promised to send five new missionaries in their place. Alas, I fell shy of the attempt! But the evangelistic practices of graduates expanded rapidly under Jerry Reed's tutelage.

Few had greater impact on the students than John Weborg. His academic research focused on the history of Pietism, and the Covenant Church flourished as a result of these studies and connections. He also became involved in the spiritual development of seminary students and their spouses. Taking a cue from the Roman Catholics, we saw spiritual formation as essential training for seminarians. John soon developed a strong emphasis on spiritual formation at North Park. At first none of the sixty-odd evangelical seminaries had any such emphases. It had been assumed that anyone in graduate seminary would be adequately mature, spiritually. We had all succumbed to the state church and modernist assumption that seminary was purely academic. Every spring I would have the forthcoming graduates to our home for desert and hear their reflections, both positive and negative, on their trailing. Without exception, I clearly observed the experience of spiritual maturity and formation. Not that there were no such examples among earlier graduates, but the whole tenor of spiritual fellowship and maturity increasingly emerged each year.

The internationally recognized biblical journal *Ex Auditu* had been published by Princeton Seminary for many years. To our surprise, the journal asked to be moved to North Park Seminary. Under the leadership of Klyne Snodgrass, foremost scholars from around the world came each year to lecture for articles to be published in the journal. The journal had been established by the president of Pittsburgh Seminary as something of an alternative to the Society of Biblical Literature. The journal's move to North Park Semiary did much to advance this. This did so much to deepen and broaden us. I feasted there every year with the world's best believing scholars. Since the publishers of *Ex Auditu* wanted the lectures to be open even to help the laity grow in their understanding, I soon had all the council of administrators attending, and many members of the Covenant Church executive board. In a sense, *Ex Auditu* put our seminary significantly ahead of many such schools in America.

THE BOARD OF BENEVOLENCE

From its birth in 1885, the Covenant Church has sought to care for the least, the last, and the lost. The immigrants in Chicago were without adequate medical care. Every year cholera would sweep through the immigrant communities killing, disabling, and orphaning many of them. On the North Side, the churches chose Pastor Henry Palmblad to find help. In the second year of its existence they built the Home of Mercy on the unpaved Foster Avenue. On the first floor they housed the acutely ill; on the second floor they housed the dependent elderly; and on the third floor they housed orphans. The first floor became the historic Swedish Covenant Church Hospital—a landmark on Chicago's North Side. The second floor became the Home of Mercy itself, which housed senior citizens. The top floor became the Covenant Church Children's Home in Princeton, Illinois. Eventually hospitals were built in Turlock, California, and Omaha, Nebraska. The latter did not survive the depression. Later, retirement communities were established in New York, Connecticut, Minneapolis, Seattle, and Spokane, Washington. Nils Axelson, the administrator who so successfully led this whole department, told us that the total size of the Covenant Church's benevolent institutions was actually the same size as America's Episcopalian institutions.

In 1986, when I became president, the economy was in a swoon. Three kinds of businesses were hit the hardest—banking, hospitals, and colleges. The Covenant Church had a small reserve fund. National Covenant Church Properties was a church bank; North Park could barely meet payroll, and our two hospitals appeared doomed. We were told that a chain would buy both of our hospitals for $25 million dollars. Upon investigation, all they offered was one seat on their board of directors. It was a hoax. Evangelical (congregational) Systems began talks with us, but they felt it was only the Covenant Church ties that made the hospital viable. They would not assume ownership even if we threw them the keys. I held a private meeting with the key healthcare partners of our auditing firm, Deloitte and Touche. They came to my office and told me that most of the surrounding hospitals would fail. The only survivor would be Swedish Covenant Church. If we wanted to sell or dispose of it, then divestiture was possible. But under no circumstances should we abandon the hospital as if in a fire sale. Despite internal opposition, I held out. Then we were asked by the new Northwest Healthcare System to become the anchor hospital on Chicago's North Side. The other anchors were the Northwestern University and Evanston hospitals. At first we were told we could remain a Covenant Church affiliate—but then discovered we would lose all control. After intense negotiations they agreed we could control the nominating committee recommendations for the hospital's board of directors. I became a member of the board of directors of the nation's fifth-largest healthcare chain. In seeking funding for a new outpatient care building, bond counsel (who represented our bond holders) advised us to remove the statement "Man is created in the Image of God." The counsel ruled that it was a religious claim disallowed by the first amendment. I rebeled and called it off. Finally, bond counsel gave in. It was a win/win.

We were then able to build the first hospital-affiliated life care health facility in the U.S. The Galter family made the strategic gift, proud that the Jewish community could give to a Christian hospital. Later they added a second floor. We were featured on the cover of *Hospital Management Magazine*. We were then made the North Side anchor for internationally known Chicago Rehabilitation Hospital for stroke victims. We also then became an extension of the cancer treatment program of Evanston Hospital. Hearing that the local hospital agency was opening a number of new psychiatric hospital beds, I urged that we add them. We then proceeded to build the nation's first outpatient surgery center, bridged over the streets to our other facilities. It was a $60-million-dollar, seven-story high-rise structure.

EMANUEL HOSPITAL

While I was chair of the Emanuel Medical Center in Turlock, California, I had spurred the consolidation of the hospital with the national church. I strongly supported its relocation to a new and modern facility. I also pushed for the building of the Aurelian Psychiatric Unit. Then I pushed to establish a long-term care facility—against both internal and external pressure. The opposition claimed that this was socialism horning in on free enterprise by a group of doctors who wished to run it as a profit-making unit.

Again, the financial pressures led to the industry-wide need to consolidate all hospitals into chains. This would mean our surrender of control of the Christian mission. Strangely, Memorial Hospital in Modesto brought us a surprising proposal. It also was under pressure from the Tenet Hospital in Modesto, part of a nationwide chain. It had a small board of directors that controlled the hospital. They too were frightened. They felt that they could escape the crisis by giving their hospital outright to the Covenant Church, making a small multi-hospital system. Smaller hospitals in the surrounding areas were also discussing proposals to join our leadership at Emanuel. The Emanuel board of directors decided to reject the offer, fearing that we could not manage it well. After my leaving office, Stanford University Hospitals entered an agreement to establish a Stanford Cancer Treatment Center with Emanuel, covering much of California's Central Valley. So despite financial pressures, the Covenant Church held on to its relationship with our Emanuel Medical Center.

RETIREMENT COMMUNITIES

The Home of Mercy eventually became the Covenant Church Home right across the street from the hospital, serving the elderly for its lifetime. After the Second World War a generous gift allowed Covenant Church Palms to join the community of affiliates. Then conference facilities became affiliated with the Board of Benevolence. Bethany Home in Turlock, California was relocated and became the Covenant Church Village of Turlock. Elim Home in Tujunga, California was moved to San Diego as a part of Mount Miguel Covenant Church Village. Then came the relocation of Covenant Church Village of Florida to Plantation (Ft. Lauderdale). We also opened Covenant Church Village of Golden Valley, Minnesota, Covenant Church Village of Colorado, as well as one in Cromwell, Connecticut. The Seattle community on Mercer Island came close to insolvency. Paul Peterson appealed to me, saying he could save it. He got the chance and, through building an extended care center and a great deal of hard work, made it one of the premier retirement communities of the Covenant Church. As I mentioned earlier, I was part of the rescue of the Samarkand of Santa Barbara. The work of Nils Axelson and Paul Brandel transformed it into the flagship of our centers.

Covenant Church Home in Chicago needed replacement. A strong movement developed to close it and send its residents to either Northbrook Covenant Church Village or the Holmstad, west of Chicago. I found out that funds had been given to Covenant Church Home through contributions, which created a huge fund held by Covenant Church Home. But it had been lent at no interest to other Covenant Church retirement facilities. It amounted to enough funds to completely rebuild the facility, debt free. Marc Olson, the first clergy chair of the Covenant Church Executive Board, worked to proceed with the proposal. Subsequently, a fine new Covenant Church Home was raised on the old site.

Meanwhile, newly built Windsor Manor—large and elegant—on the west side, close to Wheaton College, was unable to survive financially. Its board approached the Covenant Church about taking ownership. Taking it over as a covenant retirement center was the last official signature that I made as president of the Covenant Church.

COVENANT CHURCH ENABLING RESIDENCES

Covenant Church Women's executive director Deirdre Banks began to propose a residence for developmentally disabled adults. Thus, the first Covenant Church Enabling Residence was completed on Chicago's southwest side. Other such homes followed.

Remarkably, all of these institutions survived and flourished—primarily under the guidance of Nils Axelson, followed by Roland Carlson, and then by Paul Peterson. Rather than a millstone and financial drain on the church, we were at last funding reserves for depreciation, that is, building up funds to replace obsolete and aged facilities.

REDUCING CENTRAL OVERHEAD TO ZERO

By 1994, our reserves nearly reached the sum of our total indebtedness. Doing so would reduce central overhead to zero. Attaining that goal made us the envy of most major religious organizations. In addition, we negotiated a small fee of .02% on the assets of each Covenant Church entity. This enabled us to cover all central administration expenses with special contributions and these fees, which offset 100 percent of the administrative costs of the Central Covenant Church Budget. Thus, no deductions came out of money sent directly to the Covenant Church budget. The Covenant Church fees from our institutions and my President's Fund could assure donors that every penny sent would go directly to our ministry. I came to understand that only the American Bible Society, with its huge endowment, could claim that. The Gideons, similarly, covered overhead costs directly from its own members. This significant achievement relieved my heart from the pain of thinking that any Covenant Church giving would be applied to the central Covenant Church overhead. Now every dollar given to the Covenant Church would go 100 percent to our coordinated budget!

STRUCTURAL REVIEW

By 1996, the executive board concluded that it was time to review the organizational structure of the Covenant Church. More than a generation had passed since the last such study. The board appointed a study committee to comprehensively review the constitution and by-laws. Even since I had become president in 1986, the Covenant Church's assets had doubled, and attendance had grown by nearly 50 percent. Moreover, the culture was experiencing rapid change. Federal and state laws governing churches and other nonprofit organizations were continually changing. The executive board named representative members from each conference, institution, and administrative board. It then retained a not-for-profit organizational expert consultant from Deloitte and Touche to assist us in updating our constitution and by-laws. It met regularly in the remaining two years of my tenure and beyond. Two proposals were developed. One was a series of modest revisions. The other involved more substantive changes. The substantive changes were adopted two years after my retirement.

BEYOND THE COVENANT CHURCH

The Evangelical Leaders

Soon after I became president, Bob Rickers of the Baptist General Conference contacted me. When we met, he suggested that we have a small accountability group together with Paul Cedar of the Evangelical Free Church. We were, according to studies of religious sociologists, the "three sisters." Studying the cultural demographics, secular sociologists noted that the three denominations were so nearly identical that they could be lumped together for purposes of sociological analysis. Yet we have been three denominations from the beginning. Born of the nineteenth-century pietist revivals in Sweden and Swedish-immigrant America, they have striking similarities. George Bernard Shaw once said that England and America are two nations divided by a common language; in our case the three sisters were divided by their common heritage. All revival movements tend to diversify. So it has happened over the last 100 years.

The three of us began meeting together with our spouses every year for two to three days for fellowship, accountability, and problem solving. We decided to expand the group to include mid-sized evangelical denomination presidents. This came to include Ed Davis of the Evangelical Presbyterian Church, David Rambo of the Christian and Missionary Alliance, Paul Gilchrest of the Presbyterian Church of America, Harold Binders of the North American (German) Baptists, and Dennis Jones of the Conservative Baptists. We each came with our differences and still pulsing with the power of the Spirit. Our friendships grew deep.

At first we met each year in a different place: in Minneapolis, the Cove of Billy Graham in North Carolina, Covenant Church Harbor in Wisconsin, and in the Palm Desert area in our gated community of Rio del Sol, near Palm Springs, California. It was so delightful there in the spring that we began to meet there every year. Paul and Ginny Cedar actually bought a second home in our gated community. Eventually, they moved there as their permanent home after assuming the leadership of Mission America full time. We shared numerous problems and ideas. Among them was the issue of the decline of denominations. In the changing cultural environment, sociologists noticed the steep decline among mainline denominations. This time also saw a rapid rise of the so-called megachurches, which were either independent or quasi-independent churches. While each of our denominations had some of these churches, the vast majority were independent. Their pastoral leaders often had no seminary training.

Their success led them to hold training seminars for lay people and pastors throughout the country. Often they functioned as patriarchal bishops, advising pastors and laypersons that denominations were in the latter stages of extinction and only the megachurches would flourish. Because so many of our members attended these often-helpful seminars, they returned home with a dim view of the future of their denominational families.

As we reflected together and looked over the statistics, it became clear that each of our mid-sized denominations were in significant growth patterns. Hundreds of thousands of smaller Protestant churches amounted to more than 90 percent of all churches. The news of our passing was entirely premature. I, to put a tongue in my cheek, had never quite forgiven God for not making me one of those megachurch pastors. Praise be to God for each of them and the wisdom they can share even with small churches! Megachurches and their gifted pastors are a blessing upon the whole Christian movement. But they experience rise and fall, conflict, and scandal like the rest of us small fries. We needed to share our growth stories with our people, and sought ways to do so.

A second source of discussion was the problem of the mid-judicatories. Each denomination had a series of regional conferences. Even mainline denominations noticed that if there were less than thirty churches in a conference, then even financing their work became extremely difficult. If, however, a region had more than fifty churches, the greater number of churches tended to lead to inadequate care for each of the churches.

We then faced the fact that district leaders, like our superintendents, were often in a double bind. He or she needed to represent the concerns of the national church to the local churches, and at the same time represent the concerns of the local churches and pastors nationally. The traditional role of the superintendent was to be a pastor of the pastors, as well as leader of the congregations. When conflict arose between pastors and their churches, how would the superintendent care for the pastor and the welfare of the church at the same time? This dilemma remains to this day. It is especially great now that pastoral misconduct has serious and legal implications. How does a superintendent protect the pastor and the church at the same time? These church bodies are each increasingly finding new ways to alleviate if not eliminate the impossibility of the role the superintendents must play.

A third area of discussion concerned the role of women in the church. Here the Covenant Church was the outlier as we had officially accepted the ordination of women pastors and leaders. The others had not. Then other leaders in good will warned our policy might lead us toward liberalism. Yet they all admitted that conflicts regarding the role of women were occurring in all their denominations. The changing culture made such a change inevitable—and they thanked God that they would at least be retired before these issues came to a head. Feeling somewhat lonely there, I relaxed with a smile, thanking God that he had already led us through this change with little conflict.

At a prayer summit of church and parachurch leaders in Portland, Oregon, Paul Cedar and I had special times of prayer together with our spouses. As we knelt and prayed, we wondered if some year we might have all "three sisters" hold their annuals together at the St. Paul Civic Auditorium. Each ministerium and business meeting would be held separately. General teaching and worship gatherings would be held jointly. It had never happened. The year after my retirement, in 1999, the first such family reunion occurred. At the climax assembly, a massive crowd worshipped together with much media coverage.

United States Church Leaders[3]

In 1972, the titular heads of all United States church leaders convened under Covenant Church President Milton Engebretson. This included the churches of the National Council of Churches, the National Association of Evangelicals, denominations not affiliated with either, the Roman Catholics, and the Orthodox. Milton was named chair of the meeting and remained so for the next fifteen years. While many leaders felt that matters of doctrine or public advocacy would make such a meeting impossible, it was nevertheless possible, even on controversial issues, because people felt it was important to begin annual conversations. They met for two days every year. After Engebretson, Dr. Harold Bennett of the Southern Baptist Convention continued in the role of chair until I was named chair a few years later. I served in that role for twelve years. Milton's role was decisive, building ties of goodwill and pastoral concern for each leader. This kept a bond of community and dialogue going for the ensuing years. It built ties and promoted harmony despite theological differences. Milton's skills ultimately provided the key to goodwill and openness, even as his unequivocal evangelical convictions remained uncompromised. When Harold Bennett retired as head of the Southern Baptist Board of Management, he was honored by their General Assembly, and the videos played included only two non-Southern Baptist leaders. They were of President George H. W. Bush and Milton B. Engebretson—a great honor!

The dozen years I served as chair were some of the more enriching experiences of my life. I continued to bring a preponderance of evangelical scholars and leaders and teachers to the meetings. We developed significant friendships with many. Cardinal Bernardin of Chicago extended his friendship with Milton to me. One of the most moving moments that I experienced during those years occurred during one of the sessions when Cardinal Bernardin of the Catholic Church and Augie Mieneke of the Missouri Lutheran Church each shared their own spiritual journey. This was astounding because the Missouri Lutheran has been the strictest of the Lutheran bodies. Yet each of them shared how they had come to put their faith in Christ. Then each described their daily office, that is, their daily devotionals. A sensitive tenderness came on all of us. It seemed that as we each in our own way knelt at the foot of the cross, we discovered surprising fellow church leaders kneeling together with us. I might also add that Cardinal Bernardin, while dying of pancreatic cancer, wrote to me a personal letter of prayer and condolences when my daughter Kathleen passed away.

3. Meeting of U.S. church leaders.

Later, Cardinal Keeler of Baltimore, as president of the Council of Catholic Bishops, served on my steering committee. We began years of communication and worked together on church-owned hospital issues in which these hospitals fought off mandatory abortion procedures. He then called me "Son of Thunder" (like James and John). He and Bernardin got me an audience with the pope in Rome. He was shot by an assassin just prior to my coming, but I was given several days of consultation and free run of the Vatican and its treasures. They helped me with regard to the Free Evangelical church in Bulgaria, an IFFEC member, in gaining the return of church properties that had been seized during communist rule. I tried to keep the meetings open so that Catholics and evangelicals could meet face to face with National Council leaders. Attending one of our meetings, the religion editor of *Time* suggested that our annual off-the-record meeting was probably the most significant church meeting every year.

In the middle of the hospital crisis following the Supreme Court's legalization of abortion, federal assistance with even the poor was to be denied unless we allowed abortions. It put two Lutheran hospitals, one Orthodox hospital, 810 Seventh-Day Adventist facilities, and the Covenant Church's two hospitals in jeopardy. I was invited to address the matter before the Chicago Bar Association, which occupied their own high-rise building in downtown Chicago. They said that meeting had the largest attendance in memory. Attorneys for the Catholic bishops later said that our struggle then set the pattern for maintaining our historic stance.

When the cardinal joined the steering committee, he told me that he would leave every two hours for a half hour. He told me that this was not due to pressing business but that "on the day of my ordination to the priesthood I vowed to spend thirty minutes of every two hours on my face before my Savior." I had never heard of such devotion in the Covenant Church or elsewhere. Even after retirement, Keeler wrote to me personally time again in longhand and signed his name, "Bill." A rare affirmation. Brother Jeff Groh, of the National Council of Catholic Bishops, who regularly attended our meetings, on two separate occasions informed us that the executive committee of the Council of Catholic Bishops had instructed him to convey to me that they considered my role, as well as the Covenant Church's, to be "Magisterial to the Whole Christian Church." It was the finest affirmation that I have ever received.

It was good to be together with the evangelical church leaders and deepen our ties with each other. Every year I had a private dinner with Jim Andrews of the United Presbyterian Church. We were far apart theologically, but deeply enjoying the give and take of theological interaction. I developed a friendship with Herb Chilstrom of the Evangelical Lutheran

Church. He and his wife had Elizabeth and me over for dinner at his home, together with the eminent church historian Martin Marty and his wife. This further extended that relationship over the years. Joan Campbell of the National Council of Churches also became a friend. Politically she was far to the left of me, but she had strong ties to Billy Graham, and she shared the night that her granddaughter went forward at a Billy Graham Crusade and received Christ as her Savior.

Twice I sat next to Senator Albert Gore of Tennessee. At one meeting on defense policy during the Bush years, I advanced to him an idea that I heard had been proposed by Henry Kissinger: all our atomic weapons in the U.S. and Europe were first-strike weapons, meaning the U.S. would be the first nation to use them in war. I objected to such a stance. Kissinger had suggested that mid-range mobile missiles could be routinely moved around to secret places in the U.S. They could never be all destroyed in a first strike by Russia. Thus, they would be a deterrent even as a second-strike weapon. I doubted that Senator Gore was convinced by my arguing the case. So I was pleased to see him openly advance this proposal until the collapse of the iron curtain made such deployment unnecessary. The senator shared his faith with me concerning his personal relationship with Christ. He and his wife were the cleanup crew at their local Missionary Baptist church. Things have changed since then, and I do not know much about his current faith.

I remember Richard Hayes, the world-class New Testament professor at Duke Divinity School. He lectured on his new book on 2 Corinthians. He was asked a question concerning the rising tide of gay ordination in the mainline denominations. He replied, "I do not wish to advise you on your policies, but I will state plainly that no honest interpreter of the New Testament can come to any other conclusion but that homosexual practice was wrong."

Most interesting was a meeting with Supreme Court Justice Anton Scalia. In a rollicking dialogue for over two hours with me in the chair and he on the dais, we had a lot of strong repartee. When I mentioned that local city zoning commissions were denying churches the right to open in their cities, I argued that this was an infringement on the first amendment. He stoutly replied contrarily that the cities had every right to deny them access. Only voters, not the courts, could instruct their cities to admit such churches. And this from the most conservative justice on the Supreme Court!

N. T. Wright, later bishop of Durham, was our chief speaker one year and addressed us on the theme of "Christianity in the Post-Christian World." It was stunning. I was able to get multiple copies of the lecture run off during the noon hour. It amazed me to see all the leaders line up to grab a copy, including bishops and cardinals.

We also heard from Martin Marty and Earl Palmer, as well as a number of others. Two presenters in different years were professor Paul Leroy Holmer of Yale Divinity School and Elmer Johnson, executive vice president counsel of General Motors. Both had Covenant Church roots! I was pleased that Wesley Granberg-Michelson of the Reformed Church of America succeeded me as chair. He had been a Covenant Church pastor before moving to the Reformed Church later in his career. Perhaps most important of all was the opportunity for bishops, presidents, and chief executives of a vast number of churches to form common bonds on the taxing struggles and fulfillment of leadership. As such, two church heads each year shared their personal and professional journey down to current highlights and crises.

At the last meeting of U.S. church leaders that I led, we met at the Cove—the Billy Graham Retreat Center near Ashville, North Carolina. The prior year, the steering committee unanimously voted to honor Billy Graham for his faithful lifetime of proclaiming Christ throughout the world. The president of the Roman Catholic Council of Bishops requested a room for their bishops to celebrate Mass each morning. I had to negotiate with the highest level of the Graham Association to allow for Mass at this redoubtable stronghold of Protestant conviction. With that agreed, all elements of American Christianity—Roman Catholic, Orthodox, Mainline, Pentecostal, and Evangelical—united to give thanks and honor to the man who had preached the gospel to more people than anyone else in history: Billy Graham.

THE DECISION

As my third term as president was drawing to a close, Elizabeth and I began to talk and pray about standing for another four-year term. I would turn sixty-five years of age only thirty-five days after my current term would end on September 1, 1998. Should I seek to serve an additional term, as I would still be eligible under Covenant Church by-laws?

To step down this time would allow me to enter a new mission for up to twenty years. Having had fulfilling careers as both a pastor and a denominational church leader, I could launch my ship again on the sea of new adventure. Such a move would involve the temptation of a new venture. It would also feed my anxiety about the unknown.

To pursue a fourth term would enable me to further pursue my vision for the Covenant Church. As a rising young pastor, I was often shushed by aging leaders who told me that I would surely someday become a good leader. I was now an aging leader. Was I becoming a barrier to gifted and godly younger leaders whose vision for new times had surpassed my own? Literature on leadership underscored this concern with its suggestion that longer-term leadership often results in diminished effectiveness and resistance to change.

Still uncertain, I decided to respond to the nominating committee's request for an interview. I responded with extensive answers to the written interrogatives. I particularly emphasized moving the Covenant Church further toward a conscious embrace of globalization. This would mean increasing multiethnic local congregations and a new thrust for evangelism and justice throughout the global village. I further suggested a new emphasis on training lay leadership. I envisioned the local church as one of the most complex of all communities. It shapes the lives of all those within its care and significantly affects communities outside its walls. I further suggested that the structure and effectiveness of local churches would be an important area of courses and teaching in the undergraduate curriculum at North Park University. Certificates could be awarded by extension throughout the whole Covenant Church.

I was also now experiencing new health issues. Suffering from asthma since childhood, specialists in allergies had given me constant help. I had taken antigen shots faithfully for fifty years. Newer medications had also continually enabled me to lead a normal life. Now my struggles with asthma took a downward turn. I could not fight off colds and bouts with the flu, and was continually coughing because of my asthma. My longtime allergist, Dr. Paul Kentor of Evanston, finally told me that he had exhausted all the medical assistance he could render. High stress and constant travel had weakened me too much.

More decisive was our concern for our daughter Kristi, still struggling with the death of our daughter Kathy.

THE DARKEST VALLEY

When Elizabeth and I were entering the last two years of what would be my final term as president, we were struck by the deepest tragedy of our lives. Our younger daughter, Kathleen, was taken from us suddenly. Loving, brilliant, a social leader and devout follower of Jesus, she had graduated from Westmont College. She spent a summer session at North Park. There she studied sociology among the poor at Jesus People Covenant Church in Uptown. She committed her life to work among the poor and was offered a teaching assistant role at a major Eastern university. She did graduate work at both Fuller Seminary and the University of California Santa Barbara.

That summer she went on a visit to her boyfriend in Phoenix. Mystery still surrounds the circumstances of her death. Her automobile was found abandoned in Mexico. The police were seeking a named suspect but advised that he had also disappeared there as well. We were advised that few such crimes were ever solved.

Our pain and grief were overwhelming. Elizabeth dreaded waking every morning. My morning devotions were overwhelmed with grief. I remember weeping aloud every morning for nearly two years. We sought counseling from Dr. Bill Schmidt, a grief counselor from Loyola University. As shock numbs great pain in physical injuries, so deep an injury to the soul blots out any sense of God's presence. We could only sense him through the loving touch of friends.

Taken in for Christmas by Elizabeth's brother Donald and his wife Wilma, we stopped at Kathy's grave as we fled the desert. It was a completely clear day, with only a tiny cloud hovering at the peak of Mount San Jacinto. Then a rainbow appeared. Elizabeth spotted it and cried out, "The rainbow surrounds the throne of God" (Rev 4:3–4)! When our hearts are crushed beyond all feeling, God can show himself through our eyes. Over the next few years God showed himself again and again through the unexpected visits of his rainbow.

People from around the Covenant Church gave memorial gifts to Jesus People USA to build a lovely playground in Kathy's memory. It was built on the roof of their family outreach center as the ground level was unsafe for children.

The memorable day of dedication dawned with a cloudless sky. Among the homeless residents a little boy suddenly broke free and ran forward, pointing and crying, "There's your rainbow! There's your rainbow!" We have the photographs of that rainbow to this day. Professor Klyne Snodgrass of our seminary checked with the weather service and learned there were no normal atmospheric conditions to create rainbows that day!

As our hearts began to heal, the sense of the Spirit's presence became stronger and stronger. The sign of the rainbow appeared less and less often. Elizabeth and I experience deep pain from time to time. But that pain is precious, and to lose it we would have to banish Kathy from our memory. Like the spiritual fathers and mothers of the early church, we have learned to kiss the wounds.

When Elizabeth and I were assessing whether I should seek another term or step down, one morning Elizabeth simply said, "We need to go to the desert to encourage Kristi." I pondered her words as I drove to the office and throughout the day. As I was driving home past St. Ignatius High School, Ira Sankey's old hymn suddenly flooded my mind:

There were ninety and nine that safely lay
In the shelter of the fold;
But one was out on the hills away,
Far off from the gates of gold.
Away on the mountains wild and bare;
Away from the tender Shepherd's care.
There arose a glad cry to the gate of heav'n,
"Rejoice! I have found My sheep!"
And the angels echoed around the throne,
"Rejoice, for the Lord brings back His own!"[4]

I wept as I entered our home. I simply said, "Elizabeth, let's leave our Covenant Church oversight flock and go to Kristi in California!"

I appeared before the nominating committee at the appointed hour. I briefly outlined my vision for the years ahead. I then told them that I believed that they should now seek a new president, which they proceeded to do.

FAREWELL

The next two months as my term was ending were busier than ever before. Selling our home, making arrangements for the move, and an endless round of farewell dinners made the time pass quickly. On top of this I had to faithfully execute the duties of my office. My last official act was to sign the final documents assuming the Covenant Church's ownership of Windsor Manor, a large, modern retirement facility near Wheaton College. Windsor had a sound balance at the time, and the Covenant Church made no payments. It was a satisfying final act.

My final address at the June Annual Meeting contained three parts. The first section briefly summarized our progress toward the vision I had set forth in my 1984 Centennial volume, *The Mission of a Covenant*. That progress was a gift of God, led by a united team of leaders. I had often declared that a leader invariably achieves success by building a team, each member of which is more gifted in their specialty than the leader himself. I then expressed affirmation and gratitude to each of them publicly.

I concluded with a whimsical allegory:

> *I think of myself as the neurotic rooster who loved his role as he flew to the forecastle of the barn to proclaim the dawn to the entire*

4. Clephane and Sankey, "There Were Ninety and Nine," 197.

barnyard. Before long he began to feel that his role was not simply to proclaim the dawn. He mistakenly assumed that his task was rather to summon the dawn. He might oversleep and leave the farmyard in chaos. Such an awesome responsibility made him a neurotic wreck. He only recovered when he saw his error. His calling was not to summon the dawn. His task was simply to proclaim the dawn!

Recovering at last, today I ascend to the forecastle of the Covenant Church barnyard this one last time and cry, "Behold the dawn of God's new day!"

As the Assembly concluded with the recessional hymn, Elizabeth and I left by descending the center aisle with both gratitude and hope.

9

The Desert

THE NEXT TWO AND a half months were spent preparing to move back to California. The wonderful times we had with co-workers and friends would never be forgotten. We succeeded in selling our home. I tried to conclude my remaining days as president. As September arrived, we left by auto, along with the movers, for our little casita in the desert. It was a joy to join our daughter Kristi at our little home. Gone, of course, were the many stresses and anxieties that a leader must inevitably bear. You are now away from all the status of your leadership. It was easier than I thought. Kristi had fallen in love, and after their engagement she married Marc Baldwin. He was a brilliant young man who made a profession of faith. A year later little Cassidy Kathleen was born. She had long red hair on the day of her birth. Being nearby as she was growing up was a gift of God.

We moved to a lovely home in nearby Rancho Mirage. We also enabled Marc and Kristi to buy a home in nearby La Quinta. I continued to serve a few more years as the general secretary of the International Federation. I taught classes at Fuller and our Spanish school, CHET (Centro Hispano de Estudios Teológicos), as well as at Covenant Church Midwinter conferences. I wrote a book, yet unpublished, entitled *Turning Your World Upside Down, Personal and Social Transformation in St. Paul: A Study in the Book of Galatians.*[1] Both David Nystrom and Rob Johnston reviewed my writing. One always needs to have advice from respected and competent scholars.

---

1. Larsen, "Turning Your World Upside Down."

CORNERSTONE COVENANT CHURCH

Unfortunately, there were no Covenant churches in the Coachella Valley and Palm Springs area. We dreamed that we might be a part of starting one. Meanwhile, we visited a number of churches in the area. New shoes are never quite comfortable. A lifetime of both shaping and being shaped by the Covenant Church made it as comfortable as an old shoe. Yes, there were fine churches. We began attending a large church that had been growing regularly. But then a small group began to meet for Bible study and to pray about planting a new church. As we began, a widely publicized moral scandal broke out in the church. I was called in, but the departure of the senior pastor under the scandal had left the church with deep divisions. Our prayer group, although committed to the Covenant Church, recognized that we were a part of the larger kingdom. We then went to work to participate in the healing of that church. But when it had recovered its momentum, we began to meet again.

Marc Cedar, the son of Free Church President Paul Cedar and founder of Mission America, began leading our Bible study once again. Eventually he accepted a call to a nearby church as its pastor. Mark had been meeting with the associate pastor of a nearby Presbyterian church. This young pastor had felt led to help establish a new church in our rapidly growing area. I received a call one day from that young leader who mentioned that Mark had suggested he call me. We had lunch and I heard his story and journey. I contacted our church planting leadership in Chicago, and they invited him and his wife to an assessment gathering in Chicago. The Covenant Church was eager to engage him. Chris Hushaw had grown up in the desert and had graduated from UC-San Diego. He then studied at Fuller Seminary and graduated from Princeton Seminary. His wife, Linda, was raised in the Rolling Hills Covenant Church. A number of their friends from the Presbyterian church were seeking to join him in starting such a church. Wary of church splitting, I suggested that we meet without members of the Presbyterian church in attendance. When it became apparent that the nucleus was flourishing, then several families from the Presbyterian church joined with us. It was an exciting tie. At first, we used the theater at the nearby La Quinta High School for Sunday worship. We then rented a beautiful little coffee shop that had closed for our seven-day-a-week ministry.

Meanwhile, the housing crash of 2008 devastated our little church. Eight families lost their jobs, and seven families even lost their homes. We needed a facility for worship. Our attempts to rent vacated stores were futile because the city wanted no more churches and would not grant tax exemption.

A major realtor told us that a display warehouse development was trying to liquidate its last property, located just by Wal-Mart, Costco, and Home Depot. It was four blocks off the freeway and near the crossroads of the most-traveled north/south and east/west expressways. Over 16,000 square feet in size, with a 2,500-square-foot mezzanine, its huge floor-to-ceiling glass windows were visible to the north and west. It had been on the market for more than two years at $2.7 million. The realtor told us to offer $1 million in cash. The offer was accepted, and our National Covenant Church Properties lent it to us along with another $1 million for completing the interior. In some ways this was the stupidest thing we could do. We ventured the most when we had the least. If, however, we could sustain the first few years, we would have saved spending $1 million in land and another $1 million for a limited worship facility with little education space. I strongly supported the move, knowing that it would test us. And surely we began to fall behind, despite many gifts from other Covenant churches and friends. A member loaned us $300,000 at no interest. In May of 2016 some in the church felt we could only survive by abandoning the facility and starting again in another location. With much intense debate, the congregation voted instead to have a $300,000 fund drive over three years. Our anonymous member said if we could do that, he would forgive the additional $300,000 loan. That fall of 2016 the pledges were taken and the target was met, with all past deficits eliminated. By the end of January 2017, God had granted us $330,000 in cash receipts—two years ahead of schedule—with another $68,000 in pledges still to be met. It was a God thing! This enabled us to cut the debt by $600,000 and refinance the reduced balance over 25 years. We had survived. We lost very few families.

But that miracle was in many ways the least of it. Pastor Chris had a vision to reach the unreached. The theme was "The Church Inside Out," meaning our goal would be to reach the unreached in our community. Through unique blessings and the assistance of Todd Mackeron, we opened a thrift shop to raise funds to send poor kids to camp. Over the next seven years, we sent over 3,000 of them to camp. Many came from the poorest homes in the east valley. They worked hand in hand with the Boys and Girls Clubs of the valley. New believers found their way to Christ in our midst. I felt my spirit refreshed again as we participated in the birth of a new young church. I never took a board position or office. Elizabeth and I were more than happy to just be part of the labor, fellowship, and service. I believe my role was to be simply a benevolent uncle.

THE DESERT FATHERS

When Paul Cedar stepped down as head of the Evangelical Free Church and founded Mission America, he and his wife Jeanie had come to love the desert where our circle of evangelical denominational leaders headed each year. Forsaking the cold Minnesota climate, they bought a home near us. We began also to meet with Bob and Lynn Dugan. He had been head of the Washington Office of the National Association of Evangelicals for many years. Later we were joined by Everett Stenhouse, who had been the second in leadership for the Assemblies of God. The group included Ken Poure, head of the massive youth camp in the Sierras. So we began to meet monthly for prayer and encouragement. We decided to call ourselves the Desert Fathers, the name church historians had given to the ascetic desert dwellers in the early Christian centuries. Then we also soon had Desert Mothers. When chided by our more distant colleagues—who noted that self-denial and poverty sent the early fathers to the desert—they pointed out that we could hardly justify taking that name to describe the warm climate and easy living of the desert oasis. My only reply was, "How do you know that our only reason to gather was because of the warm climate? How do you know that the warm and lovely climate might also have been part of the motivation for those early hermits and desert communities?"

ALBERTO AND JUVENILE HALL

Within a few months of our arrival at the desert, Elizabeth and I began Tuesday night visits to Indio's Juvenile Hall. The detention facility housed and educated juvenile delinquents and miscreants. Our leaders were Alberto and Guillermo, who tried to minister every week to these troubled young people. Alberto had been a drug courier as a teenager and then became the head of a drug operation in the Coachella Valley and beyond. He was arrested and imprisoned three times. On his third conviction he became a three-time loser—meaning he would be imprisoned for life without parole. He was visited one evening by an elderly couple who welcomed him into Christ's kingdom. Almost immediately he received a court notice dismissing the drug and firearms charges against him. For some reason the evidence had mysteriously disappeared from the police inventory—or as they say, *corpus delecti*, that is, "The body is missing!" No longer a three-time loser, he had to remain in prison because he had broken his previous terms' probation. Within a short time though, he received an additional court order of dismissal from prison due to overcrowding. He could only find work as an unskilled laborer, working often in 110-degree heat. He would then go to his home, shower, dine with his wife, and then visit other jail facilities five nights a week. I noticed the skills he had in talking with young teenagers about the need for Christ. I learned more from him than any seminary course on welcoming young people into the liberating presence of Christ.

DESPAIRING TEENAGERS

Some of the stories were so tragic that Elizabeth and I sometimes felt it too painful to even return. I think of one Anglo teenager who came to me in deep despair. His father had been murdered, and his mother was in prison for drug smuggling. His aging grandparents agreed to take him and his little brother and sister into their home providing there were no drugs or crime. He was arrested for marijuana possession. The grandparents threw them out on the street. They were sleeping on the street and eating only stolen garbage from produce stores. He broke into their home one night to get a few clothes and was arrested. He now had no hope and felt that he had betrayed his little siblings. In desperation, he had been reading a Bible and told me he had found Psalm 22 as the agony of his life: "But I am a worm and not a man" (Ps 22:6a). The court had ruled that he be incarcerated at the California Youth Authority. "Due to my sin, they now have no one to feed or protect them. I betrayed them." I had him read aloud all of Psalm 22. I then had him read Psalm 51, David's penitential prayer for forgiveness. I then had him read Romans 8:1, and last, Philippians 1:3: "Being confident of this one thing, that he who has begun a good work in you, will carry it to completion until the day of Jesus Christ." The light came back into his eyes as grace showered him in the darkness of despair. He claimed to have found peace in Christ. He later disappeared into state detention facilities, and I never saw him again. Yet to this day I believe God went with him.

AN UNSHACKLED YOUNG WOMAN

At other times the transforming grace of Christ stunned us. One night I counseled two young teenage girls. One was an African American girl who had an illegitimate child. She had gotten into a fierce fight with another girl, and now was incarcerated, taking away her baby. She begged me to pray that she might be able somehow to keep her baby. The other was an Anglo girl in the seventh grade. She came in shackles. She told me that her father had molested her at ages four and five. He was imprisoned, but she was sent to a series of foster homes where she was molested again and again. Her mother was imprisoned for drug dealing. In the last home she had attempted to kill the foster parents with poison. She sobbed that she would be imprisoned until adulthood. When I asked to pray for her, she demurred. "No," she said. "I have now been able to gain secret power to put a hex on other people to make them suffer. I will not relinquish this power even to God." The other young woman begged repeatedly saying, "Unless you pray, you are going to die!"

Eventually I prayed for the young mother. As I concluded, the girl in chains asked me to pray for her also. I began a simple prayer of exorcism in Jesus' name and for her salvation and healing. Three years passed, and this same girl came back to me almost unrecognizable. She said, "Do you remember me?" I replied that I did. She said that the prayer was answered. She was no longer in shackles. She joyfully shared the deliverance from the chains. "I am now in accelerated classes to graduate from high school and will move on to college when I am 18." Her transformation amazes me to this day.

The pain, sorrow, and redemption that I witnessed in those days have sunk deeply into my heart and memory. No one has taught me more about how to touch the lives of the young and broken than Alberto. I have seen few who display so brightly the transforming power of Christ.

10

India

INDIA CAME AS A welcome surprise. Over the next decade and a half I made eighteen trips to India. From the start I wrote a daily journal with detail—sometimes two or three pages on a given day. After each trip I would make PowerPoint presentations for each trip with accompanying text. This would involve twenty to thirty slides. I did this faithfully for my eighteen trips to India over the next dozen years. Each trip lasted between twelve and fourteen days. This added up to over eight months in India. In many ways these have been the apex of my life.

INDIAN HISTORY

Prime Minister Nehru had expelled all Christian missionaries from India by 1950. The Covenant Church never had a mission field in India. Since it was a closed society, I did not specifically include it among my prayers except under the umbrella of concern for the whole world. Yet this land of more than 1.1 billion people would surpass China's total population in the next thirty years. Despite more than 300 years of Protestant mission work, less than 4 percent are baptized Christians.

For thousands of years Indian society has been frozen in a Brahminic religion that stabilizes society with an intractable caste system. During the second millennium before Christ, mass migrations from Central Asia invaded the Indian subcontinent. These hordes came on horses and with wagons, having pioneered the use of the wheel. They are known as Aryans. They brought with them the worship of their greatest god, Brahma. All Aryans are descended from his head. Thus, they are the gods on earth. The priests, the highest caste, are the Brahmins. Then the Kshatriyas emerged from the arms and torso of the god. They were the military caste. Also came the Vaishyas, the merchant caste. Together the three forward castes amount to only 8 percent of the population. In the fourth caste are the Shudras, or "slaves." Divided into hundreds of sub-castes, they amount to nearly 50 percent of India's total population, or 550 million persons. The Scheduled castes—the Dalits (untouchables) and the Tribals—constitute another 300 million. They are outcasts—non-Hindu animists. Muslims comprise over 150 million or almost 15 percent of the population:

THE FOLLOWING TABLE
SHOWS THE DISTRIBUTION[1]

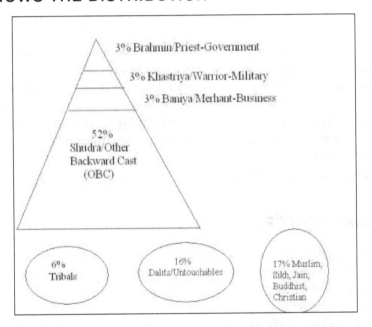

A half billion of these people are virtually untouched for Christ. Only through reincarnation in the Brahminic Hindu religion can one rise from a low to a high station. That progression ultimately takes hundreds of millions of individual reincarnations. It is therefore a religion without hope. Eight hundred million poor live on less than two dollars a day. Of these, 400 million live on less than one dollar a day. The number of the poor in just four Indian states exceeds all the poor in the entire continent of Africa.

1. This diagram was from the email notes of a student visiting as part of her course work at North Park. http.//myweekin india.wordpress.com. May 25, 2010.

ROCHUNGA PUDAITE

During the later years of my leadership in the IFFEC Executive Committee we admitted two small Indian denominations. The first was the child
of the Swedish Covenant Church's mission in the state of Maharashtra. The
second was a mission in the far northeast of India among the Mhar tribes
of the state of Manipur by the Myanmar border. This small tribal movement of 25,000 believers had never had a Western missionary. In the early
twentieth century, the slaughter of hundreds of tea planters by fierce Mhar
tribespeople had forced the British Colonial government to draw a line
of control beyond which no Westerner could travel. The son of one of the
Mhar chieftains slipped south of the line of control and encountered Watkin
Roberts. This independent pharmacist missionary discipled him. The young
man then became the leader of this fast-growing Christward movement
among the Mhar tribes. The movement grew rapidly, with another 15,000
believers across the Myanmar border. He later sent his young son Rochunga
(Ro) to a distant mission school, accessible only by walking days through
the jungle. His father wanted Ro to produce the first Mhar Bible. Doing well
in school, he finished college in Kolkata. He then finished a master's degree
at Wheaton College. He met a bright, lovely young woman named Mawii.
They raised their children in Wheaton while founding what became Bibles
for the World. Living both in the U.S. and in Manipur, they gave strong
leadership in education, health, and church planting. Their schools were the
finest, and the church was well organized.

Getting to know him well at our international conferences, he asked
to have lunch one afternoon at the Covenant Church Annual Meeting in
Chicago. He and his wife shared their desire to plant a Christian university
in India. They claimed that the prime minister had promised them permis-
sion to build. They wanted me to come and be the president upon my retirement. I replied that I would like to be of help in their work in India, but the
president of an Indian university had to be an Indian. Our friendship and
commitment deepened when I visited their Bibles for the World headquarters in Colorado Springs; Elizabeth and I had driven down at the close of the
Annual Meeting in the Colorado Mountains. They then told me of the vast
new movements emerging in northern India among the Backward castes
(Shudras) as well as the Scheduled castes (Dalits and Tribals). This was
something much bigger than their work among the Tribals of the northeast.
They had become involved with others in the vast new movement. During
an IFFEC Theological Conference at Ewersbach in Germany, I was alerted
to this vast movement by a seminary student who had been watching what
portended to be a million persons converting from Hinduism in New Delhi.

In 2003, they invited me to come to India to dedicate a new seminary building in their Mhar tribal areas in the state of Manipur. I accepted their invitation and, following a preaching mission in Holland and Belgium, flew to New Delhi and from there to Imphal in the northeast. Due to revolutionary activities, we had to get an additional passport to proceed the rest of the way. Every few miles we encountered a military encampment with bunkers and armor. I asked the driver how dangerous it was. He simply said that he had been kidnapped twice on this road over the past couple of years. I stayed with Ro and Mawii at their Indian residence and began visiting and speaking at churches, schools, and even their hospital. The students at these large schools constantly received the highest test scores of any in the region. The churches were beautifully built and run with cultural relevance and good organization. I was privileged to give the commencement address at the seminary as well as the dedication of their new classroom building. It was as fine a structure as anything similar in the West.

Before returning home, we took an auto ride up near the Bhutan border to the greatest of all Indian game parks, Kazarenga. Staying in a venerable resort, we rode elephants into the forest and savannas, observing the rare Indian rhinoceros, deer, birds, and even fresh tiger killings. In the afternoon, they took us in jeeps out onto the savannas, observing wild elephant herds. Stopping at a stream, we observed a mother elephant washing her young baby in the water. We then heard fierce trumpeting beyond the giant cane break beyond them. We had gotten out of our jeeps to take pictures, but were warned by the armed gamekeepers. Suddenly a giant bull elephant emerged in full charge toward us. The gamekeepers immediately raised their rifles, but the elephant stopped just short of us. We only felt terrified afterwards.

When we returned to Imphal, we heard that Naga tribal rebels had dynamited an oil refinery nearby. They also blew up a busload of passengers the day after we had returned on the same road. After spending the night at Imphal, we awakened to the sight of a large group of soldiers and armored cars bivouacked on the street in front of our hotel. We did not know whether this was simply a drill or an actual rebel threat—but we were glad to get from there back to Kolkata by air.

SERAMPORE

Within a short time, Ro told me that he had been asked to help with the struggling and insolvent Serampore University. It had been founded in 1818 by pioneer missionary William Carey, located across the Ganges River in the

Danish Treaty Port of Serampore, and granted a charter by the devout King Frederick IV of Denmark. The charter was to teach anything that would benefit the people of India, and it was granted the full accreditation of the Danish universities of Copenhagen and Kiel in perpetuity. It was Asia's first Western-style university. Over the years, Carey translated the Bible into seventy languages. Yet in subsequent years the school nearly foundered, even though it was the only university that could grant accredited degrees among the country's nearly seventy Bible institutes and theological seminaries. In more recent times, India's University Grant Commission had dropped it from the list of accredited colleges. Some of the affiliated schools had become so broad theologically as to be in some sense syncretistic. Then spirituality suffered, and then came virtual insolvency.

Ro told me that his nephew had been studying at Union Biblical Seminary, the best evangelical seminary in India. But it could not gain accreditation. While there he developed a friendship with another student who happened to be the son of the current Serampore principal, Dr. Lalnunchunga. He reported that sometimes his father felt that he was appointed as principal so that the eventual collapse of the school would be blamed on evangelicalism. Ro then asked me to go to Serampore to discuss the matter with the principal. Our small party included Ro, his wife Mawii, their son John, Colorado developer Ted Becket, and well-known author Joe Musser.

The dilapidated campus on the edge of the Ganges River contained the theological college and the college of arts and sciences. The old buildings were still magnificent, built 150 years earlier in the classical style with earnings that Carey and his partners made by bringing documents and books for the British Colonial government. We met in Carey's original apartment, and I was privileged to sit in Carey's original chair. There I led the negotiations for a partnership agreement. Representing the Serampore board was Dr. Mohit Pramanic, the former president of All India Steel who had become a Baptist pastor in retirement. For many years he had been chair of the school's board. Pressed by the need to depart for a flight from Kolkata to Delhi, this godly Indian leader and I finally reached full agreement on a joint partnership and charter. It was to be called the William Carey Heritage Foundation.

THE WILLIAM CAREY HERITAGE FOUNDATION

Returning to America, we incorporated the foundation with Ro as president and me as chair. Ted Beckett's wife, Audrey, was named treasurer. She had long been a supporter of a women's orphanage in India. For more than ten years she had been the chief financial analyst of World Vision. I was also named a member of the university's strategic planning committee. Joe Musser became secretary of the board.

One of the first steps was to fund the shipment of a large theological library to Serampore. We then helped in refurbishing a number of the key buildings. Salaries were so low that the professors could barely support their families. We were able to grant salary supplements. We also added Dr. Viji Nakka Cammauf to our board. Daughter of an Indian philosophy professor, she found Christ at Mills College in Oakland, California, and became missions pastor of the Oakland Covenant Church. She had completed her PhD in Theology and Culture at UC-Berkeley and founded the Little Flock Orphanage in southern India.

These were wonderful years, as I was able to meet many of the leaders of India's Protestant, Orthodox, and Mar Thomas Churches. We gradually helped bring thoroughly evangelical faculty to the Serampore school. But we were unable to reestablish accreditation. We tried every conceivable way to gain this prize, but were always blocked by what appeared to be the relentless opposition of the Hindu Nationalist Movement and its political arm, the BJP. The leadership of the college gave up. They said that it was enough to just train pastors for the existing Christian community. When Dr. Lalnunchununga and I visited the eminent missiologist Ralph Winter in Pasadena at his William Carey University we were stunned. He told us, "If you want to reach India for Christ, shut down all your Bible schools and seminaries. You are simply training chaplains to the Christian ghetto." He said that India needed training schools for doctors, lawyers, and business and political leaders who could affect the society as a whole. My heart resonated with that! But the weakness of the school and the internal survival goals of its schools led me to conclude that we needed to seek other routes for training the evangelical elite from the lower castes to lead as the new India emerged. I have a tremendous love for Serampore and continue to support and commend all that it and its seventy schools continue to do in the cause of Christ. But another door opened.

SUNIL SARDAR

While working with Ro Pudaite on our Serampore project, I met Sunil Sardar. When passing through Delhi, Ro and I met him for breakfast at a top hotel at Nehru Place. He had come to Delhi to reestablish a nineteenth-century Christian reform movement called Truthseekers. It had declined from its heyday in the latter nineteenth century. He was seeking a meeting place and home for his wife and three children who were ending a forced three-year expulsion from India. We prayed together and sought God's strength and guidance. A few months later he stopped and stayed with me for three days while on his way to New York. Those few days ended with a life partnership in the renewal of Truthseekers International.

Sunil was of the Cobbler caste—one of the lowest such castes in all India. He was a second-generation believer, the product of the missions of the Free Methodists. His father had come to Christ and worked at the Free Methodist Hospital, where his mother was a nurse. Growing up, he became the leader of all India Free Methodist Youth. Dr. David Williams, a medical missionary, had encouraged him and helped support him through college. He went into a sand and gravel business, later becoming mayor of the city.

Meanwhile tens of thousands of poor cotton farmers throughout the state were committing suicide because the state cooperative would not pay them enough to keep their families from starving. Sunil found that the Free Market Cooperative in the adjoining state of Madya Pradesh would pay the farmers substantially more for their cotton than the socialist cooperative in the state of Maharashtra. The government prohibited crossing the border to sell their product at the life-sustaining prices. Sunil led a mass movement of reported 1,000 ox-carts loaded with cotton attempting to cross the state line. Blocked by military and police, the commander threatened to shoot Sunil. He noted that there were live TV cameras. Did the military commander want to be seen killing poor farmers as they crossed the line? The commander asked for time, returning to tell them to wait until after dark. The cavalcade could then cross the line to sell their cotton at higher prices.

This drew national attention, gaining support from all reform movements, whether secular, Hindu, Muslim, or Christian. Everyone assumed that this would catapult him into national politics. He felt, however, that politics in India had failed. Instead he began a Christ followers' movement in central Maharashtra. He had relinquished his role as founder of Dinbandhu, "the Church of the Poor," which he had led over the past decade. Now more than 350 congregations had been planted among the tribal poor of the state of Maharashtra. Instead he would settle in New Delhi and revive the late nineteenth-century Truthseekers as a Christian spiritual and cultural reform movement.

JOTIRAO PHULE AND TRUTHSEEKERS

Truthseekers was founded by nineteenth-century religious and social reformer Mahatma Jotirao Phule (1827–1890). He was born in the low-caste

Mali or Gardeners' caste near Pune, Maharashtra. Because of his family's poverty, he was raised by his aunt who was a cook for a Presbyterian missionary's family. There he learned to read and write as well as learning much about Christianity. He married Savitribai when both were thirteen years old. Offended by the humiliation he kept receiving from high-caste Brahmins, he founded what he later called Truthseekers. Anyone could join regardless of caste, gender, or religion. It was strictly monotheist and repudiated the Hindu religion. He and his wife founded orphanages and the first schools for poor girls. He organized the first labor strike. He attacked Brahmanism as the root enemy. He showed his Christian origins in his famous book, *Slavery*. In a chapter of this book, dedicated to Abraham Lincoln, he argued that the Indian story of Bali Raja—the just and compassionate ancient king who sacrificed himself to save his people—was nothing less than that of the Jesus from the West. Bali Raja would one day return to establish a "City without Sorrow" (Begumpura).[2] The story of Bali Raja is celebrated annually by the greatest Indian festival of Diwali. Each year the upper castes celebrate the victory the greatest Brahman God Vishnu over Bali. The low-caste tradition of Bali Raja, however, celebrates the hope of Bali's return from hell to establish the "City without Sorrow." Phule urged Indians to welcome Christian missionaries from the West who worshipped Jesus as Savior and to receive them as brothers. He died of a stroke in 1890, and his wife, Savitribai, succeeded him as the leader. She then died a few later during a deadly plague while striving to save dying children. The movement died out almost entirely. But both Ambedkar and Gandhi, the two great reformers of the twentieth century, affirmed him as their mentor.

RELAUNCHING TRUTHSEEKERS

Not all people supported Sunil Sardar's new activism. The Brahmin upper-caste establishment charged him with undermining the social and spiritual order. Jailed and beaten a number of times, even the local Christians told him that he was bringing disgrace and danger to the whole Christian community. The enraged farmers, however, mobbed the local jail and set him free. On the way home he passed a local bookstore where he saw Phule's book, *Slavery*, on sale. He bought it and reread it again and again over the next days. He seized upon the tenth chapter of the book and saw Phule's identification of Bali Raja with Jesus. At last he had found a singular and powerful redemptive metaphor uniting the traditions of India's poor and

2. Phule, "Slavery."

the redemption through Jesus Christ. This was the foundation stone of the renewed Truthseekers International.

While this was going on, Sunil fell in love with an American school-teacher. Pam was a well-educated, deeply committed Christian. They got engaged over the telephone. Bringing his bride to India, they chose to live in the slums without running water. Over the first year, Pam nearly died during months of illness. Joining him in witness, the government expelled her, charging her with forcing Indians to be Christians. This was an exile of three years in America in which Sunil bound himself as a free slave. In the Old Testament tradition he pierced his ear with a spike. He then mounted a small gold cross through it, which he wears to this day.

He had decided to leave the Dinbandhu churches in Maharashtra in the care of his able younger brother Nitin. He relocated his wife to New Delhi, the center of India's political and cultural life. While always active in the English-speaking church at the British Embassy, he established a weekly Sunday evening gathering in the Hindi language called meaning "worship." All were welcomed here. Each week they would sing both popular songs as well as Christian Indian hymns. They would share spiritual testimonies, followed by the celebration of the Lord's Supper—in the unique Indian way. The bread was a broken coconut and the wine was always coconut milk. While bread comes from the wheat seed, in India it comes from the coconut, which is also a seed. The wine comes from the crushed coconut, even as wine comes from crushed grapes. Moreover, Indian culture often used this act to celebrate new beginnings. The Christian sacrament was always consecrated by the reading of the reading the Gospels' account of the crucifixion and resurrection of Jesus. While Satsun always had a mixture of Christian and non-Christian participants, I personally witnessed many immediate conversions at these meetings over the years.

TRUTHSEEKERS CENTER

In the southern part of New Delhi known as the South Extension or South Ex, Sunil leased a family apartment and a small center. It was within two blocks of the family apartment, and a small hotel with unbelievably low-cost rooms sat directly across the street. It had a kitchen for meals and a few rooms with modest space for gatherings and conversations.

Beginning with morning worship each day, we would welcome anyone to come and talk with us unless we departed to many places across Delhi or, ultimately, broader India. Each evening we would gather various caste leaders, political figures, and other believers in a two-hour discussion. I saw and heard things I could scarcely believe. Spaces upstairs were filled with small cots, and any out-of-town travelers could get rest for the night and meals without charge. We had guests for all three meals that often-included heads of castes, members of parliament, intellectuals, Muslims, Hindus, Sikhs, and even communists. The center clearly presented an open, loving witness of our Christian faith. Even the heads of major castes that were powerful but otherwise poor came to us from around India. So many conversions took place.

I traveled each day with Sunil, not only throughout New Delhi among its fifteen million residents, but also across north India. I walked beside him into the remote and distant slums and villages. I also accompanied him in the presence of major political and caste leaders. I did not see myself as a teacher, but simply as a listener and witness to this remarkable Christward movement. I never felt I was beyond the second grade in understanding the Indian culture.

THE CULTURAL CONTEXT OF OTHER BACKWARD CASTES

More than 550 million Shudras, or OBCs (Other Backward Castes), have never seen Christward movements, except in a small portion of southern India. Eighty percent of all Christians in India come from the Shudra, or the Dalit and Tribal, castes. The latter were both animists and never Hindus. The OBCs have steadfastly resisted Christian conversion despite the fact that they have been denied entrance to Hindu temples. They have strong monotheistic traditions. One of the obstacles is the translation into the Indian languages: William Carey and other translators used Brahmin scholars to find the words for the highest God. They were told that the name of the highest god was Peshawar, a synonym for Vishnu, the killer god who enslaved the lower-caste native people. Pandita Ramabai, the famous translator of the Hebrew and Greek Bible, chose another word, Mahadeva—The Most Holy One. It is a title, not a name. OBCs use this generic name because no Hindu god matches that name. However, even evangelical translations use the missionary translators' Peshawar or Vishnu, a name for "the Most Holy One" that is an evil god.

As we said earlier, the Truthseekers use the term "Bali Raja," the great king who was always just, but whom Vishnu crushed and sent to the underworld, who will nonetheless return and establish Begumpura, the "City without Sorrow." The Hebrew word for this savior is Messiah, the Anointed One; the Greek is *Christos*, again meaning "anointed." Bali Raja can be properly identified with Jesus because it refers to the king who sacrificed himself to save his people. The current upper-caste Hindi translation of the Bible cannot be understood by almost 80 percent of the Backward castes. Finding an accurate Jesuit translation of the Bible, Sunil and his team revised it. Analysis by Wycliffe translators confirmed the validity of these terms in translation. This Low Hindi translation referred to the New Testament as "the Law of Jesus," that is, "the Law of Bali." Zondervan permitted Truthseekers to publish a diglot version of their NILV translation with English on one side and low-caste Hindi on the other—assisting the rising OBCs to gain use of the English language, important for their education.

The English word "God," from Gud, referred to one god in the Teutonic and Norse languages of northern Europe. Through Christian teaching it ultimately became the Christian word for the one deity. So translators deem that the low-caste Hindi terms will be defined by the New Testament—an evangelical theology in and of itself.

Truthseekers has affirmed the Apostolic and Nicene creeds as well as the Lausanne Covenant as a statement of their faith. As they gather, they sing Sunil's handwritten translation of the hymn:

> The Kingdom of Bali [God] has come!
>
> The Kingdom of Bali has come!
> The Kingdom of Bali has come in me
>
> *refrain*
>
> In His kingdom, there are wells of living water;
> Drink it once. He calls you to drink.
> In his kingdom there is living bread;
> Taste it once, you will never hunger again.
> In His kingdom there is teaching of truth.
> Let us join together and be baptized together.
> In His kingdom there is no discrimination of castes.
> Experience it yourselves—the way of equality.
> In His kingdom there is freedom from hunger and fear.
> Everyone can worship him, He gives you authority.
> In His kingdom there is talk of love:
> Even enemies He tells us to love, breaking the mental bondage.
> There is sounding truth in His kingdom;
> No liar has any place or authority in this kingdom.
> The only law in His Kingdom is love;

My chains are broken, new skies have opened.

In His kingdom there is dignity for women;

Even a child has a "say"; everyone walks with dignity.

Let us join as brothers and sisters;

We will worship Him in His kingdom with truth.

—Sunil Sardar[3]

Every Sunday at Satsun, or worship, the gathering includes the Lord's Supper with the reading of the passion narrative, singing, and witness.

THE HOME TEAM

A small group of team leaders at Truthseekers Center have given constant and loyal support to Sunil and the mission.

Shiv Kumar managed all the operations and finances at our New Delhi center. A college graduate, he worked tirelessly on managing finances, schedules, and itineraries with relentless gentleness and loving care. He came from the Shepherd caste of Uttar Pradesh. Shepherds are one of the lowest and most impoverished of all the Backward castes. He always went the second mile to see that I was fed, housed, and driven anywhere I went in India. In fact, I nicknamed him my "Good Shepherd." He was also most effective in witness and ministry.

Bosker was the official driver. Trained in the army as a vehicle driver, he had become an ace racecar driver. In his newfound faith, he became an ace at getting anywhere in the horror of New Delhi's mass traffic jams and long journeys far beyond. He always met me and dropped me off in all my comings and goings.

Pranjal Torde grew up with close ties to Sunil and his family. Extremely bright, he earned undergraduate degrees in counseling and education. He later earned a master's degree in pedagogy. He speaks seven languages. Extremely devout, he left Sunil after the great tsunami that struck across southeast India and Indonesia and established a series of counseling centers to help survivors of this great disaster. As in Indian customs, he then returned to Maharashtra to care for his aging parents. It is always the duty of the eldest son to care for aging parents. I urged Sunil to contact him because we needed him so desperately for ministry. He replied that his parents took a leap of faith and sacrificed him to serve the kingdom with Truthseekers. He could effectively challenge police, politicians, and intellectuals. He was eloquent before large crowds. He could sleep on the floor of the jungle. He

---

3. Sunil Sardar. Bali Raja.

lived for years with Truthseekers for only room and board. I have seen few people anywhere in the world that show more promise for future leadership in the kingdom.

Desponde had taken a vow of celibacy in order to serve Christ's kingdom. He would travel anywhere, even alone, to share the kingdom. He often would venture alone into the red-light and gay sections of the city to give witness to Christ. One evening he came home, reporting that in rescuing a young girl from a brothel, he was beaten twelve times by the pimps. He lifted his shirt and showed the deep welts on his back. He said, "It was one of the greatest days of my life that I could suffer for Jesus." He later helped establish a small school for us among the poorest children of New Delhi.

Ram Surat was a Dalit and the first believer in his native village. He was a goatherder. His first schooling was under a mango tree. After finishing Bible school he graduated from Union Biblical Seminary, and then gained a further degree from Serampore, then followed by a master's degree from a state university. He is currently completing his PhD in Christian Studies in our PhD in Christian Studies program at Sam Higginbottom University. We have become close friends, and he serves well with his flawless English and gentle spirit. He is perhaps our best translator and interpreter.

Grant McFarland is a graduate in computer science from the University of Texas in Austin. He came over on a student tour, and he was so moved that he decided to give his life in service to Truthseekers. He raised his own support and began learning Hindi from nearly the first day. He spent evenings wandering alone on the streets of Delhi, conversing with strangers. He developed a voracious appetite for Indian history, religion, and social issues. He met and married Dimple, a young Christian schoolteacher who had been rescued from the darkest Hindu oppression. He cowrote her biography, *The God who Hears Me* which has been recently published on Amazon.[4] He is another of the most gifted young leaders I have met, who will give great Christian leadership to Truthseekers in the years to come.

A great number of others could be recounted. But my journals and PowerPoint presentations are the best that I can leave in honor of so many of them.

TRUTHSEEKERS NORTH AMERICA— NOEL AND KYLE BECCHETTI

Building a life partnership with the Truthseekers of India meant that we needed to establish an American, not-for-profit, 501c3 organization to raise

4. McFarland, *God Who Hears Me*.

funds and develop a national network of prayer and financial partners. I was limited because I did not feel it would be right for me to go to major donors whom I solicited for significant giving while I was president of the Covenant Church. Yet Truthseekers needed a donor base. Sunil and Pam had a group of personal supporters who found it difficult to fund even their ministry in India. I persuaded Sunil that we needed to establish a U.S. organization to do this. I estimated that this organization would initially need $120,000 per year to operate. This would include staffing, transportation, and administration. The nonprofit would require experienced competent staffing for the first five years. As donors increased, the overhead percentage would decrease to appropriate levels over the five years. Only God's grace could achieve it.

Elizabeth and I were down at Mount Miguel Covenant Church Village in San Diego, where I was leading a devotional series, when Noel Becchetti walked in. Noel came from a Catholic home in Redwood City. He was attracted to Christ through Bill Hayes, his high school teacher and a member of our church. He visited our church and he heard me. I was under the illusion that my eloquence had won him, but later found out that he was interested in one of our young teenagers. He later went to Chico State University, where he headed a student movement with InterVarsity Christian Fellowship and invited me to come on a preaching mission. Marvelous things happened. After graduating he became a journalist and then an editor for *Christianity Today* and its youth arm. He was also the ghost writer for Tony Campolo. He then became the leader of the Center for Christian Mission. During all of this he met and married a godly, gifted attorney, Kyle, who was then chair of the board of North Park University. They developed that organization quickly and were raising thirteen million dollars annually to help high schoolers spend time among the poor in America's cities. I instantly challenged him with this prospective role.

Noel would be the North American director, and attorney Kyle would run the back office from their home in San Diego. They wanted a new adventure and sacrifice offered to cut their income in half to carry out the mission. Seldom have I seen such godly sacrificial service as they gave over the next four years. Kyle drew up the articles of incorporation and handled the finances. I asked my friend Merlin Call, of Pasadena Covenant Church, to also help cover all the legal angles. He was a partner in a major Los Angeles law firm and had served for many years as chair of the boards of both Fuller Seminary and Westmont College. Our board included me as chair; Kyle as secretary; Paul Sweas (whom I had welcomed to Christ while I served in Redwood City); Lonnie Allison of the Billy Graham Center, formerly Covenant Church Director of Evangelism; Dr. David Williams, former medical missionary and mentor to Sunil in India; Pam's brother-in-law, teacher Dan Davis; Dan Benson, COO of a major healthcare system; and Alan Forstrom of the Covenant Church's Christian Education Department, who was also a senior partner in Arthur Anderson Company—this group helped us develop a five-year plan.

Noel and Kyle diligently went to work. They itinerated across the country developing prayer and financial support. They also recruited groups of students from various colleges, including North Park, to go on mission trips to India. Within four years we had sent over a million dollars of assistance to India—more than double that of our five-year projection. This partnership was one of the most fulfilling of my life. They then left us to provide journalism and leadership training with Asian Access, a significant missions organization to the Far East. We stay in touch and meet whenever we can for food and sharing.

As I was then turning eighty years old, I felt it time to pass the chair to younger leadership. The board members in Indianapolis felt they were then strong enough to assume the responsibilities for continuing to develop our American affiliate. Unfortunately, this led to an acute crisis, and I was called back to reorganize Truthseekers. This took nearly two years, and it is now fully reconstituted.

KEY TRUTHSEEKERS

While not a part of the central leadership, people of amazing gifts and growing faith brought to the mission much that we could never achieve ourselves. Some of these must be mentioned, with regret for the lack of space to name everyone.

Braj Ranjan Mani was a bright news columnist with *India Today*, who held a master's degree in journalism. Born and raised in poverty in India's poorest state, Bihar, when growing up he and his siblings ate rats to supplement their meager fair. As a radical low-caste activist, he embraced Neo-Buddhism as well as Karl Marx. He began a lifelong struggle against the Brahmanic caste system. Perhaps the most profound and brilliant thinker I have ever met, he was equally at home in Western philosophy and literature. When we discussed postmodern philosophy, he would supplement our discussions with a short biography of each of the leading players. He collected a massive library in his small apartment. He began to visit Truthseekers regularly. We often had lunch, and he would bring along a huge manuscript he was earnestly trying to complete, his substantive volume entitled

DeBrahmanising History: Dominance and Resistance in Indian Society.[5] The book has been reprinted four times and was completely revised in 2015. It is now required reading in many Indian secular universities. Leading European communists have admitted that his subsequent book has corrected basic assumptions of Marxist thinkers. A part of our often-daily conversations whenever I have been in India, he was the first person on my prayer list in our local Cornerstone Covenant Church in Palm Desert. I wrote his name on the big white board and prayed over him. A Marxist and Neo-Buddhist, he broke down during the sacrament one Sunday and welcomed Christ into his life. He grew to even reading high Christology by Christian theologians. One day he encountered a major caste leader at our center who was in deep grief. He called us together. He led the laying on of hands with prayer. Then Dr. Hukumsingh Deshrajan, leader of the sixty million members of the Lodhi caste, claimed the gift of deliverance. I saw this with my own eyes.

Gail Omvedt has been a strategic player since the beginning of Truthseekers. She was born in 1940 and raised in the Augustana Lutheran Church of Minneapolis. After graduating from Carlton College, she completed her PhD in sociology in South Asian Studies. UC-Berkeley radicalized her, and she moved to the secular far left. She became an active Marxist. She married a radical Indian physician and took Indian citizenship. Drawn to the Indian Buddhism of Babesab Ambedkar, she became its foremost academic authority. But she found Marx and Buddha lacking. She also had become perhaps the foremost authority of the northern Bhakti tradition of lower-caste thinkers of the fourteenth century such as Kabir, Ravidas, and Tukaram. They were devout anti-caste monotheists. She held professorships in several of India's prestigious universities. She lectured twice at Harvard.

While unable to fully return to her earlier Christian faith, she nonetheless attached herself to Sunil and Truthseekers. She became a good friend, and was always supportive of both Sunil and myself. She fully participated in Truthseekers, but never attended Sunday Satsun or celebrated the sacrament. I was most moved by her book *Seeking Begumpura*,[6] wherein she showed that lower castes had become devout worshippers of the one true God. They had rejected the Brahman and Buddhist doctrine of reincarnation and waited for the coming day when they would find the "City without Sorrow." This is a linear rather than cyclical conception of history—putting them right in the stream of the Christian worldview. In a sense, they were "pre-Christian."

5. Mani, *Debrahmanising History*.

6. Omvedt, *Seeking Begumpura*.

She wrote and polemicized relentlessly. One night, while Sunil was singing contemporary Indian hymns with Vice Chancellor Dr. R. B. Lal, she took me to the piano and we both sang together old gospel hymns like "Blessed Assurance." One night when Sunil had other commitments, we both had dinner with D. Raja, head of India's Communist Party. He was particularly enraged by the presence in India of George Bush. I didn't want to start a fight. Instead she systematically demolished his Marxism. As we continued to talk over a period, both Sunil and I sensed she was growing closer to public profession of a return to Christ. She would ask for prayer. Then one Sunday she came to worship—and took the sacrament—something she had not done heretofore. She has asked to meet with me when I next go to India. Unfortunately, health is now in decline. Pray for her.

Dr. Seddikki, upon turning to Christ for salvation, became a key leader for Truthseekers. He would always pray Muslim-style by falling to his knees with his head on the floor. His Muslim faith made him compassionate toward the poor. He established the Rajiv Gandhi Foundation for relief of the poor. He had become offended by the ignorance of the mullahs, particularly their knowledge of the Koran. He explained to me that he was a physician and always read extensively on any medicine he would prescribe. So he read through the Koran four times. In it he found many references to Jesus. He healed the sick, something Mohammed never did. The Koran clearly stated that at the end of the world Jesus would return to judge every man. Mohammed would not. He then decided to read the New Testament. This drew him to become a true follower of Christ.

He then established a school for impoverished Islamic refugees from Kashmir. He felt that no poor Muslim boy could ever rise above poverty without also learning English. In the school they were given two books—the Bible and the Koran. They could choose. This infuriated the clergy, but delighted the parents. One day a sick woman encountered him at the mosque. He told her he had no medicine, but suggested that she pray to Jesus. Startled, the woman went to the mullah who accused him then of being a Christian. He simply asked if Mohammed had ever healed a human being. Had not the Koran affirmed that Jesus did this constantly? He then asked the mullah, "Don't you think that she might properly ask Jesus for healing?" Reluctantly the mullah agreed. I never heard that the woman had been healed.

Than Singh's father was so incensed by the oppressive caste system that he repudiated Brahmanism and became a Sikh. He raised his son as a Sikh but told him to find someone who could lead him to Christ, for Christianity was far superior to Sikhism. A radical reformer, he became a Christian but continued to dress as a Sikh. He had been jailed more than fifty times as he led protests to prevent high-caste leaders from expelling Dalits from their traditional lands. I remember one week when he was featured in the Delhi daily newspapers. He would take me from time to time to meet with strong justice advocates.

Kanta was a communist trained in Moscow. She had come to lead the women's section of the Communist Party of India. Found by Christ, she left the party, but became the activist leader of more than 80,000 lower-caste people in northeast New Delhi. I remember her bringing a young woman who had been thrown out on the street by her husband. As often happens, her family would not take her back. Kanta found her hungry on the street and brought her to our Sunday worship. We prayed and Kanta took her in. This strong woman had endured much abuse and suffering, but she was steadfast. She would even take on Sunil. She helped disciple the two young teachers; one was Dimpel, Grant McFarland's future wife. She led a village foot washing one time in northeastern Delhi. The story was told of Jesus. She then invited people to come and have their feet washed by Indian and American Christians. First came the Dalit women, who were seated on the ground in the back. Then came a growing group of Backward caste women and a few men. It all angered the village schoolmaster, who stood saying, "Leave our community. We don't need your Western propaganda. Gandhi will remain our leader!" Kanta took him on strongly and demanded that he too must have his feet washed. I then saw him seated up front while Dr. Rob Johnston washed his feet. What an irony! She was fearless, remaining for more than two hours afterwards debating alone with the Brahmin leaders.

Kancha Ilaiah was chair of the Department of Sociology of the historic Osmania University in Karnataka. Born of the Shepherd's caste, he became fiercely revolutionary as a young leader. He became a Naxalite—the most violent Maoist movement in India, which still controls large segments of rural India. Rising to leadership, he had to pass the test—commit murder for the cause of the revolution. He could not and was ousted from the terrorist organization.

Kancha's brother became chronically disabled as a young man, who had a large family of children. Constantly in critical medical crisis, he was unable to even feed his family. Kancha then devoted his life to caring for his brother and his family. Meanwhile, he had become a scholar and writer. His rejection of the caste system catapulted him into open conflict with the Hindu religious and political leadership. Millions came to follow him. He continued to write books. His book *Why I Am Not a Hindu*[7] stirred national controversy. He and Sunil soon became allies, although he lived in

7. Ilaiah, Kancha, *Why I am Not a Hindu.*

Karnataka. I came to know him. We brought him to Lou Tice's Pacific Institute in Washington State. I remember when he told us, "I wish to be buried as a Christian." Our dialogue and friendship increased. One day on a phone call he declared, "I have now publicly declared Jesus Christ as my Savior." He thus became one of our strongest Truthseekers.

Dr. Dhananjai Tripati was student body president at Nehru University, the "Harvard of India." He engaged with Sunil one day after Sunil had addressed a group of students. Subsequently he became president of the student body. Sunil invited him for dinner in honor of his election. He was a brilliant high-caste intellectual, both a Marxist and an atheist. He became a friend of Sunil's over the next years and thus a friend of mine. He would often come to our center, sometimes bringing other young radical grad students with him. We began emails during the times I was back home in the States. He began to attract criticism from his fellow radicals for his frequent dialogues with us. One evening he announced that he was being isolated by his colleagues who had given me a special name: "The Virus at South Ex" (the district where our center is located).

Serving also as leader of the OBC students, he demanded more freedom from Hindu religious domination for these Backward caste students. Trying to calm the riotous mass gathering of the student body, he pleaded for everyone to moderate their language. He was then physically attacked by a dozen radical Hindu students—only to be rescued by a larger group of OBC students. That night I talked with him, and he was at perfect peace. The confrontation was covered by all the daily newspapers of New Delhi.

Then a gradual movement toward Christ emerged. He told me that he had decided that all philosophers and political leaders were inadequate. Jesus was the only true model. He asked me to pray for him. The next time I came to Delhi, he declared that he could finally affirm that Jesus was the Son of God, but he was still an atheist. He asked, "Does that make a Christian?" I said, "No, but it does make you a Truthseeker, moving toward Christ." I awoke that night, remembering Jesus' words in Matthew 10, "He who receives me, receives him who sent me." I met with him that evening and had him read the text. I took him to several other passages that clearly show Jesus was either the true God or he was an impostor. Dhananjai then said he was ready, and welcomed Jesus Christ as his Lord and Savior. In subsequent years, he finished his dissertation and it was published. Lecturing abroad again and again, he continues to talk about taking a second PhD in Christian theology with our CATS degree program through Sam Higginbottom University. He is now a full-time professor at South Asian University in New Delhi.

CHRISTWARD MOVEMENTS
AMONG THE CASTES

Throughout history a vast number of people declared themselves Christians not by individual conversion, but by "people movements." These are mass conversions led by tribal or ethnic leaders. Our Western tradition often sees conversion as essentially an individual matter. Moving a whole group of people at the behest of a leader sounds suspiciously like the cultural Christians of which Kierkegaard spoke in the nineteenth century: "In Denmark everyone is a Christian. That is why there is not a Christian in Denmark."[8] Missiologists point to many cases where small tribes and even large groups go through a converting process over years at the behest of their leaders. In India, a number of small tribes have converted virtually en masse. But Methodist bishop J. Waskom Pickett led a study by the World Council of Churches on "People Movement among a Small Group of Other Backwards Castes in South India," which led to the book *Christian Mass Movements in India*.[9] John R. Mott declared that 80 percent of all Indian Christians were converted through mass movements. Studying smaller movement throughout India, these movements ceased to grow in the post–World War II years. Sunil Sardar began to witness some newer movements among major castes shortly after 2000. Here I began to witness them among more than twenty such castes. I chose to use another term; I call them Christward Movements. Others also are now doing the same, claiming that I was the first to coin that term. Who knows?

We began to have a series of biennial gatherings of caste leaders, involving the heads of more than twenty castes—some of them with more than 40 million members each. We would give them a few days of training. I decided to teach them about Christology, first because so much of my doctoral work was in this area. The second reason was that the Trinity, including the deity of Christ, was a unique concept not present in India religious awareness. When I began, I was almost immediately interrupted by a leader of a caste of forty million. He simply said, "We are not here to learn of these things. We are here to learn how we as followers of Bali Raja can pray, marry, and bury our people." I was offended, but then came to understand that only the Brahman priests could intercede with the gods and celebrate weddings and funerals. Thus, the only access to the supernatural was through them. These were the chains that kept them in submission. I saw that the first order in liberation from idolatry required a priesthood. Then came Christ's

8. Heiser, "*Training in Christianity*," 240–42.
9. Mott, "Foreword," 5.

deity, and the Trinity. During these years Covenant Church World Relief funded these critically important gatherings.

The Butcher Caste and Tecum Singh

This caste has 6 million members. Its leader is Tecum Singh, a young man in his thirties. He was the first caste leader to initiate a relationship with Sunil, early in 2003. He soon indicated that he would like to become a believer. He kept coming, but kept stalling. Living more than five hours away in Aligar, he even missed the first appointment with me present. When we were concluding our daily worship time at the center, he walked in with several of his minions. Almost Caucasian in his coloring, he was dressed in white from head to toe. Thinking he must be a high-caste person, I noticed that he was wearing two-dollar tennis shoes. He then joined Sunil and me in the office. I joined Sunil behind his large desk while Tecum stood with his leaders. Sunil then nodded for me to begin and he would translate. I felt speechless, but simply asked:

Q: Why are you here?

A. We want to become Christians.

Q. What does it mean to be a Christian?

A. Follow Jesus: clothe naked, house homeless, feed hungry, heal the sick.

Q: What do you say to Jesus as you come?

A: He threw his whole body face-down on the desk, lifted his arms, and cried, "SLAVE!"

I have never heard a more clear-cut surrender to the lordship of Christ.

He began almost immediately to organize the caste in his area to move the entire caste nationwide toward Christ. He quickly organized five schools, one of which was among a small group of Dacoits, a bandit clan in the more rural areas. We visited the schools. We shared in a vast rally of the local membership of the caste. Again, we met just with his leaders, and a dozen strangers joined us. They claimed that they were from another caste of 5,000 who were seeking Christian baptism. Sunil was dumbstruck, simply asking them to pray that someone might be sent to them with Scripture and teaching.

Sitting on the ground during lunch, I asked Tecum's father about the life of his son. He said that as infant, the child was dying of dysentery. He began to cry out "Mahadeva! Please save my son!" Mahadeva is the title of the merciful God whose name is not known. The father went twice to the doctor who refused to come for treatment of an untouchable child. He finally got a police officer who took the doctor to help the son. As Tecum grew he became more rebellious and violent, even criminal. The father still cried out to Mahadeva, begging him to make his son a good and just man. Having become head of the caste through sometimes criminal and violent means, Tecum was changed dramatically when he came to Christ. The father lifted his eyes to heaven and said to us all, "I now know the name of Mahadeva. His name is Jesus!

One day Tecum brought Ranjit Singh, the head of the Copper and Brass caste in five states, to declare his people for Christ. He had personally presented a solid brass crucifix of Jesus that he had personally made for me. It was almost too heavy to bring home from India and sits above my desk. Eventually, another mission group hired Tecum, and we have not seen him as often. But we still remain close to the Copper and Brass Workers leadership.

The Belli Caste and Dinesh Kumar

The Weavers' caste, the Belli, has 40 million members, led by Dinesh Kumar. Raised in the greatest poverty, he did get to go to school. Because he was low caste, he could only sit outside the schoolroom during classes and gain his schooling listening from the footsteps. Nonetheless, he rose to become the chief of the state of New Delhi's Federal Tax Commissioner. As such he won the largest tax fraud case ever won in India. It was against Suzuki Motors. He became politically active, but ultimately saw that political and economic reform would not take place without a religious transformation. He had heard of Sunil, but could never locate him. While we were both away in the city of Aligar, he and Jiram Singh Jai, head of the 40 million members of the Potters' caste, asked for a meeting. We agreed to meet in Delhi as soon as we returned.

Together with Jiram, who did not handle English well, he read a long statement explaining their mass suffering and asked for the way to become Christians. They felt that the most important thing that they could gain was education and schools for their children. Yet, Dinesh said, even if we could not provide that, they would still want their castes to become Christians. It was a simple but transforming process of prayer and faith.

He soon retired from his post and gave his full time to supporting Truthseekers daily. He constantly traveled with us, sharing the Christian faith with everyone near him on trains or transit. He became a student of the word, aiding in translation. He would vehemently exclaim that the words of the Bible were entirely strings of gold and diamonds. He was an elegant spokesman with his people, but did encounter some resistance within the caste at first. But the caste then began following him in greater numbers. In Jabalpur, a city of 3 million, he publicly faced down the mayor and the district collector, who were trying to block a rally. He was charged by the police, but never prosecuted.

One interesting fact is that the name Belli is the ancestral name for the caste founder. It is in fact Bali Raja—the ancient king who sacrificed himself to save his people and who would one day bring to them the Begumpura, the "City without Sorrow."

So eloquent was his witness that he went to the great Lausanne Conference on World Evangelism at Cape Town, South Africa, celebrating the 200th anniversary of William Carey's call for the first world missions gathering. He was privileged to share the story of his conversion at the opening plenary session. He did well, despite the intimidating circumstance. Tragically, other members of the assembly from India abruptly attacked him personally. They claimed that his description of the evils of caste oppression of the poor was a shameful attack on India itself. He took it in stride. The tragedy is that many traditional evangelical communities have developed a similar shush ethic, that is, they try never to create trouble through involvement in social or political protest. Too often they harshly rebuke any who stir up trouble on the basis of social and economic injustice. This is one of the reasons the backward castes have never been drawn to Christian faith.

The Shepherds' Caste and Severi Sin Pal

The Shepherds' caste is among the poorest of all the lower castes. With no land, their sole source of income comes from their grazing sheep and goats. Ten million of them live in the state of Uttar Pradesh. Earlier in the twentieth century, there was some Christward movement among them, led by Sam Higginbottom and others. It had been suppressed, however, by Nehru and Gandhi. In our time, one young Shepherd, Shiv, who did get an education, found Christ. He became Sunil's office manager from that time on. Relentless in his work, gentle in his approach, he diligently took care of all my needs whenever I was in India. His elder brother, Severi Sin Pal, was head of the 10 million members of their caste, led from the city of Etta in Uttar Pradesh. Shiv took advantage of Samaritan's Purse and its Christmas boxes for poor children and got hundreds of these sent over the next few years. He asked Severi why they didn't worship the Shepherd God—Jesus—instead of the oppressive Brahminic deities. Severi then invited Sunil to Etta. During a Covenant Church Midwinter Conference, I received a phone call from Sunil, who said the Shepherds were most interested in his witness. Then they had asked for further conversation. The leadership decided to come to New Delhi and take a stand for Jesus Christ, the Good Shepherd.

They arrived on a Saturday, February 18, 2006. Accompanying Severi were the national general secretary of all Shepherd castes as well as the caste attorney. Severi was dressed in white, with a pistol and long ammunition belt hung from his waist—a token of his status as Head of Caste. He read a statement about their desire to become Christians. I led them in a prayer. An amazing moment! On their return to Etta, they stopped at another city where 3,000 of the caste also declared for Christ. One month later, sixty motorcycles were dispatched from the capital city of Lucknow announcing the leadership's decision to follow Christ throughout the state. They continue to have mass rallies and small group meetings. They have had their ups and downs, but the big surprise came in 2015.

The Potters' Caste and Nokalal Prajapati

Near Jabalpur, a city of 3 million people in Maida Pradesh, a young law student approached a tea stand in the year 2007. He was the first in his family to ever gain any higher education. He came from the Backward caste of Potters. When someone mentioned his name, the owner of the tea stand flew into a rage. The proprietor was high caste, while Nokalal was low caste. Raging at the young man, he took his teacup and smashed it on the ground, because the fingers of the low caste defile anything they touch. He then proceeded to wash the table on which the tea had been served, for it too was defiled. A dog then proceeded to urinate on the table's leg, but that was no caste violation. Nokalal was so enraged that he gathered thirty of his close friends and set out across the countryside on a thirty-day protest march, calling all the Potters to abandon Brahmanic Hinduism. They took no money or food but were welcomed and fed everywhere. It was estimated that more than 100,000 joined the protest. As they journeyed, they wondered what religious faith they might follow. Some felt they should become Muslim; others advocated Buddhism or Sikhism. Nokalal would have none of it. All religion meant nothing but slavery and oppression.

David Lal was the leader of Midyear Missions in the nearby city of Dohma. Hearing of Nokalal's plight, he searched and found him. Unable to make any progress with Nokalal, he took him to see Sunil in New Delhi. There Sunil welcomed him to Christ in a dramatic moment of conversion. As the movement began to gather steam, Sunil and I followed them to Jabalpur, with caution that this was a very militant Hindu city. I simply shook hands with him, among others, as we left the airport. We were followed by police. I was deposited alone in a guesthouse and told to share nothing of our purpose. That evening Sunil and other leaders came by the hotel for tea. They drove to a safe house and met Nokalal. He told his story. The next day would be the mass rally, preceded by the baptism of key leaders. He had not been gone for more than hour when we received word that he had been arrested. In the morning I awakened to read the newspaper by myself at breakfast. I read the article about his arrest. It noted that the police were looking for the American who had just arrived in the city with vast sums of money to purchase converts. The plans changed that evening. I was told to waken at 3:00 a.m. and stand outside the hotel. I was then picked up in an old SUV and driven into the countryside.

We drove far out into the country and stopped by a river. The sun was just rising, and the moon was now setting. Women threshers on a distant field were harvesting millet, bent over with hand sickles. Here thirty young leaders of this caste were baptized. We sang, in Hindi, Sadhu Sundar Singh's Indian hymn "I Have Decided to Follow Jesus"—a great hymn sung so often here. It was an unforgettable time.

It was decided that, under the dangerous circumstances, I should be hidden sixty miles away at the village of Dohma. I was placed in the now-historic residence of the house where Donald McGavran was born. Midday they said it was now safe to go to the mass meeting back in Jabalpur. The militant political leadership had forced the meeting out of the city limits. No notice was given to the masses journeying to the site. They then blocked off all the roads coming from the countryside. The area was filled with police and military personnel. A court had been set up in the open air to try any who declared for Christ. There were three empty buses to send all new believers to prison. They hid me out of sight in a windowless room of an auto dealership. The speakers spoke without fear. At the end the masses stood and took the Truthseekers Oath, declaring that they now worshiped only the one true God and Bali Raja (Jesus), who would one day return and bring the "City without Sorrow."

I was then taken by the back road to a building in the city chosen for me to wait in until I was picked up. We drove all night over the Tiger Road to safety in the city of Nagpur.

The Lodhi Caste and Hukumsingh Deshrajan

The 60-million-member Lodi caste consists of small farmers largely in the states of Uttar Pradesh and Madya Pradesh. Its powerful leader is Dr. Hukumsingh Deshrajan, a professor of political science at Aligarh University.

While doing his doctoral research into the religious traditions of his caste, he discovered that they were originally monotheist. His grandmother had told him to forsake the Brahmanic gods and worship the True Most Holy One. A Jesuit medical doctor was most helpful to him in his research. He was strangely drawn to the Christian man and his faith. He began to search for a Christian leader, but felt repelled by most Christian communities. He had heard of Sunil Sardar and Truthseekers. He found him after searching for a couple of years. He became a true follower of Christ. He eloquently exhorted large crowds everywhere to follow only Christ. He eagerly studied the Scripture. He came to me on several occasions to study the Scripture. He often came to spend several days at a time at our center. Often he came just to spend time with me.

He asked me to take a summer—three months—to train over ten top young leaders in each of three states: Uttar Pradesh, Madya Pradesh, and Tamil Naidu. Unfortunately, I was unable to do so. At one point he gathered 3,000 of his national caste leaders in a stadium in New Delhi. He later told me that the leadership had unanimously changed the charter of their caste to say no Lodhi could ever worship the Hindu gods—only the one true holy God. They later amended this to acknowledge Bali Raja as the coming deliverer. He was always gracious. But on one occasion, David Lal, our friend who heads the Mid-India Christian Services Mission, asked him in my presence if he could keep Lodhi hoodlums from trashing their hospitals and schools. Hukumsingh merely replied, "The next Lodhi who even points a finger at your mission will have no finger!" Caste leaders can be tough!

Remarkably, three other small castes in Uttar Pradesh decided to merge with Lodhi under Hukumsingh's leadership. This meant they could interdine and intermarry. Together they amount to more than 20 percent of Uttar Pradesh, with its population of 180 million. After hearing a biblical exposition from our own Dr. Rob Johnston, he cried, "Oh, come and teach us the Bible!"

The Scavengers and Belaram

Scavengers are the lowest-class outcasts. They are toilet cleaners. One afternoon while crossing the street from our small guesthouse to the center itself, I was greeted by two young men dressed in pure white. They pointed to the center and asked "Sunil Sardar?" I merely pointed upstairs. Later Sunil told me that they were sons of a village chief from outside Delhi. They were part of the championship wrestling team, winning bouts throughout the New Delhi region. Their father asked them to contact Sunil in order to arrange a meeting with him. A few days later the fog had become so dense that we had to abort our five-hour trip for a caste gathering. Sunil then called the father and asked if we could come the next day. It was only two hours away, and we drove to the rural village.

His name was Belaram. Hundreds gathered. We shared the story of the good news of Jesus Christ (Bali Raja). We then began to wash the feet of many. I knelt and washed Balarama's feet. He then got up and began to chant the caste saga in Hindi. It spoke of their terrible oppression. They had hoped in Gandhi. They then thought that Ambedkar would bring freedom. But his Buddhism changed nothing. He then said, "Today Jesus has come to our village. Every year we will all celebrate his coming on this same date because we are now all his followers."

He then invited us to dine together. As they were toilet cleaners, we felt awkward. Claiming in our hearts deliverance from snakes and fire recorded in the disputed ending of Mark 16, we timidly received bottled water and orange soda. Then came freshly baked flatbread and stewed cauliflower. We were most anxious about the desert, rice pudding. It was, however, a dead ringer for Swedish rice pudding.

We went a year later to another village also led by Belaram. It turned out that he was the chief of more than 110 such villages north and east of New Delhi. In more than 100 villages, a significant Christward movement had begun.

The Stone Carvers and Vijay Paswan

I arrived in Delhi in November 2002, and Sunil told me of a caste leader of stone carvers from Bihar, India's poorest state. It was a small caste, but they could not even afford the stone out of which they made carvings. Desperately, this young man named Vijay Paswan had traveled across north India to seek aid from its member in parliament. The leader said he had no money, but would recommend he go to find a man called Sunil Sardar in the South Extension. Arriving, he was disappointed because Sunil could scarcely pay the team's food and rent. But he did give him the message of salvation.

Vijay responded at once. Sunil said that he had no personnel funds or teachers to send to this state. Instead he gave a copy of our low Hindi New Testament, telling him to read and pray regularly with his people that the teachers would one day come. Vijay hung his head in sadness. When Sunil asked what his problem was, Vijay said he was illiterate. Sunil then asked if he knew someone who could read. Vijay replied, "My brother reads." Sunil told him to still gather his people and have his brother read the Bible and pray in hope.

Five months later, Vijay returned saying that his entire village of nearly 1,000 had not only turned to Christ, but had filed for the required notice of religious change with the local magistrate. His village was located on a main roadway through the state, and many travelers spend the night in the village. Around a fire he would gather them regularly and ask each to share the nature of the god or gods they worshiped. At the conclusion, he would share the message of Christ. Soon many from different castes had turned to Christ.

An Indian leader had donated thousands of miniature booklets, the size of a business card. It told the story of Jesus. On the back was a photo of Sharad Yadav, head of the JDP Party and titular head of all low-caste parties. Vijay would approach a person explaining that he was illiterate. Most often the person would read aloud the brief story of Jesus. They would frequently ask, "Is this not a picture of Sharad Yadav? Does he believe this too?" Very often that opened the door to the kingdom.

Over the years since, Vijay would often take the long journey across India to come and visit with us. The stories of violence and struggle were deeply moving. He gave me a small stone carving of Jesus washing the feet of a woman. Strangely, some traditional Christians mocked him, saying, "Jesus would never wash the feet of a woman." But this is authentic biblical Christianity.

The movement became viral. It spread into thirty-five districts of Bihar. Then it crossed the borders into the states of Jharkhand and West Bengal. Sometimes Vijay would bring musicians with him. I cannot forget the time that leaders of both states came. The new leader in West Bengal said they were faced with a dilemma. Eighty percent of their stone carvings were idols. He declared, "One day as we were praying, God spoke to us that we could no longer make idols." I asked them who had told them this. They replied, "No one, it just came strongly upon us when we were praying together." They then explained that they could no longer support or feed their families. If they tried to adopt another trade, they would be violently opposed by other trades for crossing the boundaries. The West Bengal leader then said, "We trust that God alone will feed and clothe us." I have never in my life seen such profound surrender to the Lord Jesus.

Somehow, they have survived and continue to flourish. Vijay continues to celebrate scores of marriages of new believers monthly. Yet these people have never had a missionary. Sunil himself has been limited in the time he can visit these people. It is the gifted and godly leadership of Pranjal Torde, who visits there whenever he has funds for transportation, that has been crucial. I have heard the numbers, but we do not, as a rule, publish them. But this may have been the most amazing of all the Christward movements I have seen in India.

Walmikis

In April 2015, the leader of the New Delhi Walmikis approached Sunil. More than 2 million of them are scattered throughout the poorest sections of this city of 15 million. They are the lowest castes of Dalits—or scavengers. The leader told us they had despaired of ever gaining justice and an end to poverty. Twenty years before, they had converted to Buddhism in the hope of deliverance; the leadership had concluded that this was a total failure. He had heard of a man who sang hopeful songs at a rally near the airport. He had a message of hope. He then went to a mass meeting. Claiming he felt he had been struck by light from heaven, he went into seclusion in absolute darkness for many hours. He finally concluded with certainty that this was an answer from heaven. He invited Sunil to one of their residences in a poor section of town. I went with Sunil and Shiv. He lived with others in a two-story, block-long, dormitory-style building. It had a room for cooking and had restrooms. Each family had a small room along a large wide corridor running the full length of the building. The room contained only an eight-square-foot bed and a few folding chairs. We sat on them, and the three leaders told us their story. They wanted to be Christ followers. I prayed with them for salvation. They then said that they were convening a mass rally the next month, May. They had reserved a town square and notified the press and media. Here they would proclaim Jesus as the Savior. They had also opened a small central office to coordinate their movement. They continue to seek training and instruction from our center to this day.

The Mali Caste

The largest of all the Indian castes are the Malis, or Gardeners' caste. Known by different names throughout India, they have an estimated 180 million members. It is the caste of Jotirao Phule and his wife, Savitribai, two of the greatest spiritual and social leaders of the nineteenth century. Even Gandhi called him "the True Mahatma." But after his death in 1890, his wife succeeded him as head of Truthseekers. Trying to save children from a dreaded plague, she succumbed to it herself in 1897. With the rise of nationalism and the hostility of the upper castes, the movement virtually disappeared. Among the Malis he was basically forgotten. As a part of the OBCs (Other

Backward Castes, or Shudras, meaning "slaves"), they never received the government financial support for their poverty as did the scheduled castes of Dalits or Tribals.

Sunil was puzzled by the fact that so few from this caste turned to Christ. Only Dr. Gaude, a Mali leader from Sunil's hometown of Yevatmal, turned to Christ. Eventually one leader of this caste was welcomed to Christ by Sunil. The vice chief minister of the state of Maharashtra, Chagan Bushbal, had somehow become an acquaintance. He had been mayor of Mumbai during its greatest period of city development and became the head of Shiv Sena, the right-wing caste. In the political turmoil, he fell from office due to legal and political conflicts. Sunil ministered to him so that he became a Truthseeker. Restored to power once again, he sponsored a mass gathering in the next state of Rajasthan. He planned a mass rally on International Women's Day in the beautiful capital city of Jaipur.

Meanwhile, Truthseekers gathered several writers to compose a short book on Phule's wife, Sevitribai. It is entitled *A Forgotten Liberator: The Life and Struggles of Sevitribai Phule*.[10] It has been reprinted again and again in ten languages. Out of print now in the U.S., Amazon will sell a used copy for USD$85. Bushbal called for a mass rally Saturday, March 8, 2008. Press reports estimated the crowd at 200,000, but Sunil felt it was closer to 100,000. Bushbal asked me to be one of the speakers. Sunil translated my impromptu response:

> Today we celebrate International Women's Day. India has long celebrated the Albanian Mother Theresa. But India had its own Mother Theresa. She was Sevitribai Phule, wife of the great Mali reformer Phule. Co-equal with him in the founding of Truthseekers, she opened India's first schools for poor girls. She wrote poems and songs about the sufferings of these people. In one of the great plagues, she tried to care for children dying of that curse. While nursing them, she contracted the disease and died shortly thereafter.
>
> India has not come as far in developing the rights of the poor and the outcaste as the United States. But we have been independent for only two hundred years. But India has only been independent for seventy years. In the vision of this great movement for universal literacy is the hope that India will not make her contribution to this world by simply providing cheap labor to the West. Through universal literacy as she envisions it, India will contribute more than any nation to the peace and prosperity of the world.

10. Mani and Sardar, *Forgotten Liberator.*

We responded to a cluster of news and television media and went back to Delhi in amazement.

In April 2015, Chagan Bushbal invited Sunil and me to a national rally of the Mali leaders. The massive auditorium was packed with thousands. Chagan was sitting in the middle of the first row of the audience with the other leaders. When he saw me, he arose and embraced me before the multitude. The program proceeded with an oral history, pictures, and drama of the life of Phule. Chagan gave out many awards. Finally, he summoned Sunil to the platform. He garlanded and turbaned Sunil and said, "This man is not of our caste. But it is he who for the first time has taught us our identity. We now embrace the Phules as our historic leaders. And thus, we offer thanks to Sunil Sardar for leading us to our identity. Jai Baliraja!"

Alas, Chagan has once again fallen on hard times. The stress of legal and political conflict has brought him very low. Sunil asks that we continue to pray for him.

CHRISTWARD MOVEMENTS

In some twenty castes of varying sizes, I encountered the leadership and watched as they came to Christ. They began leading their respective castes in a Christward direction. These processes often take years, as was noted by Methodist missionary J. Waskom Pickett in the 1930s in his scholarly research across India. Some of these and other Christward movements continue in India beyond any contact Truthseekers have encountered.

In 2009, the Evangelical Fellowship of India convened an all-India congress in Hyderabad. It was convened by its president, Richard Howell, PhD. Several hundred gathered for several days. An entire evening was given over to Sunil and Truthseekers to share God's work among and through them. Papers were presented by Sunil, Dr. Thomas Faust, Dr. Roger Hedlund, Braj Ranjan Mani, and me. My paper, entitled "Christian Mission and OBC Resistance,"[11] discussed why there had been almost no Christward movements of the half billion Other Backward Castes (OBCs). We closed the evening by all sharing in the Lord's Supper in our unique way: the breaking of a coconut and the drinking of the milk—symbols of sacrifice and bloodshed understood throughout Indian culture. Later, the entire assembly affirmed and prayed for our unique mission by acclamation, led by Dr. Howell. Our papers were later published in the volume *Living Faith: The Fragrance of Christ*.[12]

11. Larsen, "Christian Mission and OBC Resistance."
12. Larsen, "Christian Mission and OBC Resistance," 99–104.

CATS

CATS is the acronym for the Center for Advanced Theological Studies at the Sam Higginbottom University for Agriculture, Science, and Technology. The new academic program was the first university-accredited evangelical PhD in Christian Studies in India. In January of 2012, the first classes were held. By 2017, the program had more than forty PhD students. As of that year, the program's funding all came from within India, except for scholarships and transportation for us teachers.

As I mentioned earlier, our intention from the beginning and our partnership with William Carey's Serampore University in Calcutta was to provide a university-accredited PhD in Christian studies. While accredited by treaty with King Frederick VI in 1838, the University Grants Commission never recognized Serampore's degree due to Brahminic opposition. We struggled and struggled. To bring Indian scholars to America for this doctoral degree would cost a minimum of US$150,000. Most of these graduates never went back to India, which made for a terrible business model. We needed a truly academic and spiritual program taught by Indians at Indian prices. Fuller Seminary and others had tried and failed to enter into agreements acceptable to the Indian government.

My longtime colleague Dr. Robert K. Johnston had been provost at both Fuller Theological Seminary and North Park Seminary. He had also been president of the American Theological Society. Now he was professor of theology and culture at Fuller. He had worked with missiology professor Charles Van Engen in establishing a PhD program, Prodola, for all Latin America accredited through the University of Costa Rica. It drew upon the best of all the evangelical scholars in Latin America. These professors were named visiting faculty to the University of Costa Rica. Two intensives a year for two years and three years of directed doctoral research would yield a world-class accredited PhD. Rob suggested that we propose the same thing to India. He traveled with me to India and made the presentation. The university was too paralyzed financially and academically to entertain such a proposal. They felt that university-accredited PhDs were unnecessary because the seventy related schools only needed pastors for their respective churches.

Sunil noticed my frustration and told me that he was the member of the board of directors of the Allahabad Agricultural Scientific and Technical University in Allahabad. He was a close friend of its leader, Vice Chancellor Rajendra B. B. Lal. Under the British system the vice chancellor would be what we call president. With two PhDs and a devout faith, he had been mentored by the InterVarsity staff director at Kansas State University, where he received one of his PhDs. Founded in 1910 by Presbyterian missionary Sam Higginbottom, the university covered a square mile of exhausted land at the confluence of the Ganges and Jumuna rivers. So began India's first agricultural school. Over the years it had waxed and waned. Dr. Lal became its head, and a few years later it had become the number one agricultural university in India. With 12,000 students, it offered PhDs in a number of specialties. Now under the umbrella of the Church of North India, it had a small, struggling seminary.

So Rob, Sunil, and I arrived at the university in March of 2010. We sat in R. B.'s huge office with his secretaries and minions. R. B. asked me why I had come to him. I replied simply, "I need to deal with someone who can make a decision." Then began a day-long dialogue between Rob and R. B. While I have all the necessary degrees to be a part of the academy, I am not an academic administrator. David Hubbard of Fuller Seminary told me when appointing Rob as provost at Fuller, "He is the most qualified man in evangelicalism for this position." R. B. and Rob negotiated everything for more than six hours. He spoke from pure memory while Rob continued to scribble changing rules and fees. R. B. offered to carry all overhead but would not pay for American costs. Many would have paid money to watch this amazing negotiation. When the day ended, I thanked them both and suggested that his deans and academics could work out the details for final approval. R. B. simply asked, "Why? It is just now decided!" He then issued orders for each of the senior administrators to have completed reports on his desk in the morning. And so it began.

11

Other Religions in India

DURING THESE FIFTEEN YEARS I was privileged to observe Christward movements beginning in four of India's major faiths. Sunil's stand for human rights marked him as a Christian. When asked to become a member of the All India Christian Council to struggle for Christian rights, Sunil demurred. He said, "I am not interested in Christian Rights; I am only interested in Human Rights!" As other leaders of persecuted religions noticed his effectiveness, they joined in protest and action.

The Old Scots Church (Presbyterian) in Nagpur had been attacked by goons from the RSS (the "Al Qaida" of the Hindu Nationalists.) They vandalized the church, destroyed its furniture, and beat the pastor and his family. Outside they broke the windows and trashed the church's van. The Christian leaders from all churches called for a rally to protest. Sunil demurred, declaring that in a land only 5 or 6 percent Christian, these protests were futile. He said they should gather all the oppressed religious minorities and join with the oppressed backward and scheduled castes to take action against all religious violence. A mass rally was held by thousands in a city square. Leaders from all dissenting racial, religious, and political minorities joined together. I was privileged to speak, but also noted that a communist, Buddhist, and even a Muslim imam spoke against all violence. Nagpur, a city of 3 million, is the national headquarters of the RSS. So forceful was this response, I have been told, that there has been no Hindu violence since. Interestingly, Sunil became an admired hero. As a result, these groups have subsequently given this Christian the lead, and he has done more for human rights than anyone else in a given year.

Buddhism

Born in India around the time of Moses, Buddhism grew out of Hinduism with its belief in reincarnation, but it rejected the Brahminic deities. It spread rapidly until it reigned supreme under the greatest of all emperors, Ashoka. Yet Ashoka was a monotheist, while Buddha was nontheistic. The Brahmins rebelled and waged a war of extermination, forcing the survivors over the Himalayas into Tibet and the Far East. It survived in only a few places. Yet it was the great Dalit Babesab Ambedkar who was educated in the West and became the drafter of the India Constitution in 1947. Drawn first to Christianity, he ultimately embraced Buddhism instead. He struggled with Gandhi over the rights of the scheduled castes. Gandhi would not repudiate Brahmanism and was dedicated to the caste system almost until the very end. At a rally in New Delhi in 1955, he and nearly 500,000 Indians shaved their heads and converted to Buddhism. He died suddenly shortly after. This resulted in a Buddhism that organized itself politically into Neo-Buddhism, which is seldom recognized as authentic Buddhism by traditional Buddhists in India and Southeast Asia.

Prakash Ambedkar leads the Neo-Buddhist political party. The grandson of the famous Babesab Ambedkar (1891–1956), he has been a long-time acquaintance with Sunil. He was somewhat hostile to Sunil early on because he felt that Sunil's emphasis on the necessity of Christ diminished the greatness of Buddha. As time went on, they continued to collaborate in the struggles of the scheduled and Backward castes. Tom Wolfe, of the University Study Center in Delhi, argued well that Buddha was more like the prophet Isaiah, not the Redeemer, who was Christ. I remember one day at the center in Nagpur when I was alone with Sunil and a dozen men joined and reverently debated for several hours in the Marati language. I didn't know what it was about, so I occupied the time counting the holes in the ceiling tiles. After they left, Sunil told me they were Ambedkerites. They had told him that he was hurting their movements. He had repeatedly said that only Christ could lead the poor to justice. He said that as the conversation concluded, they all agreed that, as great as Buddha was, they needed Christ to lead them. One Sunday morning Sunil took me to a distant address where he had been invited by a dozen Buddhist and reformed Hindu leaders. They wanted his help in organizing the poor for human rights. He astounded me when he told them that none of them were true Buddhists—their concerns for social justice came only from Jesus Christ. They profoundly thanked him. More recently Prakash and Sunil have become the two key leaders in the Balijan Cultural Movement, which unites the marginalized for social and spiritual struggle.

Udit Raj was a brilliant Neo-Buddhist political leader. He was drawn to my longtime colleague Rochunga Pudaite of Bibles for the World. He asked if Ro and Mawii could be the adoptive grandparents to his two small children. He prayed for salvation, but the commitment was uncertain. He did lead in the organization of a one-day gathering of 1 million people in New Delhi to repudiate Brahmanism and convert to either Buddhism or Christianity. Though the army and police largely thwarted that effort, I was acutely interested in him and the movement. He would fight against the persecution of Christians. I invited him to visit with me in America. He stayed at my house with his wife, while my daughter Kristi housed their two young children. One morning while I was showering he burst in on me and handed me his open cell phone, saying that Arjun Sing was on the phone. This man was Minister of Human Resources in the Indian cabinet and the second most important leader in the Congress Party. He offered to meet with me when I was back in Delhi. And we did, riding in Udit's top-of-the line SUV. Udit's bodyguard always accompanied us wherever we went indoors and outdoors. He always carried a pistol-handled sawed-off shotgun. The bodyguard sometimes accompanied us to Christian foot-washing rallies. He invited me to attend one of his Buddhist-conversion rallies. Scattering the crowds with red lights and sirens, we traveled far to a rally of about 5,000 who were ready to declare themselves followers of the Buddha. Unexpectedly, he led me to the high platform, followed by the shotgun-armed bodyguard and seated me in the front row next to the Buddhist monks who sat on the ground as hundreds came forward to take the Buddhist conversion oath. The thing resembled a rather sterilized and dispassionate alter call. Udit then unexpectedly called on me and told me to get up and speak. I had no idea that was coming! I simply said:

> Today you have become Buddhists. I, however, am a Christian, and there is a great difference. But two truths unite us:
>
> One: In caste there is no justice.
>
> Two: Without the freedom to convert there is no freedom at all.

Afterward I was surrounded by the press, who questioned me for some time. I continue to pray for the day when he openly declares himself for Jesus Christ.

Dr. Bhalchandra Mungekar was the former head of Mumbai University. A noted economist, he became vice chair of India's planning commission, a central organizing body of the whole government. As vice chair, he presided in the absence of the prime minister himself. He was also president and chair of All India Institute of Advanced Studies in Shimla. He became a close friend of Sunil's; they had regular contact by phone. When Sunil's phone went out for several days, Dr. Mungekar told him, "I must have you right with me by phone at all times. You have prior access to me over the prime minister." When thousands of farmers in Maharashtra increasingly committed suicide because they could not repay their agricultural loans, Sunil tipped him off. Mungekar then discovered that the federal allocations had been sent almost completely to the western half of Maharashtra, with little to the eastern portion. He flew at once to that state and promptly initiated more equal distribution.

On several occasions I accompanied Sunil to visit with him in his home. We discussed Christ from time to time. I most remember the time he sat in his home and said, "I know that Buddhism, which is nontheistic, will never be able to reach the poor Dalits and Tribals. Only a living god can thus bring them hope and deliverance. I am convinced that only Jesus can deliver them." He has since retired; I pray that this truth will bring him to the feet of Jesus.

Islam

Islam has more than 150 million followers in India, making Indonesia the only state with a larger Muslim population. In the Iraqi city of Basra in AD 711, Rabia-Adawiyyo, a woman, rejected the rituals and Muslim rules. Instead she argued that the love of God was the only requirement—and to seek him is to lose yourself in him. Thus was born the most mystical form of Islam—Sufism. For the most part, Sufis are mystical and nonviolent. They would make pilgrimages to the monuments of their great saints, and both Shia and Sunni teachers rejected and persecuted them as heretical. Some Sufis even made Jesus their most hallowed saint—but not savior. In the sixteenth century, Sufi missionaries entered the subcontinent proclaiming a passive Islamic piety. The oppressed farmers in both India and Pakistan became Muslims—hence the Muslim population to this day. They remain among the poorest of all India and are constantly harassed and even murdered by both Islamic and Hindu militants.

Between 1856 and 1925, Ahma Rezid Kahn led a massive reform movement that spread among Sufi populations that today numbers an estimated 60 million Indians and more than half of Pakistan. They are called Berilwis. In 1998, however, a newer movement began among the Pasmandas, "those who were left behind." They sought to mobilize the poor. The leadership said that oppression of the poor was the greatest evil and proposed alliance with the oppressed people of other religions. Today there are twenty of these mosques in Delhi alone. It is from among these that that many have come into dialogue with Sunil Sardar. Also from these Dr. Seddikki became one of our chief Christian leaders, as noted earlier.

We had gathered nearly twenty caste leaders at one of our earliest Truthseekers multiday training sessions. We were puzzled by the fact that two bright young Muslims joined us, together with two bodyguards carrying rifles. They had come from the Berilwis. They ate, sang, and prayed with us. I was somewhat startled that they joined us in the Lord's Supper. They had made no profession of faith in Jesus. But they were young Muslim leaders in a Christward movement.

A high court Muslim judge was sitting by me at a round table at a special dinner in India's foreign minister's residence, and we had a deep discussion about human rights. I recalled my teacher Dr. Karl F. Henry's comment, "In the end God will judge a nation by the way it treats its minorities!" The judge straightened up and declared, "That is the heart of all justice!"

A Moslem Kashmiri rug merchant, Sunil's neighbor, was well to do. He constantly urged me to use his business cell phones to call America. He even offered me his unoccupied guest apartment whenever I was in town. I queried Sunil about him. He replied, "He thinks I am something of a Sufi Saint!"

Sunil and Gail Omvedt felt that we might gather the Pasmandas, or "those left behind"—whether Muslim, Buddhist, Jewish, or Christian— around the legacy of Ambedkar, Phule, Ravidas, and other Indian saints. This became the Balijan Cultural Society. I was part of the organizing committee. Many times, Muslim leaders would come to Sunil for advice on how to help their people find justice.

In the spring of 2009, we came to hold a Truthseekers rally in the Maharashtrian city of Yevatmal. But political tensions had become too intense due to the approaching elections. Sunil made some phone calls and then drove to some large hall. It was an assembly of thousands of Muslims. We were immediately called forward to sit on the platform. I was astounded that they would call on me, a Western Christian, and Sunil, an Indian Christian wearing a gold cross in his ear. Sunil translated for me as I spoke impromptu. I talked about the struggle for racial justice in America—the years of slavery, Jim Crow, and segregation. I personally remembered when many black people were required to use separate fountains and restrooms. They had to sit at the back of buses and were denied voting rights. I had to admit to the horror of lynching, which still occurred when I was younger. Then I referred to Martin Luther King Jr. and his struggle for human rights. I said I knew also of the injustices Muslim people had suffered under Brahminic suppression. I then quoted the climax of King's greatest speech, "Free at Last." I didn't know whether I should use the name "Allah" in place of

God. No, I decided, I would use our term: "Free at Last! Free at Last! Thank God Almighty, I am free at last!" So I invoked King's faith. A long applause followed. They then garlanded both Sunil and me. The following speakers all ended their speeches with the surprising words, "Thank God Almighty Allah, I am free at last." What they really meant I do not know.

A few mullahs began attending Sunday worship. The hymns were all Christian and the testimonies about Christ the Savior. The Scriptures on Christ's death for our sins and his resurrection were clearly enunciated at the Lord's Supper. I sometimes sat between them. One mullah told me that this was the only place he had ever sensed the presence of God's Spirit. Students from North Park experienced much of this kind of sharing. A touch of Sufi mysticism opened a tiny door to the work of the Holy Spirit. How I pray that multitudes of these poor Muslims will one day embrace our Lord Jesus as Savior!

These expressions of and admiration for Jesus did not make them in any sense Christian. But to them Jesus is a door to justice. In rural areas, the average lower-caste member—whether animist, Hindu, or Muslim—knows nothing of Jesus or even about Islam. I brought Dr. Dudley Woodberry, dean emeritus of Missions at Fuller Seminary and leading scholar of Islam, to India to give Sunil and me a better understanding of what had happened. The Koran teaches more about Jesus than about Mohammad himself. Virgin-born, he healed the sick and raised the dead. He is returning to judge the world. Mohammad is not. Woodberry recommended simply telling Jesus stories from the Koran and then stories from the Gospels. Increasingly, many are starting to embrace Jesus not simply as a prophet, but as the Savior himself.

The Lingayats

In the twelfth century AD, a new religion broke free from Brahmanism. It was led by the great reformer Basava. He attacked all idols and taught faith in only one good, holy God. He fought against the caste system. He and his followers would gather all castes to sit and dine together as part of their egalitarian faith. Intensely persecuted by the Brahmins, they were nearly exterminated a number of times, but later rebounded. In the nineteenth century, an important leader was born into a Christian family in the state of Karnataka: Chanappa Uttangi (1882–1965). He was trained by the Swiss Basel Mission in that state. Because he received a Western academic education, he greatly aided not only the mission, but also the renewal of the Lingayat movement. The Brahmins had used academic ridicule to shrink the Lingayats, claiming that the Basava traditions were all myths. With decisive scholarship Uttangi showed the historic reality of that religion, now of nearly 60 million, largely in Karnataka. He is honored by all Lingayats to this day. Proclaiming that Jesus was the true Lingayat, he kept the door open between Christianity and the Lingayats for nearly a century. He is honored universally as a Lingayat leader and saint. Other Christian leaders in India are reporting numbers of Lingayats turning to Christ.

Sham, a photojournalist in Maharashtra, had noticed and then followed Sunil throughout his struggles for equality and justice in the state. He was a prominent Lingayat leader, a member of its ruling council of eight. His openness to Christianity led to his clear conversion. A quiet but persistent disciple of Jesus, he traveled with us whenever we were in Maharashtra.

In 2009, Sham introduced Sunil to Dr. Moglewar, also a member of the Lingayat council of eight. He is the religion's foremost historian, author of two massive volumes. A resident of Nagpur, he founded the new Lingayat College at Nagpur University. Discouraged by the increasing Brahminization of their faith, he questioned Sunil at length. Sunil invited him to our center in New Delhi to see the vital faith, music, and sharing of our worship. He was deeply moved, concluding that Christ is the only way for the Lingayat faith to survive. He received Christ. Sunil and I met with him several times. On a few occasions, I spoke to large groups of Lingayats.

Later in 2009, Dr. Moglewar took us to Bangalore, the central headquarters of the Lingayat, and to its massive center with a university. We spent some time in discussion with the Sri Guru, who was second in leadership. He was fluent in English and shared how much they admired Chanappa Uttangi and his introduction of Jesus to them. We then went through an open door into the courtyard where the Si Sri Guru sat reclining on the floor. There were no guards. Anyone could approach him. Every day he would write small verses of blessings on palm leaves for each of its visitors. He was 103 years old. We also visited their high-rise building for social and welfare services. The fact that they had just established a Sanskrit college signaled to us the prosperity and political power of the religion and that it had been moving away from its strict egalitarianism into a more Brahminized caste system. We visited some of their temples. There was a statue of Basava. There were worship services. Solitary worshippers would prostrate themselves before his image in supplication and then leave. We now understood Dr. Moglewar's anguish over the decline of this once egalitarian movement. We could finally see his hope that Christ would bring them fulfillment of Basava's dream. Two of the eighteen leaders committed themselves to Christ's way. I have not yet heard whether the movement toward the saving faith in Christ is strengthening or failing.

Ashok Allure, a young plant geneticist, had risen to international prominence. Indian wheat had never been successful, and it was vital to feed India's people. After much research, he discovered that Mexican wheat could thrive in India's semi-arid climates. He brought it back to India with transforming success. Now he is a UN employee. He organizes farmer co-operatives to eliminate extortionary mark-ups by Banyan middlemen. At its annual celebratory mass meeting in Bangalore of the most noted Lingayats, the religious leadership chose Ashok to present the religion's annual award to Sunil as the Indian citizen who has done more than any other to advance human dignity and rights. He was drawn Christward by Sunil. He came to the U.S. on a scholarship by Lou Tice, head and founder of the Pacific Institute of Seattle, who flies national political, business, and military leadership from around the world for a four-day session at his ranch in eastern Washington for intense training. He invited Sunil to bring leading truth-seekers from India to join him. So Ashok came with us for the session and for a Truthseekers meeting at Covenant Church Camp of the Cascades for several more days. Here we led him in basic Christian thought and practice. We pray that this beginning will grow to mature discipleship in his life. He has since been named head of his university in Karnataka.

GURUDEV SEVA MANDAL

Tukdoji Maharaj (1902–1968) founded the One Lord Society in 1942. It has 2 million members, mostly in Madhya Pradesh and Maharashtra. Nagpur University, with 50,000 students, was renamed Tukdoji Maharaj University. Headquartered in Nagpur (with a population of 3 million), this religious society governs 42,000 rural Indian villages. Under a provision of the Indian Constitution, villages can organize themselves as small republics under their own constitution. The villages have their own courts, and police consist of all young men thirteen to eighteen years of age—quite the opposite of the United States!

The religion is strictly monotheistic and governs itself through their bible, the Gram Geeta. Tending toward pantheism, it nonetheless proclaims faith in only one just and loving God. Their houses of worship contain no idols. Gandhi was originally part of the movement, but left to lead a nation-wide movement. Every morning the villagers arise at 6 a.m., sing psalmlike hymns, and pray before work. Evenings include prayer meetings for the village, the nation, and the world. All are equal, and even the village leader has only advisory powers. There are altars in every community house of worship, but no idols—only an empty altar.

Sunil's brother, Nitin, is often in contact with them. He heads the 400 churches of the Dinbandhu (church of the poor), which Sunil had established earlier. Nitin always showed them respect and cooperated with them. As the third consecutive guru was dying at ninety-three, he asked to become a Christian. Sunil came over from Delhi and welcomed the guru to Christ. The dying leader called his other leaders together and told them that from henceforth only Jesus Christ could be their Guru and Savior. Thus began the process.

The political and administrative leader is Dhayneshwer Rakshak, a middle-aged businessman operating that country's first nationwide chain of grocery stores. He became a close friend and traveled with us often. A true follower of Christ, he is one of our key Truthseekers leaders. In 2016, the Maharashtra state named him the person who most supported human rights.

Every year, for a seven-day ashram, pilgrims come nearly 200 miles on foot. Wearing their small caps, they also carry an altar with no idol, emphasizing the reality of the one true god. Some of these pilgrimages take seven days each way. Each night they stay at a village and clean the whole community before they leave in the morning. Sunil, Tom Wolfe, and I joined the ashram. I spoke seven times of Jesus. At one such gathering I addressed 80,000 people at once. As the community matures, a countermove is also pulling the movement in a more Brahminic caste direction. Rakshak leads the majority opposition in the more Christward direction. In 2017, he received the award from the state of Maharashtra for doing the most for human rights in 2016.

CRISIS

Our most dramatic crisis occurred in October 2014. I had been asked to write a research paper on the question, "Who were the Assuras?" Originally the Assuras appeared to be a caste of buffalo herders. The buffaloes were kept by the outcasts, but not by higher castes. The Assuras henceforth became the term that described all the lower castes.

Nine months earlier the request had come to my friend *Jitendra Yadav*, "Jitu." He was the leader of the All India Backward Castes Students at Jawaharlal Nehru University—India's foremost academy. One of the dozen student body leaders, striking and fierce in appearance, he was finishing his PhD. I had met with him a number of times. He became a follower of the Savior.

The university had required all students to participate each year in the worship ceremonies of the multiarmed goddess, Durga. Her annual festival commemorates the legend of her winning the battle with King Mahishasura, the leader of the demons, and her finally butchering him with her sword. Thus, the triumph of Brahminic India over all its enemies would be complete. Jitu led the low-caste student reaction that forced the university to make the Durga worship optional. He then scheduled an annual celebration day in honor of the martyred King Mahishasura. This spread throughout the universities of northern India; news media covered this revolt extensively. It provoked an intense reaction from the Brahmin political and priestly leaders. They ridiculed Jitendra as trading in myths and tall stories. One evening, in frustration, he asked me directly, "My doctoral work is in another area; could you write me a research paper to answer their sneering ridicule?" I agreed.

How could I possibly write about something documented in languages I could not speak? I speak no Hindi, Sanskrit, Indo-European, or Proto-Indo-European. These sagas came from the pre-histories from between 2000 and 1400 BC. During this period the Hebrew Torah and the Persian and Aryan Vedas emerged. The account of Durga's murder of Mahishasura came to be written in the Indian Paranas. These months of research were excruciating. I had to use secondary sources because of my ignorance of the languages. Since this violated the academic standard I had always tried to observe, I felt incompetent. Nonetheless, I did find numerous translations and resources in English that were respected by scholars from the different perspectives. The Durga saga and its annual festival reinforced the triumph of the highest castes over the lower castes. Thus, the emergency of this new festival challenged the universal supremacy of high-caste perpetual domination of the lower castes. I sent my study to Jitendra and Sunil, regretting my inability to work with the languages.

Sunil sent it to his circle of scholars—Christian, Hindu, and Buddhist. They affirmed my conclusions. But I heard nothing from Jitu. Then in August I received an email from Ivan Kostka, editor and publisher of the magazine *Forward*, a color *Time*-format magazine founded by Ivan to be printed bilingually in Hindi and English. It sought to reach OBCs and others, while being useful in learning English, which was so important for economic growth. Ivan said he would like to use my research for the lead article in the October 2014 issue. He would add a few elements and follow with a series of other articles and photographs of artwork. I agreed.[1]

1. Larsen, "Who Were the Assuras?"

Before the tenth of October, the police had arrested the staff of *Forward* and issued arrest warrants for Ivan. Luckily Ivan and his wife were away in Mumbai, but the charges were pending for several years. The police raided all the bookstores and bookstands in Delhi, confiscating all copies. They got a court order forbidding possession of even single copies.

This set off a reaction on all levels, with the lower castes as well as all the Indian journals and press crying "censorship!" Political channels firmly denounced the greatest writers of all segments. More than eighty mass protests occurred across northern India as a result. I was not able to get a single print copy of the magazine. Later, in the great Lodhi Gardens Park at Easter Sunrise Christian worship, I was handed a tattered copy in a brown wrapper, now sequestered in my files.

Lower-caste protests broke out in India among many universities; Jitu and his friends had touched off a fire that would continue to spread far and wide with many student demonstrations. Their leader was charged with sedition based on a nineteenth-century law still used by the government to arrest and detain for any reason.

The contention peaked when Raul Gandhi rose to the defense of the lower castes in parliament. The turmoil climaxed in the shutdown of both houses of parliament for several days. My paper was only a tiny spark among many that set a fire going; the real incendiaries were Jitu and his friends. Now a professor at a New Delhi University, Jitu comes to pray and worship at our center.

THE WEEK THAT WAS

The week of April 8–15, 2015, was also climactic. During this week, the Walmiki leader brought us to their slum dwelling and sat us on the huge bed and gave themselves to Christ. These nearly 2 million had abandoned both Brahminism and Buddhism. I gave an account of this movement when discussing the castes. I also attended the massive rally of thousands of leaders of Mali (or Gardeners') caste in a great assembly hall. I was openly embraced by one of their chief leaders, Chagan Bushbal, before them all. They dramatized their loss of identity despite their 180 million membership. Then they dramatized the story of their caste member Phule, and then owned him and the story of Bali Raja (Jesus). They turbaned and garlanded Sunil, who, though from the Cobblers' caste, had shown them their identity by bringing the reality of Phule to them.

For the last week of that trip, I was visited again by top leaders of the Shepherds' caste of 10 million in the state of Uttar Pradesh. It became clear that their planning had reached its climax, only to find their three top leaders at loggerheads. They asked me to mediate the matter so that their amazing plan could proceed. I was taken aback. Many can attest that I have the gift of generating conflict wherever I ago. No one has ever suggested that I had gifts as a reconciler or peacemaker. The following account of what happened comes from my daily journal:

Wednesday, April 8, 2015

Three top Shepherd leaders arrive 8:30 a.m. with their minions. Two of them received Christ as I led them in prayer in 2007. They lead ten million shepherds in the state of Uttar Pradesh. The movement has uneven stops and starts. More recently they have had Christmas celebrations of 50,000. They are among the poorest of any caste. Without any land, only their herds, they are often poorer than Dalits and Tribals. But the government insists that they are just OBCs (Other Backward Castes) and thus are ineligible for scholarships and government employment that is available to the Scheduled Tribes and Castes.

In despair and frustration, they notified the government in January that if relief was not granted by April 30, they would begin converting to Christianity at the beginning of May.

Unfortunately, a three-way division among leaders had emerged. I was asked to join them in a process of reconciliation. Dumbfounded, I agreed to join them. The meeting began with the reading of John 10—Jesus the Good Shepherd. We then had a session of earnest intercessory prayer. Then followed oaths of unity and collaboration. It appears they had resolved their divisions even before we gathered. Christ had already done the work of reconciliation!

They then gave each of us a spiral notebook with photocopies of national regional news articles beginning in January. It was mostly in Hindi and some in English, with many photos.

Each of the three leaders would select three deputies, making a council of twelve. The headquarters would be established in Agra (the location of the Taj Mahal). A large CNI (Church of North India) fronting a large plaza had been procured for May 2. The masses, led by marching bands, would proceed, singing praise and adoration to Jesus, the Good Shepherd.

At this point I suggested that a mere rally was insufficient. Instead people would be asked to sign their names in official books, declaring henceforth they would follow Christ alone. They would then receive a certificate indicating the same. Baptism would later follow pending simple catechesis. They enthusiastically adopted the plan. They already had leaders in every town and city.

They would then proceed to hold similar rallies throughout
Uttar Pradesh (pop. 180 million) over the next two years, ending
April 30, 2017.

Shepherd communities in other states have decided to follow
the same structure as they observe the Uttar Pradesh process.

They spent the rest of the meeting adopting procedures, bank
accounts, etc. Meanwhile the Walmiki leadership gathered in the
next room with Sunil to further plan further for their May 14
declaration.

I left for the airport and was home at 8:30 p.m.

The first day of the decision was in fact held on May 14 in the city of Agra, close to the Taj Mahal. In the city square the roll was taken. They have proceeded, over two years, from city to city in that state of 180 million people, to call people to publicly declare their faith in the Good Shepherd. For three reasons, we do not reveal numbers:

1. These can be estimates and exaggerations.

2. Hindu nationalists will react even with violence if there is too much publicity.

3. Publicity in the United States must await their own declaration, not ours.

Two years have passed. The leadership now certifies that thousands of people have been prepared for baptism. Other "herder" casts such as the Yadavs have also begun conversion. The conflict is now intensified as the Modi government and the Hindu nationalists are moving with criminal and violent sanctions. But it is in the hands of God, whom we pray will protect them.

Large movements in other states continue to flourish. Rajasthan is seeing the massive Belai (Weavers' caste), together with the huge Meena tribal caste, coming in significant numbers. The latter is headed by Sri Mohan, who is now a key member of our India board. The state of Madhya Pradesh has 40 million citizens. There are now Truthseekers meetings in all fifty-one of its states. On March 11, 2018, more than 10,000 gathered to honor Sunil on his birthday. Large posters with his picture were displayed throughout the state. I can only trust that this Christward movement shall continue to spread in the years I shall not see.

Conclusion

As I ENTER MY eighty-fifth year, I must bring my story to a conclusion. Looking back, I confess to have had dreams and ambitions far too great for me. But God has given me a small place in his kingdom. In more than fourscore years, through success and failure, good decisions and bad, I can now see that nothing I have experienced has been lost in God's plan for my life. Elizabeth and I have had much sadness, but are not sad. Yes, and in that life, I have flourished. With my dear Elizabeth, the joys and fulfillments have been far beyond our expectations.

If this account must conclude here, our journey nonetheless continues. After a life together with Elizabeth, we find ourselves in good health and close to our daughter, Kristi, and granddaughter, Cassidy. We flourish in a small Covenant church of which we are charter members. Elizabeth continues to lead in prayer and care for the poor and the troubled. I no longer carry the burdens of office, but continue to participate both in Truthseekers and the William Carey Heritage Foundation. We no longer have the vigor of younger years, yet we share an increasing sense of Christ's abiding presence—sometimes I almost hear a voice saying, "I am with you."

Finally, I think it best to simply quote two Christian leaders who spoke succinctly:

First, the nineteenth-century Danish thinker, Søren Kierkegaard:

> Life can only be understood backwards,
> But must always be lived forwards.[1]

---

1. Kierkegaard, "Life Can Only be Understood," 306.

And a prayer by twentieth-century Swedish UN leader Dag Hammarskjöld, later killed on a peace mission in Africa:

—Night is drawing nigh—
For all that has been—"Thanks!"
For all that shall be—"Yes!"[2]

I conclude these stories with the prayer that I may soon kneel at the
feet of my Savior and hear him say, "Well done, good and faithful servant!"[3]

2. Hammarskjold. "Night Is Drawing Nigh," 89.
3. Matt 25:23.

Bibliography

Bellah, Robert N., et al. *Habits of the Heart: Individualism and Commitment in American Life*. Oakland: University of California Press, 1985.

Buber, Martin. *The Prophetic Faith*. New York: Macmillan, 1949.

Clephane, Elizabeth, and Ira D. Sankey. "There were Ninety and Nine Who Safely Lay." In *Favorite Hymns of Praise*, 197. Wheaton, IL: Hope, 1967.

Covenant Committee on Doctrine. *Covenant Church Affirmations*. Chicago: Covenant, 1976.

Emerson, Michael O., and Christian Smith. *Divided by Faith*. London: Oxford University Press, 2000.

Gustafson, James. "Pigs, Ponds and the Gospel." In *Perspectives on the World Christian Movement*, edited by Ralph D. Winter and Stephan C. Hawthorne, 670–80. Pasadena, CA: William Carey Library, 1992.

Haldane, Robert. *The History of Christianity 1650–1950, Secularization of the West*. New York: Ronald Press. 1956.

Hammarskjöld, Dag. *Markings*. Translated by Leif Sjoberg and W. H. Auden. New York: Alfred A. Knopf, 1964.

Heiser, Basil, OFM. "*Training in Christianity* by Sôren Kierkegaard, and: *For Self-Examination and Judge for Yourselves* by Sôren Kierkegaard (review)." *Franciscan Studies* 6.2 (1946) 240–42.

Ilaiah, Kancha. *Why I am Not a Hindu: A Sudra Critique of Hindutva Philosophy, Culture and Political Economy*. Calcutta: Samya, 1996.

Johnston, Robert K. *Theology at Play*. Eugene, OR: Wipf & Stock, 1997.

Kierkegaard, Søren. "Life Can Only be Understood Backward." Journalen JJ:167 (1843), Søren Kierkegaards Skrifter, vol. 18, 306. Copenhagen: Søren Kierkegaard Research Center, 1997.

King Fredrick VI, *The Royal Charter and Statutes of Serampore*, in Johnson Thomaskutty, *St. Thomas the Apostle: New Testament sand Apocrypha, and Historical Traditions (Jewish and Christian Texts and Related Studies 25)*; London and New York: Bloomsberry T and T Clark, 2018.

Ladd, George Eldon. *A Theology of the New Testament*. Grand Rapids: Eerdmans, 1974.

Larsen, David L. *The Company of the Creative: A Christian Reader's Guide to Great Literature and its Themes*. Grand Rapids: Kregal, 1999.

———. *The Company of the Hopeful: A Christian Reader's Guide to Great Literature and its Themes*. Grand Rapids: Kregal, 2004.

———. *The Company of the Preachers: A History of Biblical Preaching from the Old Testament to the Modern Era*. Grand Rapids: Kregal, 1998.

Larsen, Paul Emanuel. "Christian Mission and OBC Resistance." In *Living Faith*, edited by Richard Howell, 99–104. New Delhi: EFI Publication Trust, 2011.

———. "Convergence of Covenantalism and Interiority." *Covenant Quarterly* 44.1 (1986) 13–23.

———. "Expository Preaching in a Contemporary Suburban Congregation: A Study in the Book of Ephesians." STD diss., San Francisco Theological Seminary, 1978.

———. *The Mission of a Covenant*. Chicago: Covenant, 1985.

———. "Turning Your World Upside Down: Personal and Social Transformation in St. Paul." Unpublished Manuscript. Microsoft Word file. 2008.

———. "Who Were the Assuras?" *Forward Magazine* (October 2014) 9–14.

———. *Wisdom from Proverbs: Wise Up and Live*. Ventura, CA: Regal, 1974.

Larson, Esther E. *Tales from the Minnesota Forest Fires: An Experience of a Rural School Teacher*. St. Paul, MN: Webb, 1912.

Mani, Braj Ranjan. *Debrahmanising History, Dominance and Resistance in Hindu Society*. New Delhi: Manohar, 2005.

Mani, Braj Ranjan, and Pam Sardar. *A Forgotten Liberator: The Life and Struggle of Savitribai Phule*. New Delhi: Mountain Peak, 2008.

McFarland, Dimple. *The God Who Hears Me*. New Jersey: Pennsauken, 1916.

Mott, John R. "Foreword." In *Christian Mass Movements in India*, by J. Wascomb Pickett, 5–8. New York: Abingdon, 1933.

Olson, Karl A. *Into One Body by the Cross*. 2 vols. Chicago: Covenant, 1986.

Omvedt, Gail. *Seeking Begumpura: The Social Vision of Anticaste Intellectuals*. New Delhi: Navayana, 2009.

Persson, Walter. *Free and United: The Story of the International Federation of Free Evangelical Churches*. Chicago: Covenant, 1998.

Phule, Jitarao. "Slavery." In *Selected Writings of Deshponde Phule*, translated by Maya Pandit, edited by G. P. Deshpande, 21–101. New Delhi: Leftward, 2002.

Pickett, J. Wascomb. *Christian Mass Movements in India*. New York: Abingdon, 1933.

Prothero, Roland E. *The Psalms in Human Life*. London: John Murray, 1906.

Sankey, Ira D. "There Were Ninety and Nine." Gospel Hymns and Sacred Songs. New York: Biglow & Main, 1875.

Snodgrass, Klyne. *Stories with Intent: A Comprehensive Guide to the Parables of Jesus*. Grand Rapids: Eerdmans, 2018.